JOHN BLANCHARD

# The Beatitudes
## for today

D1056576

'a stimulating, humbling, encouraging,
practical treatment of the Beatitudes in
a very readable, accessible style.'
Evangelicals Now

DayOne

# The Beatitudes
## for today

John Blanchard

DayOne

© John Blanchard 1996
First printed 1996
Second printing 1999
Third printing 2006

All scripture quotations are from The New International Version © 1973, 1978, 1984, International Bible Society. Published by Hodder and Stoughton, unless otherwise stated.

British Library Cataloguing in Publication Data available
ISBN 0 902548 98 0

Published by Day One Publications
Day One Publications Ryelands Road Leominster HR6 0NZ
Tel: 01568 613 740
Fax: 01568 611 473
email—sales@dayone.co.uk
web site—www.dayone.co.uk
North American—e-mail-sales@dayonebookstore.com
North American web site—www.dayonebookstore.com

Designed by Steve Devane and printed by Guttenburg Press, Malta

## Dedication

*This book is gratefully dedicated to the members of the
Christian Ministries Board, in thankfulness for their
partnership in the gospel 'from the first day until now'*
(Philippians 1:6)

# Contents

This book fills a significant gap in contemporary Christian writing.

The past thirty years have seen the publication of several excellent volumes on the Sermon on the Mount, but we have lacked a full-length treatment of the Beatitudes, and I am therefore delighted that John Blanchard has undertaken this task.

The Christian world has been deeply indebted to him for his preaching and writing ministry over many years. Both are characterised by an absolute faithfulness to the text of Scripture, a deep concern to apply God's Word to today's world, and a God-given insight into the implications of biblical truth.

John Blanchard's fertile mind, wide reading, and clarity of style are all apparent in this excellent volume. There have been few eras in church history when we have more urgently needed this teaching. It is my prayer that we may be encouraged and enabled through the wide use of this book to live what Mr Blanchard calls a 'revolutionary lifestyle in a rotten culture.'

**Eric J. Alexander**
**St George's -Tron Church,**
**Glasgow.**

**February 1996**

In the course of a church-based evangelistic mission in Torquay a number of years ago, my assignment one night was to speak at a house meeting in a somewhat upper-class part of the town. When I arrived, my hosts were embarrassed to tell me that only two people, a successful young businessman and his wife, had replied to their invitation and that as the wife was already a Christian my evangelistic 'target' would be just one man.

The couple duly arrived and the five of us settled into the hosts' huge lounge, drinking coffee and chatting about nothing in particular, but as the time wore on I knew that I would soon be formally introduced and asked to 'give the talk'. As the minutes ticked by I sensed what line I ought to take, but as I looked at the solitary unconverted guest I also began to get increasing bouts of the collywobbles over what I was proposing to do. Eventually the host introduced me. I explained why I was in town, confessed that I had been very uncertain about what to speak about at this particular meeting, and then said something like this:

'Although there are only five of us here, and we are enjoying a relaxed evening together in this lovely room, I have decided to preach a sermon.' The businessman's look spoke volumes! I went on: 'To make matters worse, I want to read every word of it from a prepared script.' More eloquent looks! 'As if that were not sufficiently off-putting, I want to use a very old sermon - and it is not even one of my own.'

By now the 'target' (it was almost impossible not to think of him as such) was leaning back in his armchair with patronising boredom written all over him. I then opened my Bible and began to read Matthew 5, continuing non-stop until I reached the end of Matthew 7. At that point I had read the whole of the so-called Sermon on the Mount verbatim, without any interpretation other than an occasional pause or the emphasis of a particular word or phrase. At one stage I noticed that the businessman had hauled himself upright, then later that the bored look was giving way to interest. By the time I had reached the end of Matthew 7 he was literally sitting on the edge of his chair, leaning forward as if eager not to miss a single word, and in the discussion that followed it was obvious that the words of Scripture had come across with quite extraordinary power. In the Preface to **Letters To Young Churches**, his paraphrase of the New Testament Epistles, The British scholar J B Phillips said that in the course of his work he was continually struck by the 'living quality' of the text and that 'again and again the writer felt rather like an electrician re-wiring an ancient house without being able to "turn the mains off"'. We all felt something of Scripture's 'electric shock' that night: it was an unforgettable experience.

Over the years since then I must have quoted from the Sermon on the Mount hundreds of times in the course of my ministry, and from time to time preached on quite a number of its 111 verses. In 1989 I paid a return visit to the Moody Keswick Bible Conference in St Petersburg, Florida and based all the studies I taught that week on the first twelve verses of Matthew 5, universally known as the Beatitudes. By the time I had prepared and delivered those studies I was awe-struck by the sheer brilliance of what Jesus had said, and by the way in which he had unerringly defined genuine Christianity and exposed that which is false.

When the series was over, it was suggested that the studies might form the basis of a book. For several years I put the idea in my mental 'pending tray', where it was eventually joined by two other projects, one based on another part of the Sermon on the Mount - Matthew 6:9-13, or what we always call 'The Lord's Prayer' - and the other on the Ten Commandments. Providentially, in discussing these ideas with my good friends Brian Edwards and Derek Prime, we found that we all shared a particular interest in writing on all three subjects. As Derek Prime had already done some preliminary work on The Lord's Prayer and Brian Edwards was making similar progress on the Ten Commandments, we very happily agreed that it would seem sensible to avoid duplication and to produce one independent book apiece, while linking them loosely together as a trilogy.

As I turned back to the Beatitudes and studied them afresh I was totally unprepared for the avalanche of insights they contained and which I had previously missed. They are a perfect example of what the great sixteenth-century Reformer Martin Luther meant when he said that in Scripture 'every little daisy is a meadow'. The Beatitudes can be read aloud quite easily in less than a minute, yet the truths they contain are not only eternal but powerfully relevant to every age and I thank God for the unexpected opportunity of giving them renewed and closer attention. Nothing I have ever prepared for publication has had a greater impact on my own life.

Andrew Anderson has a busy and effective itinerant ministry, Graham Hind energetically pastors a church in South Wales and Andrew McGowan is Director of the excellent Highlands Theological Institute in Scotland. I owe a great debt to these three friends who kindly spared the time to read the first draft of the manuscript and made many helpful suggestions as to how it could be improved. I would also like to express my special thanks to Eric Alexander who has done me the honour of contributing such a gracious Foreword. Joy Leary has been my secretary for some fifteen years and she has once again risen superbly to the special challenges presented by a work of this kind.

As this fresh treatment of familiar text goes into circulation my prayer is that all who read it will reach the end of these pages grateful for the assurance that by the grace of God 'theirs is the kingdom of heaven' (Matthew 5:3) and determined as never before to demonstrate the fact by the quality of their lives.

**JOHN BLANCHARD**
Banstead
Surrey

**March 1996**

# Chapter 1

# Setting the scene

'Now when he saw the crowds, he went up on a mountainside and sat down. His disciples came to him, and he began to teach them...'
(Matthew 5:1-2)

The temptation in preaching or writing on the Beatitudes is to jump in at the deep end and begin expounding the text with little or no reference to the context in which we find it. I can hardly think of any part of Scripture where this would be a greater mistake. While it is true that each one of the Beatitudes is capable of standing on its own, their combined relevance and significance come much more sharply into focus if we see them in their biblical and theological contexts. I therefore make no apology for taking several chapters to set the scene for the astonishing words we shall be studying together.

## THE CROWDS AND THE CHRIST

Matthew tells us that the Sermon on the Mount was prompted when Jesus 'saw the crowds', yet that is not the whole story. We can begin to understand who they were and, more importantly, why they were there, when we realize that this sermon was preached near the beginning of Jesus' public ministry. After some 30 years of silence he suddenly burst on the scene like a meteor. After his dramatic baptism, at which God the Father had attested him with the statement, 'This is my beloved Son, in whom I am well-pleased' (Matthew 3:17, New American Standard Bible) and his traumatic encounter with Satan in the Judean desert, he went to live in Capernaum, where 'he began to preach' (Matthew 4:17). Soon afterwards, he called his first disciples, who joined him on an extensive tour of the region:

'Jesus went throughout Galilee, teaching in their synagogues, preaching the good news of the kingdom, and healing every disease and sickness among the people. News about him spread all over Syria, and people were brought to him who were ill with various diseases, those suffering severe pain, the demon-possessed, those having seizures, and the paralysed, and he healed them. Large crowds from Galilee, the Decapolis, Jerusalem, Judea and the region across the Jordan followed him' (Matthew 4:23-25).

We should hardly be surprised at such an ecstatic response, especially to the miracles. It is not impossible that Jesus performed more miracles in one day than were performed in the whole of Old Testament history! Be that as it may, news of what was happening spread like wildfire and huge crowds flocked after him. Excitement mounted, people's expectations went through the roof, and it seemed that everybody wanted to be part of what was happening. It was at precisely that moment, when Jesus saw the crowds and sensed the emotional surge of their support, that he made his way up a mountainside to deliver the landmark message which Matthew records for us.

It would have been easy to capitalize on his popularity and to enlist thousands of supporters for his cause. Instead, he wanted to make it crystal clear before he went any further that Christianity was not a bandwagon but a battle and that the Christian life was serious and demanding. There was to be no blurring of the issues, no small print, no hidden agenda - and no easy ride. Jesus was about to shatter the illusions of those who may have been easily satisfied with superficial answers to their spiritual needs.

The lesson here is obvious. There is something essentially dishonest about 'easy believism', about a so-called 'gospel' that promises peace, joy and happiness but demands nothing in the way of repentance, self-crucifixion and holiness. The Sermon on the Mount delivers a death-blow to the idea that a person can have Jesus as Saviour without having him as Lord, and can have forgiveness without holiness. Instead, Jesus said that Christians are 'the salt of the earth' and 'the light of the world' (Matthew 5:13-14), with the clear implication that, regardless of what they claim, those whose ethical quality of life is not both a moral antiseptic and a reflection of true Godliness in a polluted and darkened world are not Christians but hypocrites.

## SERMON OR SUMMARY?

One question which has been endlessly debated is whether the Sermon on the Mount was in fact a sermon at all! Some scholars suggest that Matthew took fragments of teaching given at different times during Jesus' ministry and lumped them together for the sake of convenience.

Some of those who think that Matthew is giving us a summary of our Lord's teaching, rather than a report of one particular sermon, point to the closing words of Matthew 4. They suggest that just as those words could be said to be a summary of the ministry of Jesus in general and not merely a report of its opening days, so the Sermon on the Mount is a summary of his teaching in general and not notes of one particular sermon.

A second argument is based on the fact that statements very similar to parts of the Sermon on the Mount are to be found elsewhere in the Gospels. After calling Christians 'the light of the world' Jesus said that people do not 'light a lamp and put it under a bowl' (Matthew 5:14-15) - and elsewhere he asked 'Do you bring in a lamp to put it under a bowl or a bed?' (Mark 4:21). Again, his statement that '...if you do not forgive men their sins, your Father will not forgive your sins' (Matthew 6:15) sounds very much like 'And ... if you hold anything against anyone, forgive him, so that your Father in heaven may forgive your sins' (Mark 11:25). These examples, and others like them, have led to the theory that Matthew was nothing more than an editor compiling a list of quotations, many of them taken from the writings of others. These arguments have some appeal but neither of them offers real evidence. On the other hand, there are several reasons why we should probably take the structure of the Sermon on the Mount at its face value.

The first is related to the fact that the words we have here form one of the five major segments of teaching recorded in Matthew's Gospel. These are chapters 5-7 (the Sermon on the Mount); chapter 10 (a kind of 'ordination address' for the twelve apostles); chapter 13 (a series of seven major parables); chapter 18 (teaching on the subject of the kingdom of heaven, underlined by two further parables); and chapters 24-25 (an extended statement about events surrounding the end of the world). These five statements stand out quite clearly as the highlights of Matthew's Gospel - but not as edited highlights. Instead, each one of them is placed into a specific context.

As we have already seen, the Sermon on the Mount comes towards the beginning of Jesus' public ministry. In chapter 10, Matthew gives the names of the twelve apostles chosen by Jesus, then says, 'These twelve Jesus sent out with the following instructions: ...' (Matthew 10:5). The teaching in Matthew 13 is introduced with the words: 'Such large crowds gathered round him that he got into a boat and sat in it, while all the people stood on the shore. Then he told them many things in parables, saying: ...' (Matthew 13:2-3). The teaching in Matthew 18 is sparked off by a specific question from one of the disciples: 'Who is the greatest in the kingdom of heaven?' (Matthew 18:1). The major discourse recorded in Matthew 24-25 comes soon after Jesus and his disciples had visited the temple in Jerusalem. As they were walking away from it, Jesus prophesied that one day it would be razed to the ground. Later, when he was resting on the Mount of Olives, the disciples asked him, '"Tell us ... when will this happen, and what will be the sign of your coming and of the end of the age?"' (Matthew 24:3). In each case, the impression given is that the segment of teaching was presented as a whole.

But there is an even more striking piece of contextual evidence. Matthew concludes each of these teaching segments with an almost identical phrase: 'When Jesus had finished saying these things ...' (Matthew 7:28); 'After Jesus had finished instructing his twelve disciples ...' (Matthew 11:1); 'When Jesus had finished these parables ...' (Matthew 13:53); 'When Jesus had finished saying these things ...' (Matthew 19:1) and 'When Jesus had finished saying all these things ...' (Matthew 26:1).

These two factors, the opening context and the closing comment, suggest that Matthew was putting historical markers in place, to make it clear why the particular segment of teaching was given and when it came to an end. Why would he have 'anchored' the teaching fore and aft in such a way had this not been the case?

What is more, the fact that teaching similar to that given in the Sermon on the Mount is found elsewhere in the Gospels cannot possibly prove that Matthew's material is not original. Since this is not a technical book there is neither need nor space to go into the fascinating discussion as to the possible sources of the Gospel writers' material. However, the insistence of some that whenever parallel teaching is found we must immediately ask who did the borrowing collapses in the face of the simple fact that every preacher with an extensive ministry inevitably repeats himself. One famous eighteenth-century minister is reported to have said that a sermon was not worth preaching until it had been preached at least 50 times! In the present century R G Lee, the well-known American preacher is said to have preached a sermon entitled 'Pay Day Some Day' over 1,000 times, including once a year in his own church! Even if those particular stories have grown with the telling, it would be amazing (strange even) if Jesus never repeated, emphasized or underlined the seminal themes found in what we could call his 'inaugural address'. Whether Jesus was speaking in the city or in the country, to huge crowds or to small groups, to the religious hierarchy or to unsophisticated country folk, the spiritual needs of his hearers were the same, as was their ignorance of the fundamental principles of the Kingdom of God. It would surely be amazing were he to have addressed these issues only once and left all his other audiences in the dark?

A further point in favour of treating these three chapters as an integrated whole is that they have the 'shape' of a sermon. It is true that neither Jesus nor Matthew actually called it one (the first person to do so was probably the famous fifth-century North African theologian Augustine) but it has all the characteristics of a formal discourse. There is an overall theme; there is an introduction (and, as we shall see, an attention-grabbing one at that!); then come several distinct but clearly related points; finally, there is a powerful and dramatic climax, facing its hearers with the inescapable issue of their own personal response to its message. Writing on this, the contemporary American preacher John MacArthur calls the sermon 'a great illustration of homiletics' and adds 'It has three points (you can't get any better homiletics than that!); the citizens of the kingdom, the righteousness of the kingdom, and an exhortation to enter the kingdom. Then, in the last part of the chapter, we see the effect of the sermon ... It flows beautifully from one thing to another with magnificent transitions.'

## MARKS OF AUTHORITY

Another clue that what we have here is a weighty, formal and integrated statement is a phrase unfortunately omitted by the NIV but correctly translated elsewhere by the words, 'And **opening his mouth** he began to teach them ...' (Matthew 5:2, NASB). As Jesus could not have taught them **without** opening his mouth, why does Matthew use such an elaborate phrase?

Some commentators have suggested that this is intended as an instruction to preachers not to mumble or mutter in the pulpit, but the idea that Jesus was giving an elocution lesson need hardly be taken seriously. The important thing to notice is that this particular phrase occurs in just two other places in the new Testament, and on both occasions the context is particularly significant. When the Apostle Philip had a remarkable encounter with an Ethiopian court official who invited him to explain a passage from the Old Testament, 'Philip **opened his mouth,** and beginning from this Scripture he preached Jesus to him' (Acts 8:35, NASB). When Peter was invited by a Roman army officer Cornelius to preach to him and to his relatives and friends in Caesarea Luke tells us, 'And **opening his mouth,** Peter said: ...' (Acts 10:34, NASB). Philip's sermon sparked off a strategic advance in the growing impact of the early church, while Peter's sermon to Cornelius marked a critical phase in releasing the gospel to the Gentiles. In both cases this 'opening of the mouth' seems to highlight the significance of the event. The same is certainly true when the phrase is used by Matthew to introduce the Sermon on the Mount. What we seem to have here is not a collection of 'bits and pieces' but a unified and structured statement which formed a launchpad for the three years of ministry to follow.

A final clue to the formality and cohesion of Matthew 5-7 is the fact that Jesus 'sat down' (v 1) before he began preaching. In our contemporary Western culture, sitting down to speak is a very informal practice, something done in a house meeting, at a picnic or in some other small group. In Jesus' day, however, exactly the opposite was true. Jewish religious leaders were in the habit of standing or walking around as they taught, but when they wanted to make an official statement, as opposed to giving less formal teaching, they sat down; as Jesus was to tell his disciples later, '"The teachers of the law and the Pharisees sit in Moses' seat"' (Matthew 23:2). One expert has suggested that every synagogue had a special chair called 'Moses' seat' which was reserved for the town's leading religious teacher. Jesus himself reflected this practice. Before teaching the series of major parables we noticed earlier, he 'got into a boat **and sat in it**, while all the people stood on the shore' (Matthew 13:2); in Mark's version of the major teaching segment recorded in Matthew 18 we are told that it was given '**sitting down**' (Mark 9:35, NASB); and the long statement about the end of the world was delivered when Jesus was '**sitting** on the Mount of Olives' (Matthew 24:3).

There are echoes of this in the way we speak of a professor's chair at a university. Matthew's deliberate inclusion of the seemingly irrelevant detail that Jesus sat down to teach is therefore a clue that the Sermon on the Mount was marked not merely by solemnity but by authority. After all, a professor's studied statements on his chosen subject carry much more weight than ideas thrown around by his students!

This sense of authority is heavily underlined in the text of the sermon itself. Time and again Jesus opened up a subject with phrases such as 'You have heard that it was said ...' and 'It has been said ...' (Matthew 5:21, 27, 31, 33, 38, 43), then clinched his own teaching with the words, 'But I tell you ...' (Matthew 5:22, 28, 32, 34, 39, 44). What is the significance of these phrases? To put it very simply, Jesus was contrasting Jewish rabbis' interpretation of the Old Testament with his own, and making it crystal clear that his was correct. A great deal of contemporary Jewish teaching on Old Testament law consisted of a mishmash of interpretations and traditions handed down over the centuries and which had become so confusing that, as the well-known British preacher Martyn Lloyd-Jones puts it, 'It was almost impossible to tell at this time which was the law and which was the interpretation.' For centuries, most of these laws had never been put into writing but had been handed down from one generation to another by word of mouth. When they were eventually codified into the **Mishnah** in the third century AD the English version ran to 800 pages, while one commentary on them, the **Babylonian Talmud** took up 60 volumes!

Over the centuries religious leaders had gradually turned the Old Testament law into a jungle of petty rules and regulations. For example, the fourth Commandment forbad work on the Sabbath, but what did 'work' mean? The experts of Jesus' day said that, unless the situation was life-threatening, 'work' included giving medical help. Even if the situation was life-threatening, one could do only enough to prevent a patient getting worse; nothing could be done to make him any better. For example, if a wall fell on someone, just enough rubble could be removed to see whether the person was dead or alive. If the victim was dead, the body had to be left where it was since removing it would constitute work. If the victim was alive, another batch of regulations came into play. A fractured limb must be left unattended. A wound could be bandaged, but no ointment could be used. If a sprained ankle was diagnosed, not a drop of water could be applied to it. Another example underlines how ludicrous the interpretation of Sabbath law had become: if a hen laid an egg on the Sabbath, this constituted work, so the egg could not be eaten; if, however, the hen was being reared for the table, an egg laid on the Sabbath could be eaten with a clear conscience, as egg-laying was not deemed to be the hen's main occupation!

### THE LAST WORD

The contrast between that kind of nonsense and the clear, penetrating statements Jesus made could hardly have been greater. Indeed, his words demonstrate that 'he was claiming a unique authority'. Even Old Testament prophets were in the habit of prefacing their sermons and teaching with phrases such as 'Hear the word of the Lord' (Isaiah 1:10), 'This is what the Lord says' (Jeremiah 51:1) and 'Listen to what the Lord says' (Micah 6:1). There was never any suggestion that they were speaking on their own account, formulating their own principles, issuing their own commands, making their own promises or giving their own warnings. Instead, they were frequently at pains to insist that they were only messengers. Yet when Jesus spoke he went one gigantic step further and said, '**I tell you**'. Since he never once contradicted Old Testament teaching - on the contrary, he specifically said, '"Do not think that I have come to abolish the Law or the Prophets; I have not come to abolish them but to fulfil them"' (Matthew 5:17) - we are driven to the conclusion that he was claiming the exclusive right to interpret what the Word of God said, and to do so infallibly.

But surely this is God's prerogative? Precisely! And the claim Jesus made for his exposition of the Old Testament is nothing less than an affirmation of his deity. Martyn Lloyd-Jones makes the point well: 'He was not a mere man; he was not a mere expounder of the law or just another scribe or Pharisee, or prophet. He was infinitely more than that, he was God the Son in the flesh presenting the truth of God ... Everything we have in this Sermon on the Mount must be accepted as coming from the Son of God himself ...'

One of the New Testament writers strikingly confirms this: 'In the past God spoke to our forefathers through the prophets at many times and in various ways, but in these last days he has spoken to us by his Son, whom he appointed heir of all things, and through whom he made the universe' (Hebrews 1:1-2). God had revealed himself progressively through many Old Testament servants; now in the person of the Lord Jesus Christ he was giving a revelation that is unique, final and complete. As the American scholar Simon Kistemaker comments, 'When Jesus finally came, he brought the very Word of God because he **is** the Word of God.' That being so, we should hardly be surprised to read that at the end of the sermon, ' ... the crowds were amazed at his teaching, because he taught as one who had authority, and not as their teachers of the law' (Matthew 7:28-29).   As we study the Beatitudes, we must do so on the understanding that the One who spoke these words has the same divine authority today.

# Chapter 2

# The Congregation

'Now when he saw the crowds, he went up on a mountainside and sat down. His disciples came to him, and he began to teach them ...' (Matthew 5:1-2).

There is fairly general agreement that the 'mountainside' on which Jesus delivered this sermon lies on the northern shore of the Sea of Galilee. When standing on the spot traditionally assigned to it, it is easy to imagine Jesus and the crowds being there (especially if one can turn a blind eye to the trappings which have been added for the benefit of modern tourists) but the precise location is virtually irrelevant. Some commentators have suggested fascinating links with the giving of the Old Testament law on Mount Sinai, but these owe more to a lively imagination than to intelligent insight, and nowhere does Matthew draw a parallel between Jesus and Moses. However, there are other issues worth examining.

## LUKE: COMPARISONS AND CONTRASTS

The arguments we touched on in the first chapter in favour of seeing the Sermon on the Mount as a single segment of teaching almost (but not quite) answer another interesting question that has often been asked: Is this sermon another version of the one we read in Luke 6? Although Matthew's account is three times as long as Luke's, there are obvious comparisons. Each begins with a series of similar (though not identical) 'blessings'; some of the same subjects (passing judgment on others and loving one's enemies, for example) are covered; and both sermons end with a metaphor based on the wisdom of building one's house on rock and the warning against building it on sand. These and other similarities certainly convince the American commentator William

Hendriksen: 'It is clear that the sermon recorded by Matthew and the one reported by Luke are one and the same'.

On the other hand, there are differences. Matthew says that Jesus 'went up on a mountainside and sat down', while Luke says he 'went down with them and stood on a level place' (Luke 6:17). That is why this passage is sometimes called The Sermon on the Plain, though the great sixteenth-century reformer John Calvin dismisses this particular issue as 'a light and frivolous argument'. Matthew says Jesus began the sermon when he had 'sat down', whereas Luke makes a point of saying that he 'stood'. Matthew places his report of the sermon **before** he became one of the disciples (an event which he records in Matthew 9), whereas Luke places it **after** Matthew's appointment, although this difference is diminished by the fact that Matthew is not always strict in his chronology.

The issue may not be as clear as Hendriksen suggests. Only some 26% of material is common to both sermons; 44% of the Sermon on the Mount is not in the Sermon on the Plain, though about 30% of similar material can be found scattered in other parts of Luke's Gospel. But statistics can prove anything - or nothing. The only safe conclusion on the issue of whether Matthew and Luke are giving their versions of the same sermon would seem to be the Scottish legal verdict of 'Not Proven'. This would certainly leave room for the very natural explanation that, in the course of his three years of public ministry, Jesus often restated and emphasized those themes which formed the bedrock of his message.

This is all very interesting, but at the end of the day it is not critically important. Not even the greatest biblical expert knows for certain whether the whole Sermon on the Mount was delivered at once, or whether Matthew and Luke are giving their versions of the same incident - and it makes not the slightest difference to the importance and relevance of what Jesus said. These issues have their place in any introduction to the Beatitudes, but it is important not to fall into the trap of concentrating too much attention on them. As Martyn Lloyd-Jones confessed: 'I do feel constantly the need to warn myself and everybody else against becoming so immersed in the mechanics of

Scripture that we miss its **message**. While we should be concerned about the harmony of the Gospels and similar problems, God forbid, I say, that we should regard the four Gospels as some kind of intellectual puzzle. The Gospels are not here for us to draw out our perfect schemes and classifications; they are here for us to read in order that we may apply them, that we may live them, and practise them'.

In a completely different context, someone has said: 'The main thing is to make sure that the main thing remains the main thing' - excellent advice for everyone who studies Scripture. Technical questions have their place, but they are not 'the main thing'. If the Bible's primary appeal is to the mind, we must always remember that its ultimate appeal is to the heart. We are to come to the Bible not merely as students who need to be informed but as patients who need to be healed, as wanderers who need to be restored, as weaklings who need to be strengthened and as children who need to be led.

As we do so, it is a great encouragement to know that the Bible is a book from which all the hammers of criticism have never chipped a single fragment and that we are 'entrusted with the very words of God' (Romans 3:2).

## DISCIPLES AND 'DISCIPLES'

We have identified the preacher and seen something of the context in which his sermon was preached - but who were the hearers? Matthew tells us that after Jesus sat down 'his disciples came to him, and he began to teach them', a statement which seems to exclude everyone else. Yet at the end of the sermon 'the crowds were amazed at his teaching', which could hardly have been the case had they not been within hearing distance. So who were the hearers?

At a practical level the answer seems simple and obvious. As Jesus made his way up the mountainside, many people followed him. When he sat down, his inner circle of followers, the disciples, would have settled down closest to him. Others, including some of those who had been struck by his earlier teaching, would have sat as near as possible. Beyond them, other people would have spilled out over the mountainside, exactly as we would expect. Those closest to Jesus would have heard every word, caught every gesture, seen every expression. Those further back might have missed some of what was said, while those on the outer fringes may have heard very little. What we do know is that sufficient people heard enough to produce the astonished reaction which Matthew records.

That seems to be the straightforward answer to the question at a practical level, but it raises a more important question: for whom was the sermon intended? Some suggest that it was meant solely for the disciples, and that the crowds only heard what they did because they happened to be there. But this suggestion involves too narrow an inter-pretation of the word 'disciples'. If we read the New Testament carefully, we find that the word is not limited to Jesus' 'inner circle' (sometimes called 'apostles'). In fact, it is not even to those who had committed themselves to Christ. The Greek word used - **mathetes** - literally means 'a pupil, or learner' and does not necessarily imply obedience to what is being taught. The New Testament gives a clear illustration of this. On one occasion, after Jesus had underlined the sovereignty of God in salvation by declaring that 'no-one can come to me unless the Father has enabled him', we are told that 'many of his disciples turned back and no longer followed him' (John 6:65-66). As these 'disciples' became deserters, we can be sure that they were never genuine believers in the first place.

There is, therefore, a sense in which we could say that virtually all of those present on the mountainside on that day were disciples. To one degree or another they all wanted to hear something of what Jesus had to say; **and Jesus had something to say to all of them**. There were certainly occasions when Jesus held closed sessions with the apostles, for example, to explain the inner meaning of his parables, but this was not one of them. This is confirmed by the fact that the discourse includes exactly the kind of challenge we would expect to hear at the end of an evangelistic sermon: 'Enter through the narrow gate. For wide is the gate and broad is the road that leads to destruction, and many enter through it. But small is the gate and narrow the road that leads to life, and only a few find it' (Matthew 7:13-14). Those words can hardly be addressed to those who had previously committed themselves to Christ and were already on 'the road that leads to life'.

What Jesus preached was what we call a 'double-barrelled' sermon. It was crammed with meaning for believers, challenging their lifestyle and testing the depth of their commitment. But it also had a devastating message for unbelievers, shattering their illusions as to the kind of life which is pleasing to God and satisfying to man.

## THE NEW PEOPLE

This all has contemporary impact. The words Jesus spoke then he speaks now, and he intends them to be heard by everyone, regardless of their spiritual condition. To begin with, the sermon has a powerful message for the modern Christian, which can be summed up in one simple phrase: **'Do not be like them'** (Matthew 6:8). The subject at that point was prayer and Jesus had exposed the folly of the Pharisees who were in the habit of praying on street corners to attract attention to themselves and who believed that the longer they prayed the more likely they were to be heard. Jesus torpedoed this hypocritical nonsense and went on to teach his followers the Lord's Prayer, a model of simplicity and profundity.

It is important to notice, however, that the principle 'Do not be like them' is a recurring theme in the sermon and in some ways it is the key phrase. If the overall theme of the sermon is the kingdom of heaven (of which more in later chapters), the subordinate theme is the principle that those who are in the kingdom are to be **different** from those outside of it - different not only from outright pagans but different from nominal Christians, different from religious hypocrites, different from those described by Paul later in the New Testament as 'having a form of godliness but denying its power' (2 Timothy 3:5). The British theologian J I Packer comments: 'There is no single paragraph of the Sermon on the Mount in which the contrast between Christian and non-Christian standards is not drawn. It is the underlying and uniting theme of the sermon; everything else is a variation of it ... The Sermon on the Mount is the most complete delineation anywhere in the New

Testament of the Christian counterculture. Here is a Christian value system, ethical standard, religious devotion, attitude to money, ambition, lifestyle and network of relationships - all of which are totally at variance with the non-Christian world. The sermon presents life in the kingdom of God, a fully human life indeed but lived out under the divine rule.'

In other words, the Sermon on the Mount is not a set of regulations which a person must obey in order to become a Christian, but a description of how a person is meant to live as a Christian. Nowhere does this come across more clearly than in the Beatitudes. They are not directions but descriptions. In them, as we shall see in detail in later chapters, Jesus says that true believers are poor in spirit, they mourn over sin, they are meek, they hunger and thirst after righteousness, they are merciful, they are pure in heart, they are peacemakers. These definitions go right to the heart of things, are indications of character, not a set of laws. Yet their challenge becomes even greater when we realize two things. The first is that **all Christians are meant to display these characteristics**. Jesus nowhere suggests that they are required only of Christian leaders, or preachers, or those in full-time Christian service or those holding office in the church. Nor are these the characteristics of particularly zealous believers. The Beatitudes reflect the qualities of the normal Christian life, not the abnormal, and they are meant to be seen in the life of every Christian without exception. The Bible is relentlessly insistent on this: 'If **anyone** is in Christ, he is a new creation; the old has gone, the new has come!' (2 Corinthians 5:17). Theologian R V G Tasker fleshes this out: 'Anyone who claims to be God's son, or to know him, or to belong to his kingdom, or to be a member of his body, the church, in whom these qualities are conspicuous by their absence, is "a liar and knows not the truth"'.

The second thing to notice is that **all Christians are meant to display all these characteristics**. The Beatitudes are not like a buffet bar from which we are invited to pick and choose whatever takes our fancy. There are obviously some character traits which are not found in all Christians. Some are extroverts, others introverts; some are naturally adventurous, others naturally cautious; some are positive in their approach to problems, others tend to be negative. Nobody would seriously suggest that these should somehow be ironed out so that all Christians become identical in temperament. Nor does the Bible suggest that all Christians have the same natural abilities or the same spiritual gifts. Scripture is quite specific about this: 'But each man has his own gift from God; one has this gift, another has that' (1 Corinthians 7:7). But the Beatitudes are not about gifts, they are about graces, and God expects all his people to manifest all of them. By this means they are to demonstrate to a sceptical and cynical world not only that they belong to the kingdom of heaven but they are under the dynamic, life-changing influence of the King. Jesus did not suggest that only some believers should be poor in spirit, only some pure in heart, only some meek, but said that every single one should be so. How searching this is! Friends of mine in the United States have produced a little booklet entitled **Personal Revival Checklist**, designed to help Christians in praying through the Sermon on the Mount. Here are the questions they suggest should be asked when reading the Beatitudes:

▶ Do I have a genuine poverty of spirit? Do I consistently recognize my own inability and the critical need for God in my life?

▶ Am I continually mourning over the sin of my life? When I sin, is there a godly sorrow that leads to a repentance without regret?

▶ Am I meek? Am I willing to be governed by God alone? Is the quality of brokenness clearly visible in my life?

▶ Am I hungry and thirsty for rightness in every realm of my life? With God? With others? In every situation, circumstance, decision?

▶ Am I merciful toward others? Do I exhibit a spirit of forgiveness?

> Am I pure in heart? Are my motives pure? My thinking not double-minded? Have I laid down other allegiances and affections that I have cherished more than Jesus? Do I have single-minded devotion to Jesus Christ?

> Do I seek to be at peace with all men without compromising my convictions? Do I make peace when it is within my power to do so?

> Am I standing so visibly for Christ that I am in opposition to the world, the flesh and the devil and, because of that, suffering persecution? Am I rejoicing when men revile me and say all kinds of evil against me falsely for Christ's sake?'

These challenging questions are based directly on the Beatitudes, illustrating what it means for members of the kingdom of heaven to live a revolutionary lifestyle in a rotten culture. And it can be done! In the second century a Roman writer by the name of Aristides told the Emperor Hadrian about the distinctive lifestyle of the Christians of his day. He commented on their integrity and morality, the quality of their family life and the way they handled pressure, but the final sentence in his moving and impressive letter contained his most telling observation: 'Truly this is a new people, and there is something divine in them'. As a pagan, Hadrian may have understood this to mean no more than that these 'new people' must have been strengthened in some way by the supernatural power of the gods. The real truth, however, is that they had been born into God's heavenly kingdom and the secret of their moral superiority lay in their being 'strengthened with all power according to his glorious might' (Colossians 1:11).

It is important for Christians to realize this if they are not to be intimidated when they study the Sermon on the Mount in general and the Beatitudes in particular. The only person who can demonstrate these qualities is the one whose heart has been changed by the saving power of Christ - and every person who has truly been saved has the resources to live up to the standards God has laid down. Peter says, 'His divine power has given us everything we need for life and godliness through our knowledge of him who called us by his own glory and goodness' (2 Peter 1:3), while Paul encourages us to remember that 'it is God who works in you to will and to act according to his good purpose' (Philippians 2:13). Thoughtful Christians will certainly find the Beatitudes demanding, but should never be led to despair.

## RESCUE THE PERISHING

Yet the Sermon on the Mount was not aimed exclusively at believers, and we make a serious mistake if we limit its application in this way. It gets its message across to unbelievers by exposing their ignorance on two critically important issues: the holiness of God and the sinfulness of man. John Calvin once wrote: 'Nearly all the wisdom we possess, that is to say, true and sound wisdom, consists of two parts: the knowledge of God and of ourselves', and it is precisely in these two areas that unbelievers are fatally ignorant.

To many people, God is no more than a distant deity, vaguely remote and unconcerned with the details and struggles of human life. To others, he is an easy-going father figure who takes a pretty relaxed view about man's misdemeanours, knowing that everything will eventually be swept under the carpet. As the American theologian R C Sproul puts it: 'A prevailing notion is that all we have to do to enter the kingdom of God is to die. God is viewed as being so "loving" that he really doesn't care too much if we keep his law. The law is there to guide us, but if we stumble and fall our celestial grandfather will merely wink and say, "Boys will be boys".' The Sermon on the Mount relentlessly disabuses us of that idea and reveals a God of awesome holiness who requires that his people reflect that holiness in every area of life.

Another 'blind spot' unbelievers have concerns not God's nature and character, but their own. By nature, man is stubbornly self-confident. The most radical modern expression of this can be seen in the so-called New Age Movement, which says that there is no deity but humanity. To quote Randall N Baert, at one time a prominent New Age spokesman: 'Spiritual humanism assigns man to a throne that spans the heavens and the earth in a divine heritage of universal lordship, omnipotence and self-created glory'. The Sermon on the Mount cuts through that kind of nonsense like a knife through butter. In showing its readers what God expects of mankind; it shows us how far we have fallen and how utterly powerless we are to remedy the situation.

The sermon is not a manual on the way of salvation. Instead, it shows the way salvation works out in a person's life. It does not say, 'Live like this in order to become a Christian' but rather, 'This is how Christians are meant to live'. At the same time it is made clear that living out the Sermon on the Mount is impossible outside of a right relationship to Jesus Christ. The qualities listed in the Beatitudes are never found in the natural man; they are all fruits of the new birth. All of this is meant to drive the unbeliever to the place where he recognizes his utter helplessness and calls upon God for saving grace.

## THE GOLDEN RULE

The irony is that many who stand condemned by the teaching of the Sermon on the Mount hold it in high esteem. Indeed, many people base their whole religious position on their understanding of what it says. Yet those who say, 'My religion is the Sermon on the Mount' (and I have heard it said countless times) are on very shaky ground. They are usually referring to the so-called 'golden rule' - 'So in everything, do to others what you would have them do to you', which Jesus said 'sums up the Law and the Prophets' (Matthew 7:12) - and what they mean is, 'I think the golden rule is what Christianity is all about; I try to keep it, and I hope that at the end of the day God will accept my attempt'. Humanly speaking that may sound quite reasonable, but the whole notion leaks like a sieve.

In the first place, there is no indication in the Sermon on the Mount that obeying the golden rule is the way of salvation. If we read the rule in context, we can see that it refers to our relationships with others rather than our relationship with God. It is a brilliantly simple way of telling us how to treat our fellow men. In effect, we are to change places with them and ask questions like these: What would I most want if I was in this person's place? What are the things that please me, help me, encourage me? What are the things that annoy me, offend me, discourage me? If we asked questions like these and let the answers guide our actions, then there would be a revolution in our personal relationships. That is the thrust of the golden rule. It is all of a piece with 'Love your enemies and pray for those who persecute you' (Matthew 5:44).

In the second place, if the golden rule is treated as a test to gain salvation nobody would ever pass the test. The whole idea that they might is smashed to smithereens by the Bible's insistence that 'all have sinned and fall short of the glory of God' (Romans 3:23). Nobody keeps the golden rule, or even comes close to doing so. What is more, all who hope that their attempts to do so might be acceptable are faced with the uncompromising fact that: 'All who rely on observing the law are under a curse, for it is written: "Cursed is everyone who does not continue to do everything written in the Book of the Law"' (Galatians 3:10). Notice the 'everything'! The attempt to gain salvation by morality or religion is an exercise in futility.

In the third place, it is implicit in the Sermon on the Mount and explicit elsewhere in Scripture that salvation is entirely by the grace of God. As Paul wrote to Christians of his day, 'For it is by grace you have been saved, through faith - and this not from yourselves, it is the gift of God - not by works, so that no-one can boast' (Ephesians 2:8-9). The law of God can show how godless we are, but it cannot make us godly. The function of the law is to make us conscious of our sin and of our need for salvation. In Paul's great phrase, it is meant 'to lead us to Christ that we might be justified by faith' (Galatians 3:24). No amount of rule-keeping (not even the keeping of the golden rule) can atone for sin, and nothing in the Sermon on the Mount suggests that it can do so. Instead, it shows us how helpless and hopeless we are, and in so doing points us to the only remedy for our spiritual sickness. As Martyn Lloyd-Jones puts it, 'There is nothing that so leads to the gospel and its grace as the Sermon on the Mount'.

As we study the text of the Beatitudes we do so on the basis that, in common with the remainder of the sermon, they are addressed to everyone. They have a powerful message for the unconverted, tearing away false religious concepts and revealing genuine Christianity. They have an equally powerful message for the converted, showing what true kingdom living is like and challenging them to ensure that their conduct matches their claim.

# Chapter 3

# Nothing to do with us?

'Now when he saw the crowds, he went up on a mountainside and sat down. His disciples came to him, and he began to teach them ...' (Matthew 5:1-2).

W e can safely say that the Sermon on the Mount has been more widely acclaimed than any other sermon ever preached. The seventeenth century preacher Thomas Watson wrote of it: 'Here is both usefulness and sweetness; here is a garden of delight; here is the golden key which will open the gate of Paradise.' William Perkins, one of Watson's contemporaries, wrote: 'These words are a key of the whole Bible, the sum of the Old and New Testaments.' The nineteenth century Welsh preacher David Thomas said that the Sermon on the Mount ushered in 'the dawn of a new era in the mental history of the world', while one of his peers, John Monroe Gibson, said: 'It stands alone as the grand charter of the commonwealth of heaven.' The contemporary British writer Michael Green refers to it as 'The supreme jewel in the crown of Jesus' teaching', while John Stott simply calls it 'The greatest sermon ever preached'. These accolades, and countless others like them, make it all the more remarkable that there are many Christians who say that the Sermon on the Mount is not directly applicable to us today, and that the only benefit we can get from it is by way of inference or reflection. Let me illustrate this before going into the technicalities.

## DISPENSATIONS

Some years ago I was the guest speaker at a Christian holiday centre in the South of England and taught a week-long series on the Lord's Prayer. After one of the sessions a man came to me and said, 'That was very interesting, but of course it has nothing to do with us today. The

Lord's Prayer doesn't apply to us; it will only come into force after Jesus returns to the earth and sets up his kingdom'. This man was not a liberal, someone who felt qualified to edit the Bible at will. He was a thoroughly conservative evangelical, rightly believing the Bible to be 'the living and enduring word of God' (1 Peter 1:23). Why then did he dismiss the Lord's Prayer (and, by implication, the whole of the Sermon on the Mount) as no more than 'interesting' and believe that it had no direct, contemporary relevance to his life? The shorthand answer is that he was a rigid dispensationalist. The explanation will take a little longer, but it is worth pursuing, because if the Sermon on the Mount is not directly relevant to today's world, but something that can be put on ice until after the Second Coming, our study of the Beatitudes will lose most of its relevance and all of its urgency.

To unravel the problem we need to begin with the Greek word **oikonomia** (the basis of our English word 'economy'), which occurs in one form or another about ten times in the New Testament. For example, Jesus used it several times in a parable about a 'manager' **(oikonomos)** and the 'management' **(oikonomia)** of his master's property (Luke 16:1,2). More importantly, the Apostle Paul writes about 'the dispensation **(oikonomia)** of the fulness of times' (Ephesians 1:10, Authorized Version), of 'the dispensation **(oikonomia)** of the grace of God which is given me' (Ephesians 3:2, AV) and of 'the dispensation **(oikonomia)** of God which is given to me' (Colossians 1:25, AV). The picture in every case is one of the ordering, dispensing or carrying out of a plan. On the one side, it has to do with God's eternal purposes for his creation, and especially his plan for the salvation of sinners. On the other side (the parable is a perfect illustration of the point), it has to do with man's responsibility, the exercise of his stewardship, the management of his master's possessions.

In God's plan for the salvation of sinners, God has always acted on the basis of grace. In one of the earliest direct biblical references to anyone's salvation we are told that 'Noah found **grace** in the eyes of the Lord' (Genesis 6:8, AV) and the Bible makes it clear that the same is true of every Old Testament believer. Abraham was saved by grace - the Bible specifically says of his salvation that 'God in his grace gave it to

Abraham...' (Galatians 3:18) - as were Moses, Joseph, David, Isaiah and all the countless others. Later, Moses made clear to the Israelites that God did not set his affection on them and choose them for any merit of their own but 'because the Lord loved you ...' (Deuteronomy 7:8). Even Moses could go no further than God's declaration to him: '"I will have mercy on whom I will have mercy, and I will have compassion on whom I will have compassion"' (Exodus 33:19). In not one case did any Old Testament believer make even the slightest contribution to his or her salvation. Instead, just as was the case in New Testament times and has been ever since, they were saved by 'the riches of God's grace ...' (Ephesians 1:7). What is more, all of God's people - Old Testament, New Testament and since - have the same Saviour, the Messiah promised immediately after Adam's fall into sin, progressively revealed as the Old Testament unfolded and finally appearing when Jesus came into the world to fulfil and inherit all of God's salvation promises. There is one plan of salvation, one Messiah, one people of God.

What is equally clear is that God's gracious plan for the salvation of sinners was revealed in two dispensations, which we commonly call the Old Testament and the New Testament. Under the old, or first, dispensation God's plan of salvation was presented in types, shadows and symbols, with the sacrifices and ceremonies pre-figuring the saving work of Christ. The intricate details of these may seem like so much religious rigmarole to the casual reader today, but they were all part of God's gracious provision at that time. Those who responded were truly saved by the One foreshadowed by the Old Testament systems.

In the new, or second, dispensation God's plan of salvation is presented in all its fulness in the person of the Messiah. It is important to realize, however, that this new dispensation is the carrying out of the same covenant of grace made by God with Abraham. As the British theologian Ernest Kevan puts it: 'The New Testament has more to say about grace than the Old, but it introduces no fundamentally new principle.' Today, as has always been the case, God dispenses salvation on the basis of the substitutionary death of Christ, to all those he chose 'in him before the creation of the world' (Ephesians 1:4) and he does so without any reference to quality or merit in the persons concerned. 'The salvation of the righteous comes from the Lord ...' (Psalm 37:39); he dispenses it entirely by grace.

To summarize: at the very moment of man's sin, God promised salvation through one who would, as he told Satan, 'crush your head' (Genesis 3:15). God endorsed this by means of a covenant made with Abraham and has continued to fulfil it ever since in the salvation of untold millions of his chosen people. Some benefitted from this covenant under the old dispensation, when man's knowledge and understanding of God's covenant promise were very limited and some under the new dispensation in which we have the wonderful privilege of having 'the light of the knowledge of the glory of God in the face of Christ' (2 Corinthians 4:6). In Old Testament times, God's people were saved through faith in the Christ of prophecy; from New Testament times onwards they have been saved through faith in the Christ of history. These two dispensations were God's way of revealing and executing his one gracious purpose of salvation, through which he is gathering to himself 'all those everywhere who call on the name of our Lord Jesus Christ' (1 Corinthians 1:2). So far so good - but complications are on the way!

## MR DARBY AND MR SCOFIELD

Cyrus Ingerson Scofield was born in Michigan in 1843, raised in Tennessee, and won the Confederate Cross of Honour for distinguished service in Lee's Army in the American Civil War. Some years later he was converted and became the pastor of a small Congregational church in Dallas, Texas. In 1895, at the request of the well-known evangelist D L Moody, he became pastor of the Moody Church in East Northfield, Massachusetts, but in 1902 returned to serve the Dallas church for a further five years before launching into an extensive Bible teaching ministry. An avid student of Scripture, Scofield was also very taken with the teaching of John Nelson Darby (1800-1882) who resigned his curacy in the Church of Ireland in 1827 and became the outstanding teacher of an unofficial grouping which later became known as the Plymouth Brethren. In studying the Apostle Paul's statement about 'rightly dividing the word of truth' (2 Timothy 2:15, AV) Scofield took this to mean that the Bible could not be properly understood until it had been divided into sharply distinguished 'dispensations' and that correctly interpreting Scripture meant correctly dividing these dispensations from one another. In other words, he concluded that God's **oikonomia** was not a means of dispensing his grace, but **a period of time** during which God revealed certain truth in certain ways. In Scofield's own words, dispensation was 'a period of time during which man is tested in respect of obedience to some **specific** revelation of the will of God'.

There are two important weaknesses in this interpretation of 2 Timothy 2:15. The first is that nowhere in Scripture does **oikonomia** refer to a period of time. The second is that Paul's word **orthotomeo**, which the AV translates 'rightly dividing' means 'to cut straight' and has the general sense of 'rightly dealing' with a thing. As W E Vine says in his **Expository Dictionary of New Testament Words**: 'What is intended here is not dividing Scripture from Scripture, but teaching Scripture accurately'. Writing in **The Evangelical Quarterly** in 1936, Bible scholar Oswald T Allis makes this fuller comment on Paul's words: 'This exhortation does not mean to divide up Scripture into dispensations and set each one at variance with the others, but so to interpret it that by a study of each and every part, the glorious unity and harmony of the whole shall be exhibited and the correctness of the exposition of the one part be established by its perfect agreement with every other part of Scripture as the God-inspired word.' This explanation is reflected in translations such as 'correctly handles the word of truth' (NIV) and 'handling accurately the word of truth' (NASB). Scofield side-stepped these issues and by the time his first Scofield Reference Bible was published in 1909 he had come to the conclusion that all of human history - past, present and future - is divided into seven compartments or 'dispensations': the age of innocence (from Creation to the Fall), the age of conscience (from the Fall to Noah), the age of human government (from Noah to Abraham), the age of promise (from Abraham to Moses), the age of law (from Moses to the death of Christ), the age of grace (from the death of Christ until his second coming) and the kingdom age (from Christ's second coming for 1,000 years). Those who accept Scofield's views are usually called 'dispensationalists'.

There is obviously a great deal to be said in favour of this as a general outline of human history. The period before the Fall was clearly an age of innocence, conscience was obviously a prominent factor between the Fall and Noah, as was human government from Noah to Abraham, and so on. The difficulty comes when we divide Scripture and limit the direct relevance of revelation to the particular 'dispensation' in which it was given. Unless one is very careful this tends to produce what the contemporary American author Grover Gunn has called 'hardening of the categories'. Writing as someone who had once been an enthusiastic dispensationalist, Gunn goes on to say that, in his view, 'consistently interpreting Scripture through the rigid grid of dispensational assumptions has the potential for turning biblical bread into theological shredded wheat'. Theologian George Murray is equally trenchant and says that dividing the plan of salvation into dispensations 'is not "rightly dividing the word of truth", but wrongly dividing the Word of God'.

## THE PARENTHESIS THEORY

The Sermon on the Mount is an excellent illustration of how this works out in practice. Dispensationalism teaches that when Jesus began his public ministry by 'preaching the good news of the kingdom' (Matthew 4:23) what he had in mind was the political kingdom that Jews had been expecting ever since the last of the Old Testament prophets had spoken. In that context, the Sermon on the Mount was Messiah's manifesto of the kingdom he would have set up if Israel had accepted his terms. But Israel did not accept; in the Bible's words, 'his own did not receive him' (John 1:11). In judgment on this rejection, Christ postponed the promised Jewish kingdom and inaugurated something dispensationalism calls 'the church age' (a kind of dispensation within a dispensation) and delayed the implementation of his manifesto until a future kingdom age, when God's people will come into their own.

Dispensational theologians place the change of policy towards the end of Matthew 12 and say that at that point Jesus rejected the Jews and postponed the blessings he had intended to bring them.

According to this scenario, we are presently living in a parenthesis within the Jewish kingdom programme of which the Old Testament prophets spoke, and we must therefore read the New Testament through this previously unrevealed grid. When we do, we see that the Sermon on the Mount, with its frequent references to 'the kingdom of heaven', relates to the future kingdom age and not the present church age. In his contribution to **The Wycliffe Bible Commentary** the American theologian Homer A Kent puts it like this: 'Hence, the Sermon on the Mount is not primarily a statement of principles for the Christian church (which was yet unrevealed), nor an evangelistic message for the unsaved, but a delineation of the principles which would characterize the Messianic kingdom which Jesus was announcing.'

There are two major reasons why the dispensationalist approach is defective. The first is that **it limits the kingdom** by reserving it entirely for the future. Now it is obviously true that the kingdom of heaven is not yet fully established on earth. Whatever one's views may be about a future millenium (a crucially important factor in dispensationalism), we have clearly not reached the time when, as the prophet Habakkuk promises, 'the earth will be filled with the knowledge of the glory of the Lord, as the waters cover the sea' (Habakkuk 2:14); it is not yet true that 'The kingdom of the world has become the kingdom of our Lord and of his Christ ...' (Revelation 11:15). But is it true to say that the kingdom of God does not exist on the earth at this time? Surely not? As we saw in an earlier chapter, 'Jesus went throughout Galilee, teaching in their synagogues, preaching the good news of the kingdom, and healing every disease and sickness among the people' (Matthew 4:23). Here was kingdom preaching, kingdom teaching, kingdom power, and it was operating there and then. When Jesus was accused by his enemies of casting out demons by the power of Beelzebub, the prince of demons, he challenged their logic by saying that Beelzebub would hardly engage in activity guaranteed to wreck his own kingdom, and then added: 'But if I drive out demons by the Spirit of God, then the kingdom of God has come upon you' (Matthew 12:28). Here is a clear statement indicating that the kingdom of God was a present reality, not merely a distant future hope.

If anything, the picture is clearer still when we come to the Epistles, because by the time they were written the King had left the earth. Was the kingdom programme abandoned or postponed because the King was no longer present? There is no doubt that the writers do sometimes emphasize the future kingdom. For example, Peter urges Christians to make every effort to make their calling and election sure, so that 'you will receive a rich welcome into the eternal kingdom of our Lord and Saviour Jesus Christ' (2 Peter 1:11). Here Peter is obviously referring to the believer's full experience of the kingdom, something that lies in the eternal future and therefore beyond our present knowledge or experience. However, in his letter to the Colossians Paul gives them the following motivation for 'joyfully giving thanks to the Father' (Colossians 1:11-12): 'For he **has rescued** us from the dominion of darkness and **brought** us into the kingdom of the Son he loves, in whom we **have** redemption, the forgiveness of sins' (Colossians 1:13-14). My emphasis of Paul's verbs makes it clear that just as redemption, the forgiveness of sins and rescue from sin's dominion are blessings that Christians living on earth have here and now, so is a place in the kingdom of God. There are dimensions of God's kingdom that lie on the other side of the grave and are so wonderful as to be beyond our imagination, but we are in the kingdom **now**. We are already under the authority and rule of Jesus Christ, our Saviour and King.

## THE TIN MINER

Billy Bray was the son of a tin miner from Truro, in Cornwall. His father had been converted during a memorable visit to the area by John Wesley in 1743. Billy followed his father down the local tin mine, but rebelled against his Christianity, eventually becoming a violent, immoral alcoholic. When he was nearly 30 years of age he came across a copy of John Bunyan's book **Visions of Heaven and Hell** and was gloriously converted. 'Everything looked new to me' he was to write, 'the people, the fields, the cattle, the trees. I was like a new man in a new world.' He eventually became a passionate preacher of the gospel and was so exuberant in style and in his shouts of praise and worship that he became known as 'the glory man'. Yet his favourite description of himself was not 'the glory man' but this: 'I am the son of a king.' Every Christian can give the same testimony. The Bible tells us that 'our citizenship is in heaven' (Philippians 3:20). Christians are not children of this world trying to get to heaven, but children of heaven making our way through this world. We are already members of the Kingdom of God. The rule of God has broken into history and the Sermon on the Mount is not a set of laws designed for some future dispensation but a mosaic of what happens when people come under the gracious Kingship of Christ.

## RELEVANCE AND RESPONSE

The second major reason for rejecting the dispensationalist 'parenthesis' theory is that **it limits the teaching** Jesus gave in the Sermon on the Mount by suggesting that it does not apply directly to the present time. The parenthesis theory says that the sermon applied to the disciples and the other people who heard Jesus preach it, and that it will apply at some time in the future, when the 'kingdom age' is brought in, but that it has no direct application to people living at the present time. The theory is intriguing, but surely it falls apart as soon as one begins to read the sermon? Take these words: 'You are the salt of the earth. But if the salt loses its saltiness, how can it be made salty again? It is no longer good for anything, except to be thrown out and trampled by men' (Matthew 5:13). This is not a command, but a statement of fact; Jesus was telling his disciples that in becoming Christians they had become 'the salt of the earth'. The most obvious use of salt in those days was as a preservative, and the disciples were being reminded that they were to permeate their corrupt culture with the sheer quality of their lives.

How can it be said that this teaching is not directly relevant to Christians today? Moral standards are collapsing, immorality is rife, the popular media is increasingly polluted and vulgar, and even common decency is an endangered species. Not that any of this should surprise us. As Martyn Lloyd-Jones notes: 'The world, left to itself, is something that tends to fester. Far from there being a tendency in life and the world to go upwards, it is the exact opposite. There are these germs of evil, these microbes, these infective agents in the very body of humanity and, unless checked, they cause disease.' As that festering, rotting process is going on all around us, surely the teaching that Christians are to be a preserving, antiseptic influence in society has powerful and practical relevance **today**, and cannot possibly be shunted off into some future age? The Sermon on the Mount is not merely to be praised, but to be practised - here and now.

The same kind of relevance can be seen in the very next sentence of the sermon: 'You are the light of the world. A city on a hill cannot be hidden. Neither do people light a lamp and put it under a bowl. Instead they put it on its stand, and it gives light to everyone in the house. In the same way, let your light shine before men, that they may see your good deeds and praise your Father in heaven' (Matthew 5:14-16). How can we possibly say that these words apply only, or even primarily, to some future age and have no direct relevance to Christians living today? Just as Christians are called by God to have a negative influence in the world, seeking to counteract moral and spiritual corruption, so they are called upon to have a positive influence. They are to live in such a way that unbelievers will see something of the darkness and futility of sin, sense something of the purity and clarity of light and, by the grace of God, turn from one to the other. Could anything be more contemporary, relevant and urgent?

Other sections of the Sermon on the Mount could be examined in the same way, but the point about its contemporary relevance can also be demonstrated by noting that the essence of its teaching can be found in the Epistles. These were written after the King had returned to heaven, with the obvious implication that this teaching is intended to be obeyed here and now. For example: 'Simply let your "Yes" be "Yes" and your "No", "No"' (Matthew 5:37) is repeated at James 5:12; the instruction to 'store up for yourselves treasures in heaven' (Matthew

6:20) has its counterpart at 1 Timothy 6:19; and the warning 'Watch out for false prophets' (Matthew 7:15) has a powerful echo at 1 John 4:1. The point is clear. If the Sermon on the Mount is only, or at best primarily, for some future age and largely irrelevant to us at the present time, so are at least some of the writings of James, Paul and John. If this is the case, who is to say that the same might not be true of everything they wrote?

This is what makes the issue so serious, and why I have deliberately taken so long to lay it out before turning to the text of the sermon. If the Sermon on the Mount is of use to Christians today only in the sense that it contains some admirable principles, then it loses virtually all of its practical relevance and impact. Think of its commands: Jesus told his hearers, 'Love your enemies and pray for those who persecute you' (Matthew 5:44); 'Do not store up for yourselves treasures on earth ... But store up for yourselves treasures in heaven' (Matthew 6:19-20); ' ... seek first (God's) kingdom and his righteousness' (Matthew 6:33). Can we safely ignore these and say that they do not apply to us? And what about the so-called golden rule: 'So in everything, do to others what you would have them do to you' (Matthew 7:12). Can we look on this as no more than an admirable principle and then postpone it to some future age?

Again, if the 'parenthesis' theory is true, the Sermon on the Mount's warnings lose their force. Jesus made it clear to his original hearers that 'unless your righteousness surpasses that of the Pharisees and the teachers of the law, you will certainly not enter the kingdom of heaven' (Matthew 5:20). Can today's readers of the sermon safely ignore that warning? He said that 'if you do not forgive men their sins, your Father will not forgive your sins' (Matthew 6:15). Does that have no direct relevance today? He warned his hearers, 'Do not judge, or you too will be judged' (Matthew 7:1). Does that have no contemporary meaning? The same point can be made about the many gracious promises made in the sermon. The Beatitudes alone say of those to whom they relate that 'they will be comforted ... they will inherit the earth ... they will be filled ... they will be shown mercy...they will see God ... they will be called sons of God'. Is there no point in today's Christians taking Jesus at his word and resting in the assurance and enjoyment of these promises?

In the Introduction to his **Exposition on the Sermon on the Mount**, first published two years before he died, the British author A W Pink made this comment on the issue: 'The older we grow, the less do we approve the drawing of hard and fast lines through the Scriptures, limiting their application by insisting that certain parts belong only to such and such a class and, under the guise of "rightly dividing" the Word, apportioning segments of it to the Jews only, the Gentiles only, or the Church of God only. Man makes his canals rigidly straight, but God's rivers wind in and out.'

## THE CORNELIUS FACTOR

How then should we approach our study of the Beatitudes? There is a perfect model recorded in Acts 10, one made all the more telling because of its background. As the early church began to permeate society the question arose as to whether the gospel should be preached to the Gentiles or whether it was solely intended for the Jews. The cultural cleavage between Jews and Gentiles was massive and had existed for centuries. The devout Jew would not dream of entering a Gentile's house or even buying food from one, for fear of contamination.

One day an angel appeared to a God-fearing Roman army officer by the name of Cornelius living in the town of Caesarea and told him to send for the Apostle Peter, who was at that time staying with a friend in Joppa, about 30 miles away. As Cornelius's men were approaching Joppa, Peter fell into a trance while waiting for lunch. In a vision, something like a large sheet containing a great variety of animals, reptiles and birds was let down to earth and God's voice told him: 'Get up, Peter. Kill and eat' (Acts 10:13).

Knowing that Old Testament dietary laws only allowed Jews to eat meat from animals specified by God as being 'clean', Peter objected: 'Surely not, Lord! I have never eaten anything impure or unclean', but God replied, 'Do not call anything impure that God has made clean' (Acts 10:14-15). The vision was repeated three times and, while Peter was thinking about its meaning, Cornelius's messengers arrived at the house and God told him to go with them.

By the time he reached Caesarea he had realized the implications of the vision; under the new dispensation God had removed laws he had previously imposed and there was to be no barrier to Christian salvation. Introduced by Cornelius to a large gathering of people in his house, Peter told them: 'You are well aware that it is against our law for a Jew to associate with a Gentile or visit him. But God has shown me that I should not call any man impure or unclean. So when I was sent for, I came without raising any objection. May I ask why you sent for me?" (Acts 10:28-29). Cornelius then told him his side of the story and in these words invited Peter to speak: " Now we are all here in the presence of God to listen to everything the Lord has commanded you to tell us" (Acts 10:33).

Here is the model we need, the example we should follow. As we come to God's Word we are in a very special sense 'in the presence of God'. That being the case, our attitude should be one of humility and submission. We should be ready to listen to everything God has to say to us. We must set aside our prejudices and reservations. We must stop being evasive or defensive. We must be prepared to have our thoughts, motives, attitudes and actions examined and corrected. Above all, we must be determined to respond in willing and loving obedience. In John Calvin's words, 'Our wisdom ought to consist in embracing with gentle docility, and without any exception, all that is delivered in the sacred Scriptures.' God desires, demands and deserves nothing less.

# Chapter 4

# The King's favour

'Blessed are the poor in spirit, for theirs is the kingdom of heaven' (Matthew 5:3).

The Beatitudes begin with a bombshell. 'Blessed are the poor in spirit, for theirs is the kingdom of heaven' may seem to have a pleasant, gentle ring to it, but that one sentence would have had a shattering impact on anyone who understood what Jesus was saying. Every word is packed with meaning and perhaps the most obvious way to unpack them is to ask and answer three questions: What is the meaning of 'blessed'? What is meant by 'the kingdom of heaven'? What does it mean to be 'poor in spirit'? Although these questions seem straightforward enough, it will take three chapters to answer them adequately, yet by doing so we will at the same time have laid the foundation for our study of the remaining Beatitudes.

## HAPPINESS IS...

The very first word of his sermon - 'Blessed' - would have guaranteed the attention of his hearers, and Jesus was to repeat it another eight times in driving home the message of the Beatitudes. Some modern versions of Scripture, such as The Good News Bible and The Living Bible, translate 'blessed' as 'happy', but this is totally inadequate to express what Jesus meant and can at times virtually indicate exactly the opposite. As the American scholar Don Carson comments: 'Those who are blessed will generally be profoundly happy; but blessedness cannot be reduced to happiness.' Even so, it may help us to gain a greater appreciation of what Jesus meant if we step sideways and look at the part happiness plays in human thought and experience.

Blaise Pascal, the seventeenth-century mathematical genius, physicist and religious thinker who has been described as 'one of the great minds of Western intellectual history', once made this telling assessment of the subject: 'All men seek happiness. This is without exception. Whatever different means they use, all men tend towards this end. Some go to war, others avoid it, but all have the same desire in view. The human will never takes the least step but towards this object. It is the motive of every action of every man, even of those who hang themselves.' David Thomas wrote of happiness as 'the master theme of human thought, and the primal end of human purpose and action'. It is difficult to disagree with this and impossible not to recognize man's restless search for happiness. The deep-seated longing in us for significance, self-esteem, satisfaction and security has happiness as the ultimate goal. Many people would agree with what the German playwright Bertholt Brecht wrote in **The Threepenny Opera:** 'The right to happiness is fundamental; men live so little time and die alone.' Over and over again I have heard people say, 'Happiness is what life is all about' or 'Happiness is what really matters' and it is hardly surprising that it is so relentlessly pursued. Many seek happiness in marriage, others in divorce. Some look for it in the birth of a child, others in abortion. Some think that wealth will bring happiness, others try to achieve it by taking a vow of poverty. Some feel that the only way to be happy is to be in life's fast lane, others take a more relaxed route. Some try to eat their way to happiness, others try to get there by dieting. The very fact that people look for happiness in such diverse directions underlines the truth of Pascal's verdict.

In modern times the use of drugs has joined the pervasive consumption of alcohol as a major means of trying to escape from the problems and pressures of life into happiness and fulfilment. Led to believe that man is no more than a chemical by-product, millions of people are turning to chemicals to solve their problems and bring release. As in all other times, many try to find a sexual solution, encouraged by psychologists, sociologists and others who tell us that the fulfilment of the human sex drive is a necessary condition of health and happiness and that sexual inhibitions are a major source of physical and psychological illness. We have reached the stage where, as far as sex is concerned, 'anything goes'. Marriage is irrelevant, chastity is ridiculed as a museum piece and faithfulness is optional; nothing must be allowed to get in the way of the testosterone tide.

Yet these are just examples. People look for happiness in sport, television, holidays, music, writing, acting and hundreds of other normal, acceptable activities. Others, sickeningly, look for self-satisfaction in rape, robbery, violence, child molestation, cruelty and the like. The list of avenues along which people travel in the search for happiness is virtually endless and, as Pascal noted, includes suicide, which is seen as the final escape from pain, pressure and every other source of chronic unhappiness.

## THE ELUSIVE EMOTION

Yet just as fascinating as the relentless drive for happiness is the fact that it remains endlessly elusive. Writing at a time when he was an atheist, the British writer Malcolm Muggeridge made the point well: 'Of all the different purposes set before mankind, the most disastrous is surely "the pursuit of happiness", slipped into the American Declaration of Independence along with "life and liberty" as an inalienable right, almost accidentally, at the last moment. Happiness is like a young deer, fleet and beautiful. Hunt him, and he becomes a poor frantic quarry; after the kill, a piece of stinking flesh.' Elsewhere, he concluded, 'The pursuit of happiness, however conceived, is the most foolish of all pursuits.' Writing in the **Daily Mail** on 8 March 1995, former Chief Rabbi Lord Jakobovits observed, 'We live in a most selfish age. Whatever we want, we must have. Today, every desire exists for one purpose only: to be gratified.' Yet towards the end of a penetrating analysis as to the outcome of such hedonism, he came to the same tantalising conclusion as Malcolm Muggeridge: 'But he who pursues happiness will never reach it.'

History is packed with proof of what these men have said. One of the most telling testimonies comes straight from the pages of the Old Testament. King Solomon was a brilliant administrator, able politician and shrewd military commander. In addition, he was a knowledgeable naturalist, a prolific lyricist (he wrote over 1,000 songs) and a distinguished savant, known for some 3,000 proverbial sayings. The wealthiest king alive, he owned 1,400 chariots and 12,000 horses and his annual income included 23 metric tons of gold. His rampant libido can be gauged by the fact that he had 700 wives and 300 concubines, part of his indulgence in a sumptuous lifestyle of which others could only dream. Yet when he reflected on it all, this was his conclusion: 'I denied myself nothing my eyes desired; I refused my heart no pleasure. My heart took delight in all my work, and this was the reward for all my labour. Yet when I surveyed all that my hands had done and what I had toiled to achieve, everything was meaningless, a chasing after the wind; nothing was gained under the sun' (Ecclesiastes 2:10-11).

Some 3,000 years later, the longing for happiness is just as intense and the goal just as elusive. After attending a New Age 'Festival for Mind and Body' in 1978, the British journalist Bernard Levin wrote, 'What the world lives by at the moment just will not do. Nor will it; nor do very many people suppose any longer that it will. Countries like ours are full of people who have all the material comforts they desire, yet lead lives of quiet (and sometimes noisy) desperation, understanding nothing but the fact that there is a hole inside them that however much food and drink they pour into it, however many motor cars and television sets they stuff it with, however many well-balanced children and loyal friends they parade around the edges of it ... it **aches**.' It is not difficult to confirm Levin's diagnosis. Lauded for his spectacular hits, and equally well-known for his womanising, drinking and drug-taking, American film director Robert Altman gave this telling assessment of his 'success' when interviewed for The **Observer** in 1994: 'I am sitting here today in this bleak atmosphere in the middle of winter making this silly movie and to me it is an adventure. I have no idea what it will be like. But even if it works, it will all be for nothing. If I had never lived, if the sperm that hit the egg had missed, it would have made no difference to anything.'

These testimonies, and countless others like them, confirm the verdict of the British writer Aldous Huxley's famous book **Brave New World.** Published in 1931, it portrayed a population saturated with drug-induced good feelings, free sex galore, a never-ending stream of entertainment, and technological fixes to stave off negative thoughts. Yet even Huxley realized, that that scenario would not produce lasting happiness, and **Brave New World** is predominantly pessimistic. Why should this be so? Why is the 'feel good factor' so difficult to capture and so easy to lose? Why is the American philosopher Eric Hoffman frustratingly right when he says, 'The search for happiness is one of the chief sources of unhappiness'?

One clue is to be found in the very etymology of the word. 'Happiness' like 'haphazard' is based on the old Middle English word **hap**, which meant 'chance' or 'luck'. This points us towards the simple fact that happiness is circumstantial; it depends on happenings - and the problem lies in the 'hap'! By and large, men's happiness depends on circumstances over which they have little or no control. Think of some of the things that induce the 'feel good factor': the state of the stock market, the rate of inflation, the political situation, the weather, personal health, sports results, family news, other people's words or actions. These, and hundreds of other things, exercise a powerful influence on how people feel, yet they can often do little or nothing about them. With happiness so closely tied to capricious circumstances no wonder it is so difficult to capture or to keep.

The second reason why happiness is so elusive is that, by and large, people are looking for it in the wrong places. They are trying to find inner satisfaction while ignoring the only One who can meet their need. The well-known scholar C S Lewis puts it perfectly: 'We try to be our own masters as if we had created ourselves. Then we hopelessly strive to invent some sort of happiness for ourselves outside of God, apart from God. And out of that hopeless attempt has come human history ... the long, terrible story of man trying to find something other than God to make him happy.' Solomon was a tragic example of what Lewis says. By the world's reckoning, his indescribable wealth, outstanding ability, enormous power and the means to satisfy all his carnal desires should have made him supremely happy. Yet he summed it all up in one word: **meaningless**. Solomon's case illustrates the relevance of two questions which Jesus asked some 2,000 years later: 'What good is it for a man to gain the whole world, yet forfeit his soul'. (Mark 8:36). The deepest longings of the human soul can be met only by God himself; and 'our heart is restless until it repose in thee.' Whilst it is true that God graciously grants us pleasures in the beauty of nature, a job well done, friendship, family ties and many other experiences, none of these is ultimately satisfying. Prosperity, success, popularity and good health are hopeless substitutes for a heart at rest in God, nor can any amount of physical or mental stimulation make the slightest contribution towards this. It is impossible to meet spiritual need in these ways. Thomas Watson put it perfectly: 'A man may as well think to extract oil out of a flint, or fire out of water, as blessedness out of these terrestrial things.'

Nor can religion meet the need. The outward trappings of religious observance can sometimes numb the mind into thinking that all is well, but an anaesthetic is no substitute for medicine. The Pharisees of Jesus' day were meticulously religious, yet Jesus was scathing in his condemnation of their hypocrisy. In the Sermon on the Mount he warned his hearers that 'unless your righteousness surpasses that of the Pharisees and the teachers of the law, you will certainly not enter the kingdom of heaven' (Matthew 5:20). As we shall see later in this book, the Beatitudes tear away every vestige of religious veneer and make it clear that God requires what the Bible calls 'truth in the innermost being' (Psalm 51:6 NASB).

## BLESSEDNESS IS...

Having looked at the subject of happiness in general, we can now examine the more specific and precise word Jesus used no fewer than nine times as a focal point of the Beatitudes. The word translated as 'blessed' in our English Bible comes from the Greek word **makarios,** and the culture of New Testament times gives us a fascinating clue as to its meaning. Because of its geographical location, balmy climate, fertile soil and rich mineral resources, the Greeks believed that anyone living on the Mediterranean island of Cyprus had everything necessary for a life of perfect happiness and fulfilment. There was no need to import anything, and not even the most catastrophic events elsewhere could affect the self-contained bliss the island provided. As a result, they called the island **he makaria** (the feminine form of the adjective **makarios**). They used a similar word when speaking of their gods, whom they believed to be free from moral restraints and human restrictions and unaffected by poverty or weakness. They also used it as a synonym of 'dead', the idea here being that only when they were dead could people fully and finally escape from the woes of this world. The Greeks had a different word for what we call 'happiness', but as its literal meaning was 'under the protection of a good genius or demon' none of the biblical writers ever used it. Instead, they took the word **makarios** and invested it with a spiritual significance which went far beyond anything the pagans could ever imagine.

Grammatically, the plural adjective Matthew uses - **makarioi** - is an anarthrous predicate, which means that it appears without a definite article and makes an assertion about those of whom it is speaking. Far from being a tiresome technicality, this gives us an important clue to understanding the real meaning of the word. It indicates that blessedness is related not to emotions but to character. When the Bible tells us that someone is 'blessed' it is not telling us what they feel but what they are. That is why it is misleading to translate **makarioi** as 'happy'. Happiness is a subjective state, whereas blessedness is an objective state. As John Stott says of those referred to in the passage we are studying, 'The Beatitudes are not an indication of their feelings but a declaration of God's assessment of them.' We can take that one step further and add that the Beatitudes are not conditional promises to the people concerned, but descriptions of their inner, spiritual condition in the sight of God. The Bible tells us at least five things about this.

**Firstly, blessedness is something only God can give.** We simply do not have the resources to generate a spiritual condition that makes us acceptable to God, nor even to produce the true happiness that follows. As Blaise Pascal wrote, 'Happiness is neither within us only or without us. It is the union of ourselves with God.' Of all Scripture's statements about blessedness none is more fundamental than this: 'Blessed are the people of whom this is true; blessed are the people whose God is the Lord' (Psalm 144:15).

**Secondly, blessedness is a condition which God longs for his people**

**to enjoy.** In the opening chapter of Genesis we read, 'So God created man in his own image, in the image of God he created him; male and female he created them'; and the very next words are, 'God blessed them' (Genesis 1:27-28). This speaks of God turning full-face to Adam and Eve and graciously assuring them of his favour. There is the same kind of language in the priestly blessing which God instructed Aaron to pronounce on the Israelites: 'The Lord bless you and keep you; the Lord make his face shine upon you and be gracious to you; the Lord turn his face towards you and give you peace' (Numbers 6:24-26). Again, we see God's blessing as an assurance of his favour and of his concern for the well-being of his people.

A beautiful illustration of the meaning of being blessed comes in Mary's song of praise after the angel had told her that she would give birth to Jesus: '"From now on all generations will call me blessed, for the Mighty One has done great things for me - holy is his name"' (Luke 1:48-49). Here again the emphasis is not on Mary's emotions (joyous as they were), but on the amazing fact that, in the angel's words, she had '"found favour with God"' (Luke 1:30). Before leaving his disciples and being taken up into heaven, Jesus 'lifted up his hands and blessed them' (Luke 24:50). Shortly afterwards, in one of the earliest sermons preached in the New Testament church, Peter spoke of Christ's coming into the world and assured his hearers, 'When God raised up his servant, he sent him first to you to bless you' (Acts 3:26). Although the verb in these last two quotations is **eulogeo** rather than one based on **makarios** their meanings are closely related and reinforce the sense of divine concern and favour.

These examples are all expressions of a truth beautifully captured in The Amplified Bible's rendering of a phrase towards the end of the New Testament, in which James urges his readers who sense their lack of spiritual discernment to 'ask of the giving God' (James 1:5). Unbelievers often see God with clenched fists, but believers see him with open hands, longing to bless us in ways 'immeasurably more than all we ask or imagine' (Ephesians 3:20).

**Thirdly, blessedness is independent of circumstances.** The illustration about Cyprus gives us a secular model of a spiritual truth and helps us to understand that whereas happiness is an emotion, blessedness is an endowment. Because blessedness (unlike happiness) is not tied in to happenings, it is not affected by the changing circumstances of daily life. So often one comes across Christians who seem to be constantly bubbling over with excited happiness, only to have their happiness punctured the moment something goes wrong.

Several years ago, while preaching in the United States, I stayed in the home of a very successful young couple who were surrounded with the trappings of success and growing wealthier by the day. They were enthusiastic members of a church which majored in an effervescent approach to all its activities and my hosts seemed to be on a permanent 'high'. As the husband started the car before leaving for church one night there was a startled squeal from under the bonnet. When he opened it up, their pet cat was sitting there, looking decidedly frightened and minus several patches of fur. Instantly, my hosts were in a frenzied panic. All their confidence and cheerfulness vanished. Frankly, they were in worse shape than the cat! It took several hours before they recovered and the whole incident was a bizarre illustration of how flimsy and fragile happiness is when divorced from true blessedness and of the truth of Thomas Watson's assertion that 'Blessedness does not lie in externals.'

This does not mean that Christians are meant to be in a permanent lather of excitement regardless of the circumstances. The idea that spirituality means getting into some kind of ecstatic overdrive and going through every day bubbling over with obvious happiness regardless of the circumstances has no biblical basis. Not even Jesus lived like that; in fact, the Bible calls him 'a man of sorrows' (Isaiah 53:3). Christians are called to 'mourn with those who mourn' as well as to rejoice with those who rejoice (Romans 12:15), and the Bible warns us that personal holiness needs to be pursued 'with fear and trembling' (Philippians 2:12).

On the other hand, this does not imply that the Christian life is meant to be one of unrelieved misery. The Bible may not have a word for 'happiness', but it does speak of a deep, inner joy that is the privileged possession of those who know the blessing of God on their lives. Jesus promised his followers that after his resurrection they would rejoice, 'and no-one will take away your joy' (John 16:22) and the truth of his words were confirmed again and again. When the apostles were flogged for preaching the gospel, they 'left the Sanhedrin, rejoicing because they had been counted worthy of suffering disgrace for the Name' (Acts 5:41). When Paul and Silas were flogged and jailed at Philippi, the middle of the night found them 'praying and singing hymns to God' (Acts 16:25). Paul testified to the Corinthians that 'in our troubles my joy knows no bounds' (2 Corinthians 7:4) and even went so far as to tell the same readers, 'I delight in weaknesses, in insults, in hardships, in persecutions, in difficulties' (2 Corinthians 12:10). How could he do this? Because his joy was rooted in the assurance of having found favour with God, something that even the direst of circumstances could not possibly affect in any way.

**Fourthly, blessedness is meant to be a continuous, contemporary experience.** This is something else brought out by the grammatical construction of the Beatitudes. For example, a literal translation of the first would be 'Blessed the poor in spirit', because in Greek the predicate adjective omits the verb. However, when our English translations insert the verb 'are', as in 'Blessed **are** the poor in spirit' they are not only maintaining the flow of the sentence but expressing the truth of what is meant. There is no hint of a future tense in this part of the sentence, a fact which underlines the error of pushing the Beatitudes off into some hoped-for future age. The principles they lay down are replicated all over the New Testament and are meant to produce a response here and now as God's people seek to live godly lives in an ungodly world. As one scholar has rightly said, 'The greatness of the Beatitudes is that they are not wistful glimpses of some future beauty; they are not even golden promises of some distant glory; they are triumphant shouts of bliss for a permanent joy that nothing in the world can ever take away.'

**Fifthly, blessedness is related to a person's spiritual condition.** In making this statement I am going far beyond what John Calvin called the 'common grace' by which God blesses mankind in general. Jesus spoke of this later in the Sermon on the Mount when he reminded his hearers that God 'causes his sun to rise on the evil and the good, and sends rain on the righteous and the unrighteous'(Matthew 5:45) and Paul underlined the point when he told the Athenians that God "gives all men life and breath and everything else" (Acts 17:25), These are certainly great blessings – we could literally not live without them – and God graciously grants them indiscriminately, pouring them out on downright sinners as well as on upright saints. Yet these are blessings associated with creation, whereas the Beatitudes are associated with salvation. A person may be blatantly godless, and even deny the very existence of God, yet enjoy to the full God's gracious provision of everything he needs in order to be able to lead a healthy, wealthy, popular, rewarding - and sinful - life. But this is certainly not the blessedness spoken of in the Beatitudes, in which God graciously grants the assurance of his favour. God never smiles at sin.

## OBEDIENCE; RIGHTEOUSNESS; FAITH

In the course of the New Testament, the word 'blessed' is used some 47 times in relation to man's spiritual condition, and it is interesting to notice that these references fall into three general groups. One example of each will be sufficient to make the point. Some 22 of these references are in the context of **obedience**: when a woman in the crowd called out, 'Blessed is the mother who gave you birth and nursed you', Jesus replied 'Blessed rather are those who hear the word of God and **obey** it' (Luke 11:27-28). In 13 cases blessedness is associated with righteousness, and we need go no further than the Beatitudes for a clear example of this: 'Blessed are those who hunger and thirst for **righteousness,** for they will be filled (Matthew 5:6). The remaining 12 references are directly associated with **faith:** when 'doubting Thomas' was finally convinced that Jesus had been raised from the dead and cried out, "My Lord and my God!" Jesus told him, 'Because you have seen me, you have believed; blessed are those who have not seen and yet have believed'. (John 20: 28-29).

While we must never think of God's blessing as something he owes us or as something we can earn, we dare not miss the point that the Bible repeatedly links God's marked favour to his people with obedience, righteousness and faith. These are the hallmarks of the person who has biblical grounds for looking to God for his blessing. As we read the scriptures daily, we should constantly be searching our hearts and adjusting and aligning our lives, seeking to bring every part of them into grateful submission to God's 'good, pleasing and perfect will'. (Romans 12:2).

We can summarize this chapter by saying that, in the sense in which Matthew uses the term, to be blessed by God is to know his gracious favour in a marked way. That favour is related to (but not a reward for) spiritual characteristics such as obedience, righteousness and faith, yet in the Beatitudes one further element is added: God blesses the people concerned in ways that specifically reflect their spiritual characteristics. In the first of the Beatitudes the blessing God bestows is the privilege of belonging to 'the kingdom of heaven'. In the next two chapters we will discover something of what this means.

# Chapter 5

# Concepts of the Kingdom

'Blessed are the poor in spirit, for theirs is the kingdom of heaven' (Matthew 5:3).

In Chapter 1 we looked at a number of reasons for believing that the Sermon on the Mount was an integrated passage of teaching and not a collection of 'sound bites' taken from Jesus' ministry in general. Another indication that the Beatitudes form a self-contained introduction to the sermon is that the first and last of them make the same promise. The first says, 'Blessed are the poor in spirit, for theirs is the kingdom of heaven', and the last says, 'Blessed are those who are persecuted because of righteousness, for theirs is the kingdom of heaven' (Matthew 5:3,10). This is a stylistic device known as inclusion, which tells us that everything between the two statements relates to the same subject. But we can take this a stage further by noting that Jesus mentions 'the kingdom of heaven' or 'the kingdom' another seven times in the remainder of Matthew 5-7, leaving no doubt that the kingdom of heaven is the great theme of the entire sermon.

## KINGDOMS GALORE?

If we were to widen our focus even further we would find that the Bible contains over 100 direct references to 'the kingdom of God' and 'the kingdom of heaven', in addition to scores of other passages where these concepts are implied. There is a regal thread running through the whole of Scripture, holding it all together and thereby teaching us that it is the key to understanding the history of the world.

Yet these impressive facts raise two obvious questions: Is there any difference between 'the kingdom of God' and 'the kingdom of heaven? And why does Matthew almost always refer to 'the kingdom of heaven' and almost never to 'the kingdom of God'? The idea that the two kingdoms were distinct used to be very popular among dispensationalists. They believed that the kingdom of heaven was what Jesus meant by 'the good news of the kingdom' (Matthew 4:23), something which would be established when Jesus returned to the earth, whereas the kingdom of God was the sphere of eternal salvation. Insisting on this rigid distinction is somewhat out of fashion today, and in the next chapter we will take a closer look at the implications of the issue, but before going any further it will be helpful if we can discover whether there is any essential difference between 'the kingdom of heaven' and 'the kingdom of God'.

One particularly important clue can be found in a comment Jesus himself made when a rich young man balked at the challenge of abandoning his riches: 'Then Jesus said to his disciples, "I tell you the truth, it is hard for a rich man to enter the kingdom of **heaven**. Again I tell you, it is easier for a camel to go through the eye of a needle than for a rich man to enter the kingdom of **God**"' (Matthew 19:23-24). It is perfectly obvious that Jesus was using the two terms synonymously. He was not talking about two kingdoms, but one, and when his stunned disciples reacted by asking, 'Who then can be saved?' (Matthew 19:25) they were clearly not thinking in terms of an earthly kingdom to be established at some time in the future.

The same point can be established by looking at parallel passages in the Synoptic Gospels. 'Blessed are the poor in spirit, for theirs is the kingdom of **heaven**' is clearly identical in meaning to what Luke records elsewhere: '"Blessed are you who are poor, for yours is the kingdom of **God**"' (Luke 6:20). In telling his disciples that they were being given a privileged insight into spiritual truth, Jesus said 'The knowledge of the secrets of the kingdom of **heaven** has been given to you' (Matthew 13:11), whereas Mark records him as saying, 'The secret of the kingdom of **God** has been given to you' (Mark 4:11). Again, the writers could hardly have had two distinct kingdoms in mind. The same truth is brought out in the records of an incident in which Jesus scolded his disciples for discouraging parents from bringing their children to him. Matthew writes, 'Jesus said: "Let the little children come to me, and do not hinder them, for the kingdom of **heaven** belongs to such as these"' (Matthew 19:14), while Mark's account reads, 'He said to them, "Let the little children come to me, and do not hinder them, for the kingdom of **God** belongs to such as these"' (Mark 10:14).

Another line of approach leads to the same conclusion. In speaking of the events that would precede his Second Coming, Jesus said: 'And this gospel of the kingdom will be preached in the whole world as a testimony to all nations' (Matthew 24:14). Mark's account reads, 'And the gospel must first be preached to all nations' (Mark 13:10), and it is difficult to see how this 'gospel' could refer to an earthly kingdom. References in Acts and the Epistles provide more evidence. When imprisoned in Rome, Paul taught and preached 'the kingdom of God' (Acts 28:23,31) and we are given no impression that this 'kingdom' had been postponed. Elsewhere, he expressed confidence that God would deliver him from his enemies 'and will bring me safely to his heavenly kingdom' (2 Timothy 4:18) and there can be no reasonable doubt that Paul was referring to full and eternal salvation. These and other examples show that there is no biblical basis for claiming that the 'kingdom' mentioned in Acts and in the Epistles is different from that in the Gospels. On the basis of all the available evidence, we can safely conclude that 'the kingdom of God' and 'the kingdom of heaven' are synonymous. What is more, there are other biblical terms, such as 'the kingdom of the Lord' (1 Chronicles 28:5), 'the kingdom of Christ and of God' (Ephesians 5:5) and 'the kingdom of light' (Colossians 1:12) which relate to the same subject. There is one true God and one divine kingdom although, as we shall now see, the Bible speaks of it in a number of different ways.

## UNIVERSAL AND ETERNAL

Firstly, the Bible speaks of the kingdom of God as being eternal and timeless, what Michael Green calls 'God's standing sovereignty over his world'. One of the clearest expressions of this comes in a remarkable statement by Nebuchadnezzar, King of Babylon: 'His dominion is an eternal dominion; his kingdom endures from generation to generation. All the peoples of the earth are regarded as nothing. He does as he pleases with the powers of heaven and the peoples of the earth' (Daniel 4:34-35). In a great Psalm of praise, David addresses God with the words, 'Your kingdom is an everlasting kingdom, and your dominion endures through all generations' (Psalm 145:13). The same theme runs through the opening of his final charge delivered to the people of Israel at the dedication of the temple: 'Praise be to you, O Lord, God of our father Israel, from everlasting to everlasting. Yours, O Lord, is the greatness and the power and the glory and the majesty and the splendour, for everything in heaven and earth is yours. Yours, O Lord, is the kingdom; you are exalted as head over all' (1 Chronicles 29:10-11).

The New Testament is equally emphatic about the universal sovereignty of God. Paul writes of 'the King eternal, immortal, invisible, the only God' (1 Timothy 1:17) and in the same letter speaks of God as 'the blessed and only Ruler, the King of kings and Lord of lords, who alone is immortal and who lives in unapproachable light, whom no one has seen or can see' (1 Timothy 6:15-16). These and many other passages can be summed up in three words, 'The Lord reigns' (Psalm 93:1). God is actively, sovereignly, powerfully, wisely, eternally and unchangeably in control of every atom in the universe. His kingdom was not gained, nor can it be lost; it never had a beginning and it will never come to an end. God 'works out everything in conformity with the purpose of his will' (Ephesians 1:11) and nobody and nothing can escape from its all-embracing impact. As the eighteenth-century hymnwriter Isaac Watts put it:

Through all his mighty works
Amazing wisdom shines,
Confounds the powers of hell,
And breaks their dark designs;

> Strong is his arm, and shall fulfil
> His great decrees and sovereign will

The universal, eternal kingdom of God is the ultimate fact. His absolute, unqualified sovereignty is the foundation of all other biblical truth and no understanding of history or theology is possible until this is in place.

## THE KING

The second aspect of God's kingdom can be seen when we turn from Old Testament praises to Old Testament prophecies, which focus on the One who would establish God's eternal kingdom on earth. Examples of these prophecies are among the most magnificent statements in Scripture. In a remarkable vision, Daniel saw someone 'like a son of man' to whom was given 'authority, glory and sovereign power; all peoples, nations and men of every language worshipped him. His dominion is an everlasting dominion that will not pass away, and his kingdom is one that will never be destroyed' (Daniel 7:13-14). Isaiah also pointed forward to this kingdom - and to this King: 'For to us a child is born, to us a son is given, and the government will be upon his shoulders. And he will be called Wonderful Counsellor, Mighty God, Everlasting Father, Prince of Peace. Of the increase of his government and peace there will be no end. He will reign on David's throne and over his kingdom, establishing and upholding it with justice and righteousness from that time on and for ever. The zeal of the Lord Almighty will accomplish this' (Isaiah 9:6-7). This prophecy is all the more remarkable because it was made when the house of David was in serious decline.

The connection between David's dynasty and the coming kingdom was made equally emphatic when God spoke to David through the prophet Nathan: 'Your house and your kingdom will endure for ever before me; your throne will be established for ever' (2 Samuel 7:16). Other prophecies added particular details, not the least of these being one which pinpointed the place of the King's birth: 'But you, Bethlehem

Ephrathah, though you are small among the clans of Judah, out of you will come for me one who will be ruler over Israel, whose origins are from old, from ancient times' (Micah 5:2). As the years went by this coming king began to be given the title **Messiah**, which means 'the Anointed One' (Daniel 9:26). The term had previously been used of kings and priests anointed with oil at their inauguration, but it gradually took on special significance; the coming King would be **the** Messiah. Yet even this was not his greatest title. The last of the Old Testament prophets joined with others in telling those eagerly waiting the coming King that '**the Lord** you are seeking will come to his temple' (Malachi 3:1). But when would he come? No precise timing was given, but Isaiah prophesied that he would be preceded by a special messenger sent by God to prepare for the great event: 'A voice of one calling: "In the desert prepare the way for the Lord; make straight in the wilderness a highway for our God"' (Isaiah 40:3). Then, in the last paragraph of the Old Testament, God gave one final clue as to when this would happen: 'See, I will send you the prophet Elijah before that great and dreadful day of the Lord comes' (Malachi 4:5). Immediately before Messiah was revealed, a messenger in the mould of Elijah - austere, uncompromising and dynamic - would appear to announce his imminent arrival. For four hundred years that was God's last word on the subject.

## THE MESSENGER

With this background in place, we can begin to sense something of the stupendous significance of the angel's message to Mary some nine months before she gave birth to Jesus: '"Greetings, you who are highly favoured! The Lord is with you ... you have found favour with God. You will be with child and give birth to a son, and you are to give him the name Jesus. He will be great and will be called the Son of the Most High. The Lord God will give him the throne of his father David, and he will reign over the house of Jacob for ever; his kingdom will never end"' (Luke 1:28,30-33). Although a few people were let into the secret, this was essentially a private message. It was some 30 years later that John the Baptist suddenly burst on the scene with the dramatic public announcement, 'Repent, for the kingdom of heaven is near' (Matthew 3:2).

After four centuries of silence, his words had an electrifying effect and it was not long before the nation's religious authorities sent their agents to ask him who he was. He immediately assured them, 'I am not the Christ' (John 1:20) and when the question was rephrased, 'Are you the Prophet?' (John 1:21), he repeated his denial. The suggestion that he was a reincarnation of Elijah (expected by those who took Malachi's prophecy literally) was also rejected. When finally pressed to give a positive answer, John left no room for doubt: 'I am the voice of one calling in the desert, 'Make straight the way for the Lord' (John 1:23). Nobody with a knowledge of Isaiah's prophecy could misunderstand what John was claiming; he was preparing the way for the promised King, the Messiah. Nor would people have long to wait before the King made himself known and inaugurated his kingdom. When he was asked why he was baptizing people since he was neither Christ, Elijah or the Prophet he replied, 'I baptize with water ... **but among you stands one you do not know.** He is the one who comes after me, the thongs of whose sandals I am not worthy to untie' (John 1:26-27). John could not have been clearer; the Messiah had already been born. The next day John saw Jesus coming towards him and said: 'Look, the Lamb of God, who takes away the sin of the world!' (John 1:29). To the Jewish people, with their knowledge of Old Testament history, and especially of the prophets' message that the coming Messiah would bring a deliverance far beyond that effected by their religion's sacrificial system, this could mean only one thing - John was saying that Jesus was the One of whom the prophets spoke.

## THE KING AND THE KINGDOM

It was not long before Jesus confirmed John's claim. The first recorded words in his public ministry were, 'The time has come ... The kingdom of God is near. Repent and believe the good news!' (Mark 1:15). As he began to travel throughout Galilee he went 'preaching the good news of the kingdom' (Matthew 4:23). When he sent out the twelve disciples, giving them authority to drive out evil spirits and heal every disease and sickness, he specifically told them what the core of their message was to be: 'As you go, preach this message: 'The kingdom of heaven is near' (Matthew 10:7). Some time later, when the Pharisees suggested that he was using satanic power to cast out demons, Jesus showed them the absurdity of Satan working to frustrate his own purposes and added, 'But if I drive out demons by the Spirit of God, then the kingdom of God has come upon you' (Matthew 12:28). Again, the signal was clear. The amazing miracles Jesus was performing at will, in what someone has called 'a wholesale onslaught on the forces of evil', were evidence that the awesome powers of heaven were being unleashed on earth; the long-promised kingdom had come, the King himself was present.

Nor did Jesus leave people in any doubt that he was the very King of whom the Old Testament prophets had spoken. Commenting on his rejection by so many people in spite of the miracles he had performed, he told them, 'But this is to fulfil what is written in their Law: 'They hated me without reason' (John 15:25). When he was arrested, he said that this was taking place 'that the writings of the prophets might be fulfilled' (Matthew 26:56). After his resurrection he assured his bewildered disciples, 'Everything must be fulfilled that is written about me in the Law of Moses, the Prophets and the Psalms' (Luke 24:44). Bible students sometimes speak of certain Old Testament passages as being 'Messianic' because they make clear and specific references to the coming Messiah, but it would be more biblical to say that the whole of the Old Testament is Messianic. Every part of it points forward in one way or another to the One who could say of all the sacred writings, 'These are the Scriptures that testify about me' (John 5:39).

What then was the kingdom Jesus came to inaugurate? It is obviously not identical to the kingdom the Bible has in mind when it refers to God's eternal sovereignty over the entire universe. That kingdom can never be said to have been inaugurated and by definition includes everyone in human history and embraces their eternal destiny (whatever that might be) as well as their earthly life. The kingdom Jesus inaugurated and which is almost always in mind in the New Testament is clearly not universal in the sense that it includes all mankind. In the first place, it is one in which Christ rules not merely as Creator but as the 'mediator of a new covenant' (Hebrews 9:15) on behalf of those for whom he died, those the Bible describes as 'God's chosen people' (Colossians 3:12). The American theologian Louis Berkhof puts it well: 'No one is a citizen of this kingdom in virtue of his humanity. Only the redeemed have that honour and privilege. Christ paid the ransom for those that are his, and by his Spirit applies to them the merits of his perfect sacrifice. Consequently, they now belong to him and recognize him as their Lord and King.'

What is more, and as we shall see more clearly in Chapter 6, Jesus said that the only people who enter it are the 'poor in spirit'. Later in the Sermon on the Mount he emphasized that something much more than outward religious observance is needed: 'For I tell you that unless your righteousness surpasses that of the Pharisees and the teachers of the law, you will certainly not enter the kingdom of heaven' (Matthew 5:20). On another occasion he singled out the need for radical humility: 'I tell you the truth, unless you change and become like little children, you will never enter the kingdom of heaven' (Matthew 18:3). It is clear from these and similar statements elsewhere in the New Testament that when Jesus spoke of the kingdom of heaven he was speaking of a kingdom within a kingdom, what Don Carson has called 'a **subset** of the universal kingdom'. Countless volumes have been written on the subject of the kingdom of God; we can do no more than touch briefly on a few facets here.

**Firstly, it is a supernatural kingdom.** In making this point we can take on board the second question we asked at the beginning of this chapter: Why does Matthew almost always refer to 'the kingdom of heaven' and almost never to 'the kingdom of God'?

The straightforward answer is that Matthew wrote primarily for Jews, many of whom studiously avoided using the word 'God' (which they felt too exalted to be spoken out loud) and often resorted to euphemisms, of which 'heaven' was one. There is a good example of this in the well-known parable of the prodigal son who returned home crying 'Father, I have sinned against heaven and against you' (Luke

15:21). Matthew uses 'heaven' in exactly the same way and British citizens do much the same kind of thing today (though not for the same reason) when they sometimes speak of 'the crown' instead of 'the Queen'.

Our English translation of Matthew's phrase hides an interesting point of emphasis, which is that whenever he used the word rendered 'heaven' it is always plural: he writes of 'the kingdom of the heavens'. The Bible uses the word 'heavens' in three major senses: the envelope of air surrounding the earth, what we now think of as 'outer space' and the immediate dwelling place of God, what the nineteenth-century American scholar James Alexander delightfully calls 'the local residence of God'. The relevant point about all these is that all three are extra-terrestrial. They extend far beyond the earth, literally and metaphorically, and 'the kingdom of the heavens' is one which does not originate on earth, is not earthly in character, does not employ earthly means and has no earthly limitations.

**Secondly, it is a spiritual kingdom.** Old Testament prophecies about the coming kingdom - and King - were often double-barrelled. They had an immediate relevance as well as an ultimate one; they referred to contemporary politics as well as distant future events. Yet as the centuries rolled by, and as their political and economic problems strangled the Jews' spiritual aspirations, they increasingly focused their hopes on the Messiah as an earthly ruler, one who would put an end to their grinding poverty, throw out the occupying forces and restore the nation's former greatness. By the time Jesus appeared on the scene these earthbound ideas had become virtually endemic.

The New Testament gives a vivid illustration of this. Luke tells us that after his resurrection Jesus appeared to the apostles over a period of nearly six weeks 'and spoke about the kingdom of God' (Acts 1:3). Yet in spite of this extended seminar, and all they had seen and heard over the previous three years, including an occasion when Jesus had deliberately turned away from those who 'intended to come and make him king by force' (John 6:15), their minds were still set on one thing: 'Lord, are you at this time going to restore the kingdom to Israel?' (Acts 1:6). They were still looking for a political, territorial, national kingdom - and they wanted it immediately. John Calvin was hardly exaggerating when he suggested, 'There are as many errors in this question as words'! They were so besotted with the idea of an earthly kingdom that neither all that Jesus had said and done, nor his resurrection from the dead, nor the weeks of teaching he had given to them afterwards, could shift them.

Yet at no time had Jesus promised to set up a political empire. As the American preacher Curtis Crenshaw notes, 'An offer of an earthly kingdom that would establish his immediate reign in Jerusalem is not stated or insinuated anywhere in the Gospels.' When questioned by Pontius Pilate as to whether he was king of the Jews, Jesus had replied, 'My kingdom is not of this world ... my kingdom is from another place' (John 18:36). Like the Jews, Pilate could think only in earthly, material, political and geographical terms, and in doing so he shared in their tragic ignorance. Any thinking about the kingdom of God which concentrates only on this world, even that which focuses on the nation of Israel, is not being true to Scripture. The kingdom of God is not spatial but spiritual; its capital is not in Jerusalem but in heaven; it is not a democracy but a theocracy.

**Thirdly, it is an everlasting kingdom.** Historians tell us that the world has known twenty-one major civilizations, all of which flourished for a while and then crumbled away. To take five examples, Egypt, Babylon, Syria, Greece and Rome were all mighty powers, dominating the world's political landscape, yet each in turn disintegrated or dissolved and not one of them is a major player on today's stage. Just a few years ago Soviet Communism threatened to engulf the globe, yet today it is fragmented and discredited. These passing powers are in stark contrast to the kingdom of God. One of the Psalmists says, 'Your throne, O God, will last for ever and ever' (Psalm 45:6) and Peter writes of 'the eternal kingdom of our Lord and Saviour Jesus Christ' (2 Peter 1:11). The American preacher James Montgomery Boice makes the point precisely: 'Human powers rise and fall, but over all this seething about in human history God reigns.'

**Fourthly, it is a contemporary kingdom.** Although telling us that the kingdom of God will not be fully consummated until after the Second

Coming of Christ, the Bible also makes it clear that he inaugurated it at his first coming. When asked by the Pharisees when the kingdom of God would come, he replied, 'The kingdom of God is not coming with signs to be observed; nor will they say, "Look, here it is!" or, "There it is!" For behold, the kingdom of God is in your midst' (Luke 17:20-21, NASB). The Pharisees expected the Messianic kingdom to explode on the scene with a dramatic flourish, but Jesus wanted them to grasp that the kingdom had already come **because he had come**. We dare not miss this point and think of the kingdom of God only in future terms. The kingdom of God is not only 'there and then' it is 'here and now'.

From the upper floor of my house I can see right across the city of London, which is divided by the River Thames. Buckingham Palace, the official residence of the Queen, is on the north side of the river; so is the Palace of Westminster, including the House of Commons and the House of Lords. Yet the same Queen reigns both north and south of the river and the same government rules over both. The river happens to be a geographical dividing line between the two parts of the city, but it is not a division of sovereignty or government. So from a spiritual perspective the river of death runs through the middle of the kingdom of God, with eternity on one side and time on the other, yet God's people are as truly members of his kingdom while living on this side of death's river as they will be when living on the other side.

As we shall see more fully in Chapter 6, those who have abandoned all trust in their own goodness and committed themselves to Christ can rejoice that 'theirs **is** the kingdom of heaven'. Although Christians rightly long for the final consummation of the kingdom and the completion of their salvation, they can rejoice that they are already members of the kingdom and that through the ministry of the Holy Spirit they can continually draw upon its resources as they face the problems and pressures of living 'on this side of the river'.

## CHRISTIAN COUNTER-CULTURE

**Fifthly, it is a dynamic kingdom.** There is a sense in which the word 'kingdom' is misleading because it has so many political and territorial overtones. The Greek word, **basileia**, is primarily abstract and could literally be translated 'dominion', 'sovereignty' or 'rule'. An even better word is 'kingship', which helps us to understand that the King and the kingdom are dynamically integrated. Jesus is the embodiment of the kingdom of God and it is impossible to separate the two or to have one without the other. We read that Philip the apostle preached 'the good news of the kingdom of God and the name of Jesus Christ' (Acts 8:12). When Paul met with visitors day after day during his imprisonment in Rome he 'explained and declared to them the kingdom of God and tried to convince them about Jesus' (Acts 28:23). Again, we are told that for two years 'he preached the kingdom of God and taught about the Lord Jesus Christ' (Acts 28:31). The early church's message was not merely about the kingdom but about the King; the two were inseparable. The kingdom of God is not Christianized society. It is the divine rule in the lives of those who have a living relationship with Christ.

This helps us to realize that entrance into the kingdom involves personal submission to Christ the King. When Jesus invited into the kingdom those who were crushed by the religious rules and regulations imposed by their misguided religious leaders he called them to **himself**: 'Come to me, all you who are weary and burdened, and I will give you rest' (Matthew 11:28). What is more, citizens of the kingdom are sustained and nourished not by slavish obedience to a different set of rules and regulations, but by their dynamic, spiritual union with their Saviour and King.

This is not to say that in the kingdom of God there are no standards or ethical norms. If the Sermon on the Mount was the only surviving part of Jesus' teaching we would still know a great deal of what God requires of his people. The sermon condemns murder, unrighteous anger, an unforgiving spirit, immorality of every kind, lust, divorce, profanity, unfaithfulness, revenge, hypocrisy, pride, formalism, greed, selfishness, faithless anxiety and worldliness; and it commends humility, a contrite spirit, meekness, mercy, good works of every kind, holiness, a peaceable spirit, forgiveness, sexual purity, integrity, forbearance, love, generosity, prayer, discipline and faith. These relate to every area of a person's life, from his inner thoughts to his outward behaviour, from his relationship with God to his dealings with his fellow men. In other words, citizens of God's kingdom are called to a lifestyle which runs counter to the whole moral ethos of the world around them. As John Stott rightly says, 'The followers of Jesus are to be different - different from the nominal church and the secular world, different from both the religious and the irreligious ... And this Christian counter-culture is the life of the kingdom of God, a fully human life indeed but lived out under the divine rule.'

But how is it possible for the Christian to live in this way? Because of his dynamic, spiritual union with the King. Using a brilliant metaphor, Jesus once told his disciples: 'I am the vine; you are the branches' (John 15:5). Left to themselves, Christians would find kingdom living impossible - but they are not left to themselves. Instead, they are united to their Saviour and King, who enables them to live up to the standards he has laid down. J C Ryle, the first Bishop of Liverpool, emphasises this in his **Expository Thoughts on the Gospels**: 'In themselves, believers have no life, or strength, or spiritual power. All that they have of vital religion comes from Christ. They are what they are, and feel what they feel, and do what they do, because they draw out of Jesus a continual supply of grace, help and ability. Joined to the Lord by faith, and united in mysterious union with him by the Spirit, they stand, and walk, and continue, and run the Christian race. But every jot of good about them is drawn from their spiritual head, Jesus Christ.' The reign of Christ in and through the lives of God's people is not static but dynamic. The power which graciously brought them into the kingdom empowers them to live worthy of their calling.

### IN A NUTSHELL ...

Christians live under the gracious kingship of Christ. By the grace of God they have been 'rescued ... from the dominion of darkness and brought ... into the kingdom of the Son he loves' in whom they have 'redemption, the forgiveness of sins' (Colossians 1:13-14). They have received 'eternal life' (John 10:28). They are given privileged insight into 'the secrets of the kingdom of heaven' (Matthew 13:11). They have the honour of reflecting in their lives something of the righteousness which God requires. They are indwelt by the Holy Spirit, through whose ministry they can draw freely on divine resources. They are 'heirs of God and co-heirs with Christ' (Romans 8:17) and they can rejoice in the certainty that when their earthly life is over they will hear the King say, 'Come, you who are blessed by my Father; take your inheritance, the kingdom prepared for you since the creation of the world' (Matthew 25:34).

We are now ready to discover the identity of those who receive the King's favour and to whom these marvellous privileges apply.

# The wealthy poor

'Blessed are the poor in spirit, for theirs is the kingdom
of heaven' (Matthew 5:3).

Generations of Bible expositors have agreed that the Beatitudes
are revolutionary, and it is difficult to find another adjective to
take its place. As someone has said, 'It is as if Jesus crept into the
display window of life and changed all the price tags. It's all backward'.
One need go no further than the opening statement of the Beatitudes to
confirm this. The world says that those who find happiness are the
achievers, those with ambition, drive and thrust; the wealthy, the
popular, the gifted, the enterprising, the assertive, the so-called
'beautiful people', those with a positive image and egos to match. Yet in
a single sentence Jesus turns that whole philosophy upside down and
says that the deep, inner joy which results from knowing God's favour
belongs not to those who give every appearance of being on the top of
the human heap but to the 'poor in spirit'.

In view of what we have already discovered about true blessedness
and the kingdom of God, it is vitally important that we know what
Jesus means. In order to do so, we need to begin by eliminating a
number of misconceptions. Firstly (and this is a major issue with many
serious ramifications) **'poor in spirit' does not mean materially poor**.
Jesus does not say 'Blessed in spirit are the poor'; he does not equate
poverty with spirituality. A person can be as poor as a church mouse,
yet proudly reject the grace of God. Some years ago I was preaching in
northern France and, during my stay there, I was taken to visit some
Algerian mine-workers who were living in conditions so vile as to defy
description. The concrete walls around them and the roof over their
heads certainly provided basic shelter from the elements, but inside the
building, scarcely visible in the semi-darkness, men sat on the floor in
filthy rags, seemingly oblivious to the overpowering stench of sweat

and urine. As best I could, and with the help of an interpreter, I tried to share the gospel with them. When I had finished, one of the men looked at me through rheumy eyes and said, 'We don't need God.' Those men were undoubtedly poor but it would be stretching the imagination beyond breaking point to say that they were 'blessed'. We could go even further and say that, in rejecting the gospel, they were not only forfeiting God's blessing but guaranteeing exactly the opposite. As the nineteenth-century Scottish expositor John Brown rightly commented, 'Extreme poverty is not favourable to religion any more than extreme affluence.'

There are those to whom this kind of reasoning is objectionable, and who seem to imply that poverty is a virtue, but nowhere in Scripture is there any justification for this idea. Those who take a vow of poverty in the belief that by doing so they are obeying the Bible's teaching in general and the principle embodied in this first Beatitude in particular, are missing the whole point of what Jesus meant. There was one occasion when Jesus told a wealthy young man, 'If you want to be perfect, go, sell your possessions and give to the poor, and you will have treasure in heaven' (Matthew 19:21), but the context makes it clear that he did so because he knew that this particular man had become a slave to his possessions and needed to break free if he was to be truly converted. Jesus' diagnosis was immediately confirmed by the potential follower's response: 'When the young man heard this, he went away sad, because he had great wealth' (Matthew 19:22).

The fact is that the Bible neither commends poverty nor condemns wealth. It does not say that money is the root of all evil, but that 'the love of money is a root of all kinds of evil' (1 Timothy 6:10) - something very different. There are many examples in Scripture of people who were both wealthy and godly, and in not one instance were they asked to relinquish their wealth in order to be 'blessed'. Abraham was 'very wealthy in livestock and in silver and gold' (Genesis 13:2), yet elsewhere God refers to him as 'Abraham my friend' (Isaiah 41:8). When King David died, he did so 'having enjoyed long life, wealth and honour' (1 Chronicles 29:28), yet God called him 'a man after my own heart' (Acts 13:22). After Jesus had been crucified, a disciple by the name of Joseph was courageous enough to ask Pilate for his body so that he could place it in his own private tomb, and we are specifically told that Joseph was 'a rich man from Arimathea' (Matthew 27:57).

If material poverty is a qualification for blessing, then surely it would be cruel to give to the poor? Yet time and again the Bible commands and commends generosity to those in need, and even goes so far as to make the issue a test of genuine conversion: 'If anyone has material possessions and sees his brother in need but has no pity on him, how can the love of God be in him?' (1 John 3:17). The notion that 'poor in spirit' means materially poor is without any biblical warrant. As Scottish theologian Sinclair Ferguson rightly says, 'Jesus is speaking about life in the Kingdom of God. The poverty he describes is in a man's spirit, not his pocket.'

## BIAS TO THE POOR?

Another approach to the spiritual implications of material poverty is to say that the poor are blessed by having a special place in God's purposes. When Jesus returned to his local synagogue and was invited to read from the Old Testament Scriptures, he began with Isaiah's words, 'The Spirit of the Lord is on me, because he has anointed me to preach good news to the poor' and when he had completed the entire passage from Isaiah he told those present, 'Today this scripture is fulfilled in your hearing' (Luke 4:18,21). In a booklet written on behalf of the British-based charity TEAR Fund, Roger Forster takes the view that the words 'good news to the poor' refer to dealing with the problem of poverty 'by a total revolution of the standards and structures of society'. In doing so, he gives the words a social, political and economic content, but it is obvious from the whole tenor of the New Testament that this cannot be what Jesus (or Isaiah before him) had in mind. For example, this kind of interpretation raises obvious questions as to what 'good news' is to be offered to the poor as distinct from the gospel to the rich. The relief of their poverty would be commendable, but it would fall far short of bringing them into a right relationship with God. What is more, surely ending their poverty would disqualify them for membership of God's kingdom, or at least reduce the likelihood of them entering it?

In the same booklet, Roger Forster quotes a statement made by the Apostle Paul to the church at Corinth - 'Brothers, think of what you were when you were called. Not many of you were wise by human standards; not many were influential; not many were of noble birth' (1 Corinthians 1:26) - and he then comes to this astonishing conclusion: 'Paul was saying that the poor, the slaves, and the outcasts are in reality the rich, the kings, **the people of God.**' I have emphasized the words that make his interpretation not merely astonishing but absurd. Do we really have any biblical warrant for saying that the poor are **ipso facto** 'the people of God'? The closest Scripture might seem to get is where James asks the rhetorical question, 'Has not God chosen those who are poor in the eyes of the world to be rich in faith and to inherit the kingdom he promised to those who love him?' (James 2:5). However, the meaning of these words comes clearly into focus as soon as we read the very next sentence, 'But you have insulted the poor' (James 2:6). James is condemning the class-conscious attitude of those who despised the poor and wanted nothing to do with those whom they considered to be beneath their station. But in adopting this approach they put them- selves on a collision course with God who in choosing out a people for himself had included many of those who were 'poor in the eyes of the world'. There is no suggestion that God chose **all** the poor, nor did he choose any **because** they were poor (any more than he chose from among the wealthy because they were wealthy). Rather, James is at pains to point out that God chose them **regardless** of their poverty.

Paul makes exactly the same point in saying, 'God does not show favouritism' (Romans 2:11), a statement which directly contradicts the rather trendy modern idea that God has 'a bias to the poor'. Part of the glory of the gospel is that nobody is excluded from its blessings because of their material status. The riches of God's kingdom are neither exclu- sively nor primarily offered to the poor, but are available to all without distinction. The idea that since the poor are denied so many of this world's material possessions they can look forward to eternal riches in heaven has no biblical basis. We dare not let sentiment cloud our understanding of God's salvation. God's concern and compassion for the poor is found all over Scripture, which tells us in no uncertain fashion that those who exploit the poor will one day be brought to account; but the Bible goes on to make it clear that the poor will also be accountable to God on that awful day when he will judge each person who has ever lived, not on the basis of poverty or wealth but 'according to what he has done' (Romans 2:6).

We can actually take this one step further and say that, just as wealth can be dangerous to a person's spiritual health, so also can poverty, a truth which lies behind one of the shrewdest prayers in all Scripture: 'Two things I ask of you, O Lord; do not refuse me before I die: Keep falsehood and lies far from me; give me neither poverty nor riches, but give me only my daily bread. Otherwise, I may have too much and disown you and say, "Who is the Lord?" Or I may become poor and steal, and so dishonour the name of my God.' (Proverbs 30:7-9)

## LIBERATION

We must touch on one other subject arising from the idea that God is biased in favour of the poor, and that is what is sometimes called 'liberation theology'. This seeks support in another phrase Jesus read in his local synagogue, Isaiah's words about being anointed 'to release the oppressed' (Luke 4:18). The thinking of liberation theologians is that God is so strongly on the side of the poor, the disenfranchised and the politically oppressed that Christians are called upon to fight for their cause - literally if need be. Liberation theologians also try to find biblical warrant for their position from the story of God's people groaning under the heavy burden of slavery in Egypt, and lean heavily on the statement that 'God heard their groaning and he remembered his covenant with Abraham, with Isaac and with Jacob' (Exodus 2:24). As God then took punitive action against the Egyptians in order to release his people from their captivity and poverty so, it is argued, should Christians take whatever action is needed, not excluding physical violence, in order to release those who are enslaved in this kind of way. But this idea ignores man's basic need and evacuates the gospel of its significance. As the Scottish theologian Bruce Milne says, 'The human predicament cannot be reduced to social and political alienation.'

The fact that Jesus chose as one of his earliest disciples a man called 'Simon the Zealot' (Matthew 10:4) is further grist to the liberationist mill. The Zealots were militant reactionaries, notorious for stirring up violent rebellion against the occupying Roman forces, and some liberation theologians would have us believe that Jesus chose Simon in order to put some aggressive militancy into the other disciples and encourage them to fight for their freedom. They also promote the idea that in allowing himself to be crucified Jesus set us an example of suffering a violent death in the revolutionary cause of liberation.

These ideas are easily countered. When Jesus was arrested in the Garden of Gethsemane, one of the disciples drew his sword and cut off the ear of the servant of the high priest. Here was an ideal, high-profile opportunity to endorse militant liberation theology, but Jesus responded very differently: 'Put your sword back in its place, for all who draw the sword will die by the sword. Do you think I cannot call on my Father, and he will at once put at my disposal more than twelve legions of angels?' (Matthew 26:52-53). In refusing to avail himself of resources infinitely more effective than a servant's sword, even in the face of blatant injustice, Jesus showed himself not as the patron of liberation theology but as the 'Prince of Peace' (Isaiah 9:6).

Ministering to the needy is a responsibility to which the Christian church has responded more fully than any other grouping in human history. In his superb book **Issues Facing Christians Today**, John Stott illustrates some of the ways in which it has done so: 'Motivated by love for human beings in need, the early Christians went everywhere preaching the Word of God, because nothing has such a humanizing influence as the gospel. Later they founded schools, hospitals and refuges for the outcast. Later still they abolished the slave trade and freed the slaves, and they improved the conditions of workers in mills and mines, and of prisoners in gaols. They protected children from commercial exploitation in the factories of the West and from ritual prostitution in the temples of the East. Today they bring leprosy sufferers both the compassion of Jesus and modern methods of reconstructive surgery and rehabilitation. They care for the blind and the deaf, the orphaned and the widowed, the sick and the dying. They get alongside junkies, and stay alongside them during the traumatic period of withdrawal. They set themselves against racism and political oppression. They get involved in the urban scene, the inner city, the slums and the ghettoes, and raise their protest against the inhuman conditions in which so many are doomed to live. They seek in whatever way they can to express their solidarity with the poor and hungry, the deprived and the disadvantaged. I am not claiming that all Christians at all times have given their lives in such service. But a sufficiently large number have done so to make their record noteworthy.'

God clearly has a concern for the poor and the disadvantaged and in recent years many organizations such as Tear Fund and ECHO have reflected this in their far-reaching activities. But in the genuine concern Christians should have, not merely to share the gospel but help in meeting the clamouring social needs all around them, they must avoid identifying the one with the other and embracing the tenets of the so-called 'social gospel' which were developed by liberal theologians in the early part of the twentieth century. Building on the optimistic view of man which had been growing for some time, and relating this to material progress in the Western world, they taught that society could be improved by institutional change. That being the case, the church's major task was not to preach the need for individual, spiritual salvation (which some lampooned as 'pie in the sky when you die') but to join hands with the working class to transform the social order. These ideas have attracted a great deal of support, but they have no scriptural basis.

## FALSE TRAILS

Having explored some of the ramifications which follow from the false assumption that 'poor in spirit' means materially poor, we can turn to take a much briefer look at some other wrong interpretations of the phrase.

**'Poor in spirit' does not mean 'mean-spirited'.** Careful stewardship of one's resources is strongly commended in Scripture, but its teaching goes beyond that. It specifically condemns miserliness and commends generosity. One particular statement combines both principles: 'He who gives to the poor will lack nothing, but he who closes his eyes to them receives many curses' (Proverbs 28:27). The nineteenth-century British preacher Samuel Chadwick used to say, 'A tight fist means a shrivelled soul', and his statement can be read two ways: a tight fist results in the shrivelling of a person's soul; and the person with a shrivelled soul will have a tight fist. Either way, the person who does not reflect God's kindness to him by seeking to help those in need can hardly look to God for his blessing. The benevolent person, on the other hand, has the biblical assurance that 'A generous man will prosper; he who refreshes others will himself be refreshed' (Proverbs 11:25).

**'Poor in spirit' does not mean 'intellectually poor'.** The popular saying 'Ignorance is bliss' is more trivial than truthful. It is impossible to calculate the pain, sorrow, deprivation and evil that have resulted from people's ignorance of important facts or principles. The Bible knows nothing of the vacuous notion that people are 'better off not knowing'. Instead, it takes exactly the opposite line: 'Blessed is the man who finds wisdom, the man who gains understanding' (Proverbs 3:13). That being the case, it is hardly surprising to find the same writer urging his readers, 'Get wisdom, get understanding' (Proverbs 4:5); 'Buy the truth and do not sell it; get wisdom, discipline and understanding' (Proverbs 23:23). It is clear from Scripture that many enter the kingdom without outstanding intellectual qualifications, yet equally clear that none do so because of their deficiencies.

**Poor in spirit' does not mean having a poor self-image.** It is obviously wrong to brag about one's appearance, abilities or achievements, but it is equally sinful to go to the other extreme and to feel insignificant, hopeless and without value to God or to anyone else. This kind of thinking is not far removed from the verdict of the French existentialist Jean-Paul Sartre that man was 'a useless passion', or from the pathetic philosophy of secular humanism which says that man began as an accident and will end in annihilation. This is all vastly different from the Bible's assertion that uniquely among earth's living creatures man was 'made in God's likeness' (James 3:9). God has invested every human being on earth with a unique dignity which even his depravity has not erased. Man still has what the eighteenth-century preacher John Wesley called 'an indelible nobleness, which we ought to reverence in ourselves and others'. To deny this can hardly be pleasing to our Creator or be likely to lay hold of the blessing which comes to those who are 'poor in spirit'.

**'Poor in spirit' does not mean natural diffidence.** The key word here is 'natural', which speaks of a person's emotional constitution and has nothing to do with spirituality, nor even with religion in its most general terms. If it is nonsense to suggest that a person must be gregarious, assertive, self-assured, confident and pushy in order to know God's blessing - Paul reminded the church at Corinth that he had come to them 'in weakness and fear, and with much trembling' (1 Corinthians 2:3) - it is equally wrong to assume that the blessing promised in this first Beatitude is guaranteed to those who are shy and retiring by nature. Nobody is born 'poor in spirit'. We will never come to a right understanding of what Jesus is saying in the Beatitudes if we begin by confusing genetics with grace.

**'Poor in spirit' does not mean 'false humility'.** When people deny that they have particular gifts or that they have achieved anything praiseworthy, they are sometimes fishing for compliments, angling for someone to disagree and to commend them. In cases like this what seems like humility is nothing more than hypocrisy; it is certainly not being 'poor in spirit'. Others claim that they have no particular gifts or abilities in order to evade responsibility. Again, this may sometimes seem commendable, but it implies an oblique criticism of God; it is a veiled suggestion that he has been less than fair in the distribution of gifts. The New Testament's assumption is that nobody is deprived in this way: 'Each one should use whatever gift he has received to serve others, faithfully administering God's grace in its various forms' (1 Peter 4:10).

In his book **The Song of the Virgin** the Greek theologian Spiros Zodhiates has some trenchant comments on this: 'If you are leading a useless life, you are not being humble, you are just plain lazy ... Many a man, while seriously believing that he was exercising an acceptable humility, has buried his talents in the earth, hidden his light under a bushel, lived a useless life, when he might have been a blessing to many ... Our humility serves us falsely when it leads us to shrink from any duty. The plea of unfitness or inability is utterly insufficient to excuse us ... Your talent may be very small, so small that it scarcely seems to matter whether you use it or not, so far as its impression on the world or on other lives is concerned. Yet no one can know what is small and what is great in this life, in which every cause starts consequences that reach into eternity.' To adopt a false humility, for whatever reason, is a long way from what Jesus meant when he spoke of those who are 'poor in spirit'.

## THE INNER MAN

Having eliminated some common misconceptions of what it means to be 'poor in spirit' we can now take a positive look at the subject. The first thing we must do is to discover what Jesus meant by 'spirit'. The original Greek word is **pneuma**, and in the sense in which it is used here W E Vine defines it as 'the sentient element in man, that by which he perceives, reflects, feels, desires'. We can find ample New Testament warrant for each of these shades of meaning. Faced with the seething resentment of religious opponents, 'Jesus knew in his spirit ... what they were thinking in their hearts' (Mark 2:8); here, the reference is clearly to a sense of awareness and perception. Writing to the church at Colosse, Paul assures them, 'For though I am absent from you in body, I am present with you in spirit' (Colossians 2:5); here the emphasis is on reflection. When Mary was assured of the forthcoming birth of Jesus she cried out, 'My soul glorifies the Lord and my spirit rejoices in God my Saviour' (Luke 1: 46-47); here the emotions are engaged in an act of worship. Gently reprimanding his exhausted disciples in the Garden of Gethsemane, Jesus sympathetically admitted 'The spirit is willing, but the body is weak' (Matthew 26:41); here, the emphasis is on desire.

If we pull all of these together we see that the human spirit is everything we mean by phrases such as 'the inner man'. A person's spirit is not what we see when we assess his material worth, social standing, outward performance or intellectual capacity. It is what we would see if we could take a spiritual X-ray of the individual concerned. It is a person's true spiritual character. It is what is seen when 'the Lord looks at the heart' (1 Samuel 16:7). There is considerable overlapping of meaning in the Bible's references to the human spirit, but perhaps the best summing-up in our present context comes in a telling Old Testament statement: 'The lamp of the Lord searches the spirit of a man; it searches out **his inmost being'** (Proverbs 20:27).

## HOW POOR IS POOR?

Having seen that 'spirit' means 'inmost being', we can now ask the crucial question: 'What does it mean to be '**poor** in spirit'? There are several Greek words translated 'poor' in our English New Testament, this particular one being **ptochos**, which occurs over 30 times. Depending on its context, it covers a wide range of economic circumstances, but its basic meaning can be seen from the fact that it derives from the verb **ptosso**, which means to crouch or cower like a beggar. This particular emphasis comes across in a parable Jesus told in which a wealthy man prepared a great banquet and, after several people had declined his invitation, told his servants to go out into the town 'and bring in the **poor**, the crippled, the blind and the lame' (Luke 14:21).

The same root lies behind a word used by Jesus in the story of a man living in the lap of luxury while just outside his gate lay 'a **beggar** named Lazarus, covered with sores and longing to eat what fell from the rich man's table' (Luke 16:20-21). Again, when Jesus healed a blind man, his neighbours remembered that they 'had formerly seen him **begging**' (John 9:8). These were not people in the lower income bracket, hardly earning enough to make ends meet. They were in a state of abject poverty. They were utterly destitute and completely dependent on the goodwill of others if they were not to shrivel up and die as they lay in their rotting rags. These are powerful images, yet they reflect exactly what Jesus had in mind when he spoke of spiritual poverty. I know of no expositor who has given a finer explanation of what is meant by being 'poor in spirit' than John Brown, who wrote of such a person: 'He knows himself to be an entirely dependent being; he knows himself to be an inexcusable sinner; he knows himself to be a righteously condemned criminal; he knows that "in him, that is, in his flesh, dwells no good thing"; he knows that he has, that he can have, no hope, but in the sovereign mercy of God; that he has no righteousness to glory in, but the obedience unto death of the Son of God; and that whatever is right and holy in his sentiments and character is owing entirely to the influence of the Spirit of God; and the knowledge and faith of all this naturally produces deep, habitual abasement of spirit. He feels himself "dust and ashes", guilty dust and ashes.'

One of the clearest illustrations of this acknowledgement of spiritual bankruptcy comes in a story Jesus told of two men who went up to the temple in Jerusalem to pray. One was a Pharisee, a member of the most important religious group in the country. The other was one of many tax collectors of that time, despised not only because they collected hated polls on behalf of the ruling Romans but because of their deserved reputation for extortion. The Pharisee stood (almost certainly in a prominent place) and paraded his virtues: 'God, I thank you that I am not like other men - robbers, evildoers, adulterers - or even like this tax collector. I fast twice a week and give a tenth of all I get' (Luke 18:11,12). Not much poverty of spirit there! The tax collector behaved very differently. Standing at a distance, and not even daring to look up, he 'beat his breast and said, "God, have mercy on me, a sinner"' (Luke 18:13). By inserting the indefinite article, most of our English translations unfortunately blur the important point that the tax collector referred to himself not as 'a sinner' but as 'sinner' (in the sense of '**the** sinner'). He did not think of himself as one sinner among many, but as if he were the only one. He was so overwhelmed with the sense of his sin, his moral bankruptcy and his spiritual destitution that, as far as he was concerned, anyone else's sin paled into insignificance by comparison. In other words, he was 'poor in spirit', with the result that, exactly in line with the text we are studying, he received the greatest blessing that could ever be bestowed on anyone - he entered the kingdom of heaven or, as Jesus put it, he 'went home justified before God' (Luke 18:14).

Wherever we look in Scripture, an acknowledgement of spiritual bankruptcy is seen as the first step towards getting right with God. God's promise of salvation is not to the wealthy, the talented or the educated, nor to the respectable or religious, but to those who acknowledge that they are utterly without spiritual merit or ability. David writes, 'The Lord is close to the broken-hearted and saves those who are crushed in spirit' (Psalm 34:18). God tells Isaiah, 'I live in a high and holy place, but also with him who is contrite and lowly in spirit, to revive the spirit of the lowly and to revive the heart of the contrite' (Isaiah 57:15); and again, 'This is the one I esteem: he who is humble and contrite in spirit, and trembles at my word' (Isaiah 66:2). There is no room here for pretence, hypocrisy or reservation, nor for trying to combine some measure of humility with a lingering trust in religious observance, moral merit, respectability, or good deeds of any kind. These must all be rejected as utterly without any saving merit. As Thomas Watson rightly puts it: 'Poverty of spirit is a kind of self-annihilation.' The only way to get right with God is to abandon every iota of trust in anything else and to fling oneself instead on God's loving mercy as expressed in Augustus Montague Toplady's well-known hymn 'Rock of Ages':

> Nothing in my hand I bring,
> Simply to thy cross I cling;
> Naked, come to thee for dress;
> Helpless, look to thee for grace;
> Foul, I to the fountain fly;
> Wash me, Saviour, or I die.

The person who is seriously concerned about his relationship with God can never make any headway until he has honestly faced up to questions like these: Am I genuinely poor in spirit? Do I acknowledge that by nature I am a guilty, vile, godless wretch, utterly without merit and deserving God's righteous anger and judgment? Do I accept that none of my religion, respectability or moral efforts can make the smallest contribution to my salvation? Am I determined to turn from putting even the slightest trust in any of them? Am I prepared to trust in Christ and in him alone for my salvation? The nineteenth-century

English preacher C H Spurgeon points such a person in the right direction: 'Learn this lesson - not to trust Christ because you repent, but trust Christ to make you repent; not to come to Christ because you have a broken heart, but to come to him that he may give you a broken heart; not to come to him because you are fit, but to come to him because you are unfit to come. Your fitness is your unfitness. Your qualification is your lack of qualification.'

## ASHES TO RICHES

Just as the Bible insists on the importance of poverty of spirit, so it is full of assurances about the blessings that follow. Thomas Watson's statement, 'Poverty of spirit paves a causeway of blessedness' is borne out time and again: 'Though the Lord is on high, he looks upon the lowly, but the proud he knows from afar' (Psalm 138:6); 'A man's pride brings him low, but a man of lowly spirit gains honour' (Proverbs 29:23); 'God opposes the proud but gives grace to the humble' (James 4:6). These biblical promises can all be summed up in the principle Jesus laid down at the end of his parable about the Pharisee and the tax collector: 'For everyone who exalts himself will be humbled, and he who humbles himself will be exalted' (Luke 18:14).

In this first Beatitude, the promise given to the poor in spirit could not be clearer or greater: 'theirs is the kingdom of heaven.' We looked at the meaning of 'the kingdom of heaven' in a previous chapter; here, we need to pay close attention to the words '**theirs is**', because each has an important lesson to teach us. In the original text the word 'theirs' is an emphatic personal pronoun. If we were writing the phrase from scratch, rather than translating it from another language, we could indicate its force by underlining it or putting it in italics. The point it makes is not merely that the kingdom of heaven is promised to all those who are poor in spirit but that it is promised **only** to them. If the Beatitudes show us facets of genuine Christian character, the distinguishing marks of those who are in the kingdom of heaven, then poverty of spirit is the foundation stone of all the rest. Those who are not poor in spirit are not in the kingdom of heaven, even if their lives seem to show an occasional flicker of the graces mentioned in the other Beatitudes. 'Theirs and theirs alone' is what Jesus meant. It is therefore both a promise and a warning; a promise to those who have reached the end of their own resources and become beggars instead of braggarts, and a warning to those who cling to the hope that they can earn their way into God's favour or retain his blessing by their own unaided efforts. Everybody who is poor in spirit is in the kingdom of heaven. Nobody is in the kingdom of heaven who is not poor in spirit.

The importance of the verb 'is' lies in the fact of its present tense. For the poor in spirit the kingdom of heaven is not the hope of 'pie in the sky when you die', but something which is theirs here and now. As we saw earlier, while the kingdom of heaven extends to eternity, it is already manifested here on earth. The Bible teaches the same thing with regard to what it calls 'eternal life'. Jesus once promised that those who forsook the things of this world in the cause of the gospel would receive certain blessings here on earth, 'and in the age to come, eternal life' (Mark 10:30). But that does not mean that whenever the Bible speaks about eternal life it is referring to the future. Jesus made it clear that 'whoever believes in the Son **has** eternal life' (John 3:36) and John assured his readers, 'God **has given us** eternal life, and this life is in his Son' (1 John 5:11).

When visiting old churches I sometimes take time to read plaques commemorating local worthies from previous generations. These often give details of life and service and often add a final date preceded by the words, 'Entered into eternal life'. Almost certainly the date is wrong, because it refers to the date of death whereas (assuming the person concerned was a Christian) he had entered into eternal life on the day he was born again. Here in the Beatitudes Jesus is saying the same kind of thing about the Christian's membership of the kingdom of heaven. It is something that is entered into here and now, something to be possessed and enjoyed not merely in the future but in the present. As Paul puts it, God has 'rescued us from the dominion of darkness and brought us into the kingdom of the Son he loves' (Colossians 1:13). Elsewhere he says that 'our citizenship is in heaven' (Philippians 3:20). Christians are not children of earth trying to get to heaven, they are children of heaven making their way home, where they will enter into the sinless, deathless, endless, glorious fulness of all that their heavenly Father has in store for them, a kingdom prepared 'since the creation of the world' (Matthew 25:34). No wonder Jesus calls them 'blessed'!

# Chapter 7

# The joyful mourners

'Blessed are those who mourn, for they will be comforted' (Matthew 5:4).

We began the previous chapter by agreeing with the common assessment that the Beatitudes are revolutionary. One dictionary definition of 'revolutionary' is 'causing a revolution in a government or social system' and, while we saw earlier that the Sermon on the Mount was not a political statement, there is no disputing the fact that the Beatitudes are among the most radical and revolutionary statements in Scripture.

The point is highlighted when we think of the two key words in the sentence now before us - 'blessed' and 'mourn'. A superficial glance suggests they are poles apart. How can there possibly be any connection between mourning and being blessed? If 'blessed' merely means 'happy' in the usual sense of the word, the sentence is a nonsense, a contradiction in terms, suggesting that one can be gleeful and gloomy at one and the same time. Even if we avoid that mistake, the apparent contradiction remains. In a previous chapter we saw that to be 'blessed' was not to have some superficial emotional experience but to know God's favour in a marked way. We also saw that the assurance of knowing God's favour produces a deep, lasting, spiritual joy - which brings us right back to the eye-opening paradox we seem to have here. How can an assurance of God's unmerited favour, and the profound joy which it brings, have any connection with mourning, let alone bring it about?

## A RIGHT TO HAPPINESS?

A number of years ago, while preaching in Greece, I went to the port of Piraeus to watch a 'Blessing of the Sea' ceremony held by the Greek

Orthodox Church to celebrate the baptism of Jesus. At one point I got into conversation with two young Indian Muslims who asked me what the ceremony meant. Having told them that it had no biblical basis, I went on to share the gospel with them and to express something of the great joy there was in being a Christian. One of them reacted very strongly, and said that nobody had the right to be happy in a world where there was so much suffering. That sounds perfectly reasonable and responsible, especially when today's electronic media can bring the world's tragedies to our attention so quickly and in such graphic detail.

As I was preparing a sermon on this very text in December 1988 the world was shocked by the news of an appalling earthquake in Soviet Armenia, in which tens of thousands of people were crushed to death. Soon afterwards a transatlantic jet was blown up by terrorists over the little town of Lockerbie in the south-west of Scotland, and 250 people were hurled into eternity. A few days after that a train crashed on the outskirts of London and many more were killed. Within days a domestic flight ploughed into the M1 Motorway just three miles from where I was standing at the time, and another 40 people perished. For weeks on end our television screens and newspapers were filled with the images of grief etched on the faces of those whose loved ones had been wrenched from them, not at the expected end of a long process of illness and deterioration but suddenly and savagely. At times like these the words 'blessed' and 'mourn' seem light years apart and totally irreconcilable. Yet here they are, brought together by Jesus in a studied statement that seems to turn the world's logic on its head.

The world says that those with cause to be happy are the prosperous, the successful, those for whom the sky is always blue and who seem to know nothing of the problems and burdens, pressures, heartaches and tears with which those less fortunate are sadly familiar. Life, we are told, is all about having a good time. Entertainment is king and the amount of time, energy, money and enthusiasm spent on it is testimony to the fact. As Don Carson comments: 'The world does not like mourners; mourners are wet blankets.' Yet Jesus says that those who mourn are those who know God's blessing. In the Sermon on the Plain he went even further and added a chilling warning to those who made happiness the be-all and end-all of life: 'Woe to you who laugh now, for you will mourn and weep' (Luke 6:25). There is clearly some unravelling to be done here!

The first step in the process seems to make matters even worse, because the verb 'to mourn' - **pentheo** - is the strongest word for mourning in the Greek language, one that would be used when describing the desolation felt by someone mourning the death of a loved one. When Jacob was tricked into believing that his son Joseph had been killed, he 'tore his clothes, put on sackcloth and mourned for his son many days' (Genesis 37:34), and in the Septuagint, the first Greek version of the Old Testament, the verb **pentheo** is the one used for 'mourned'. Later, when Jacob himself died, 'the Egyptians mourned for him seventy days' (Genesis 50:3) and again **pentheo** is the word the Septuagint uses. There is an equally telling illustration in the New Testament. When Jesus rose from the dead and appeared to Mary Magdalene, she immediately went and broke the news to those 'who were mourning and weeping' (Mark 16:10), and once again the word is **pentheo**. These illustrations show that we cannot soften the impact of what Jesus said by toning down the force of the word he used. The mourning of which he spoke is not a touch of sadness, but deep, heartfelt grief.

## GRIEF AND GLORY

There is one application of this particular Beatitude which obviously makes sense, and that is if we think of it as referring to the suffering which Christians endure in this world and of the consolation that will be theirs in the next. Writing to his fellow believers in Rome, Paul rejoiced in the assurance of his standing in Christ, then added, 'Not only so, but we also rejoice in our sufferings, because we know that suffering produces perseverance; perseverance character; and character, hope' (Romans 5:3-4). Later in the same letter he wrote that suffering here on earth for the sake of Christ meant that believers would also 'share in his glory' and that such suffering was 'not worth comparing with the glory that will be revealed in us' (Romans 8:17-18).

Elsewhere, he was even more explicit: 'For our light and momentary troubles are achieving for us an eternal glory that far outweighs them all. So we fix our eyes not on what is seen, but on what is unseen. For what is seen is temporary, but what is unseen is eternal' (2 Corinthians 4:17-18).

Writing on a current issue of his time, John Calvin commented, 'A moment is long if we look at the things round us; but once we have raised our minds to heaven, a thousand years begin to be like a moment.' This is certainly one way in which this Beatitude can be seen to be true. Those who mourn, in the sense of enduring pressure, persecution, violent opposition and even martyrdom for the cause of Christ, will be comforted in the life to come. There is even a case for saying that the greater the cause for their mourning here, the greater will be their cause for rejoicing there, when, as William Hendriksen puts it, 'It will become a matter of public knowledge how much God loves them and how richly he rewards them.'

These things are wonderfully true, and there are elements here that run parallel to what Jesus is saying in the Beatitude we are studying. These elements come into clearer focus in the last of the Beatitudes, when those persecuted for the Saviour's sake are promised 'great is your reward in heaven' (Matthew 5:12). However, in the Beatitude we are presently studying the primary thrust is in a different direction altogether.

## MOURNING AND MOURNING

It is perfectly obvious that when Jesus spoke of 'those who mourn' he was not referring to all human grief, because we know from both Scripture and experience that there are many instances where mourning does not bring about God's blessing and comfort. There is mourning and mourning, and we need to be sure that we identify the one Jesus had in mind.

**Firstly, there is natural mourning.** The most obvious example of this is at the death of a loved one, with its familiar images of coffin and wreaths and the silent line of family and friends. Nowhere is human mourning more clearly focused, but do we also find the blessing promised in this Beatitude? Can we confidently assure all those attending a funeral of God's blessing, consolation and comfort, regardless of their spiritual status or that of the one whose loss they mourn? There is no biblical pledge of blessedness whenever death strikes. It is no exaggeration to say that on almost every occasion when the Beatitude we are studying is quoted at a funeral it is being taken out of context and used out of place.

If we include within the secular definition of mourning a broader range of sorrow and sadness, it is by no means limited to funerals. We mourn when we fail an examination, miss our connection at an airport or railway station, lose an important game, forget an appointment, choose the slowest lane in a queue or hit all the red traffic lights when on a tight schedule. Where is the blessedness in any of these things? Having experienced every one of them, I can ask the question with some feeling! Natural mourning is clearly not what Jesus meant.

**Secondly, there is sinful mourning.** The Bible provides us with numerous examples of this. After Cain had murdered his brother Abel, God banished him to the desert, where he was to be a restless fugitive. What was Cain's response? 'Cain said to the Lord, "My punishment is more than I can bear. Today you are driving me from the land, and I will be hidden from your presence; I will be a restless wanderer on the earth, and whoever finds me will kill me"' (Genesis 4:13-14). Notice that Cain was far more concerned about his sentence than about his sin. Guilty of the senseless slaughter of his brother, his mourning was totally self-centred, focused entirely on the suffering he would now have to face. He was overwhelmed with sorrow, but certainly not the kind that brings about the blessing of God.

When David's son Amnon developed an unholy passion for his half-sister Tamar, but realized that it was illegal for him to marry her, he 'became frustrated to the point of illness' (2 Samuel 13:2), yet his grief was carnal, not spiritual, and after tricking her into his bedroom he satisfied his lust by raping her. Two years later, having shown no signs of regret for what he had done, he was killed on the instructions of Tamar's brother Absalom. In Amnon's case his mourning was utterly without grace and equally without blessing.

The godless king Ahab provides another example of sinful mourning. Ahab coveted his neighbour's vineyard but, when the owner, Naboth, refused his offer of an exchange of property because of a long-standing religious law, the king 'lay on his bed sulking and refused to eat' (1 Kings 21:4). Frustrated at not being able to get his own way, and furious at having his pride hurt, he connived at his wife Jezebel's plan to have Naboth executed and then took what he wanted. Ahab had certainly mourned, but there was no way in which his covetous grief could lead to God's blessing and comfort. Far from being comforted, he was cursed; the prophet Elijah brought him news of God's judgment on his sin and a few years later Ahab was killed in battle.

In the New Testament, Judas Iscariot is another example of mourning that fell short of that which God seeks, even though there might at first glance seem to be some positive elements associated with what he did: 'When Judas, who had betrayed him, saw that Jesus was condemned, he was seized with remorse and returned the thirty silver coins to the chief priests and the elders. "I have sinned," he said, "for I have betrayed innocent blood." "What is that to us?" they replied. "That's your responsibility." So Judas threw the money into the temple and left. Then he went away and hanged himself' (Matthew 27:3-5). Judas openly acknowledged his sin and even made restitution of the blood money, but it seems clear that he was motivated by fear rather than by anything else, because he never sought forgiveness. Instead, his self-reproach led to a despair which left no room for God's forgiving grace. Whatever emotions may have racked Judas' heart, his was not 'repentance unto life' (Acts 11:18).

Commenting on Judas' case, J C Ryle underlines the warning it contains: 'It is possible for a man to feel his sins, and be sorry for them, to be under strong convictions of guilt, and express deep remorse, to be pricked in conscience, and exhibit much distress of mind, and yet, for all this, not repent with his heart. Present danger, or the fear of death, may account for all his feelings, and the Holy Ghost may have done no work whatever in his soul.' Nobody who reads these words should take them lightly, because they point up the need for careful, honest questions. Am I sure that my sorrow for sin is genuine? Am I grieved at my sin and not just at its consequences? Has my sorrow led me to heartfelt repentance? Have I humbly turned to God for forgiveness and cleansing?

## THE REAL THING

**Thirdly, there is spiritual mourning.** Contrasting this with natural and sinful mourning, Paul says, 'Godly sorrow brings repentance that leads to salvation and leaves no regret, but worldly sorrow brings death' (2 Corinthians 7:10). Cain, Amnon, Ahab and Judas all exhibited 'worldly sorrow', what the nineteenth-century American theologian Charles Hodge called 'the sorrow of unrenewed men, the sorrow of the unsanctified heart' - and in every case the results were not merely negative but disastrous. By contrast, godly sorrow is not a natural characteristic, nor a quality that man can produce. It is something God graciously works in the hearts of his people through the ministry of the Holy Spirit - and it always leads to positive, life-giving results. Nobody ever regrets godly, spiritual sorrow; instead, he rejoices at God's gracious dealings with him and at the blessing he receives at his hand.

In an earlier chapter we saw that the Beatitudes are not electives from which we are invited to choose those that appeal to us. The characteristics we see here are those to be found in all of God's people. They form a mosaic of the Christian's character, and are all blended together in those who have come under the gracious kingship of Christ. At this point, we can see that there is a clear and close link between the first and second Beatitude. To be 'poor in spirit' is to be convicted of one's sin, whereas to 'mourn' is to be contrite for it. Thomas Watson joined conviction and contrition together when he wrote, 'Sin must have tears', and these tears must flow before a person can enter the kingdom of God. Only those who have been humbled, wounded and broken under the crushing burden of their sin can ever know God's saving grace. As David wrote at a time of great personal crisis, 'The Lord is close to the brokenhearted and saves those who are crushed in spirit' (Psalm 34:18).

Mourning for sin, though varying in intensity, has always been a feature of true conversion to Christ, and few have expressed it more movingly than David Brainerd, a pioneer missionary to the North American Indians who died in 1747 at the age of 29. His journal, in which he wrote page after page of his terrible conviction of sin before he was converted, has become a missionary classic. One extract reads as follows: 'One night I remember in particular, when I was walking solitarily abroad, I had opened to me such a view of my sin that I feared the ground would cleave asunder under my feet, and become my grave, and send my soul quick to hell before I could get home. Though I was forced to go to bed, lest my distress should be discovered by others, which I much feared, yet I scarcely dared sleep at all, for I thought it would be a great wonder if I should be out of hell in the morning.'

Those words were written about 250 years ago, but they are a million light years away from much of what we so often see in Christian circles today. Where is the preaching likely to produce this kind of conviction? Where is the power and authority that hammers at the hearts and consciences of sinners? Where is the solemn submission to God's Word? Where are the tears of conviction, the sobs and cries of those who realize that outside of Christ they are as certain to spend eternity in hell as if they were already there? Instead, the words of the American preacher A W Tozer ring tragically true: 'In the majority of our meetings there is scarcely a trace of reverent thought, no recognition of the unity of the body, little sense of the divine presence, no moment of stillness, no wonder, no holy fear ... The whole Christian family stands desperately in need of a restoration of penitence, humility and tears.'

But what is the source of this blessedness which Jesus links to spiritual mourning, true contrition, the agony of spirit that produces inward and sometimes outward tears? It lies in the biblical assurance that God will respond in salvation. False conviction leads to agonies of doubt and uncertainty. It also leads to false conversion, which is no more than a religious milestone on the road to hell, where there will be endless 'weeping and gnashing of teeth' (Matthew 8:12). True conviction of sin leads to true repentance and faith, and the joy of release from the guilt and grip of sin. This is beautifully expressed in the prophecy of Isaiah, from which Jesus read in his local synagogue in Nazareth: 'The Spirit of the Sovereign Lord is on me, because the Lord has anointed me to preach good news to the poor. He has sent me to bind up the broken hearted ... to comfort all who mourn, and provide for those who grieve in Zion - to bestow on them a crown of beauty instead of ashes, the oil of gladness instead of mourning, and a garment of praise instead of a spirit of despair' (Isaiah 61:1-3). What greater blessing could anyone know than the assurance that God has graciously forgiven his sin and granted him a place of eternal security in his kingdom?   David's testimony expresses it perfectly: 'I waited patiently for the Lord; he turned to me and heard my cry. He lifted me out of the slimy pit, out of the mud and mire; he set my feet on a rock and gave me a firm place to stand. He put a new song in my mouth, a hymn of praise to our God' (Psalm 40:1-3). Every Christian's conversion is a glorious outworking of Jesus' words: 'Blessed are those who mourn, for they shall be comforted.'

## THE GRIEF OF THE GODLY

Yet the Christian's mourning that leads to conversion and the blessing of God that follows it lead to other experiences of the same gracious chemistry at work in the soul of the believer. In this particular Beatitude Matthew's word 'mourn' is a present active participle; we could literally translate the beginning of the sentence, 'Blessed are the mourning ...' or 'Blessed are those who are continuing to mourn ...' A participle is a verbal adjective. Jesus is pronouncing a blessing on those who are characterized by mourning. He does not mean those who are naturally negative, have a poor self-image, and who are constantly seeing the blackest side of things, but those who hearts have been so tenderized by the Holy Spirit that they grieve whenever sin raises its ugly, God-dishonouring head.

Here again we see something of the way in which Christ's teaching cuts across the wisdom of our age and the philosophy of much that passes for mainstream Christianity today. As John Stott rightly observes, 'Some Christians seem to imagine that, especially if they are filled with the Spirit, they must wear a perpetual grin on their face and be continually boisterous and bubbly. How unbiblical can one become?' He may well ask. This light-hearted attitude is in striking contrast to what we read in Scripture, where God's people are so often seen to be characterized by an acute awareness of their own unworthiness. In the Old Testament, David is a good example: 'My guilt has overwhelmed me like a burden too heavy to bear' (Psalm 38:4); 'I confess my iniquity; I am troubled by my sin' (Psalm 38:18); 'For I know my transgressions, and my sin is always before me' (Psalm 51:3). Others were equally distraught as they realized their spiritual condition. Abraham confessed, 'I am nothing but dust and ashes' (Genesis 18:27). When Isaiah had a vision of 'the Lord seated on a throne, high and exalted', with such dazzling glory that even even the angels covered their faces as they worshipped him, he cried out, 'Woe to me! I am ruined! For I am a man of unclean lips, and I live among a people of unclean lips, and my eyes have seen the King, the Lord Almighty' (Isaiah 6:5). Job had a reputation as someone who was 'blameless and upright' and who 'feared God and shunned evil' (Job 1:1), but when driven to his knees he confessed, 'I despise myself and repent in dust and ashes'.(Job 42:6)

We see the same sorrow for sin in the New Testament. Amazed at a miracle Jesus performed, Peter cried out, 'I am a sinful man!' (Luke 5:8). Later, under severe pressure, he denied that he even knew Jesus, but when he came to his senses 'he went outside and wept bitterly' (Matthew 26:75). Paul gives us a clear testimony as to what it means to be a spiritual mourner: 'For what I want to do I do not do, but what I hate I do... I know that nothing good lives in me, that is, in my sinful nature... For what I want to do I do not do, but what I hate I do ... I know that nothing good lives in me, that is, in my sinful nature ... For what I do is not the good I want to do; no, the evil I do not want to do - this I keep on doing ... What a wretched man I am!' (Romans 7:15,18,19,24). It is vitally important to notice that Paul was writing about his ongoing experience as a mature Christian. This is not morbid, self-pitying introspection. Paul is being ruthlessly honest and admitting that although the ruling passion of his heart is to obey God he is constantly dismayed at his performance and at the vileness of indwelling sin.

This is characteristic of genuine Christian experience. The more we grow in grace and the more we know of God, of Christ and of ourselves, the greater will be the depth of our mourning at how far we fall short of consistently living 'in a manner worthy of the gospel of Christ' (Philippians 1:27). It is totally out of character for a true Christian to treat sin lightly, commit sin deliberately or remember sin cheerfully. It was said of the godly Protestant martyr John Bradford, who was burned at the stake in 1555, that scarcely a day passed in which he did not weep over his sin. David Brainerd, some eight years after his conversion, and when God was blessing his ministry in a remarkable way, wrote in his journal: 'At this time God gave me such an effecting sense of my own vileness and the exceeding sinfulness of my heart that there seemed to be nothing but sin and corruption within me.' Preaching in 1889, C H Spurgeon said: 'Brethren, when I have carefully considered, and inwardly perceived, the holiness of God's law, I have felt as though the sharp edge of a sabre had been drawn across my heart, and I have shivered and trembled ... What poor creatures we are! The best of men are men at the best; and, apart from the work of the Holy Spirit, and the power of divine grace, hell itself does not contain greater monsters than you and I might become.'

There is no greater index of a professing Christian's true spiritual state than sensitivity to his own sin, but sadly it is so often lacking. Luther said in his day that mourning for sin was 'a rare herb'; today it is an endangered species. Few Christians would sing Isaac Watts' words with genuine conviction:

Lord I am vile, conceived in sin;
And born unholy and unclean;
Sprung from the man whose guilty fall
Corrupts the race and taints us all

Surely we should mourn when we think seriously about what sin is and what sin does? Sin is high treason against the majesty of our Maker, open rebellion against his rightful authority. It reeks of depravity and corruption. Thomas Watson said: 'Sin makes a man worse than a toad or serpent', while one of his fellow Puritan preachers called it 'the devil's excrement'. Surely we should mourn whenever the Holy Spirit convicts us of allowing Satan's filth to defile our lives?

Yet thoughts like these should not drive us to depression or despair. Mourning for sin is not the same as hopeless confession of guilt. God calls us to mourn in the assurance that if we do he will graciously respond in blessing. Biblical mourning for sin is not self-centred but God-centred. It does not wallow in despair, it looks for deliverance. This glorious truth is written all over Scripture, and nobody expresses it more movingly than David, whose failures are clearly on the record: 'The Lord is close to the broken-hearted and saves those who are crushed in spirit' (Psalm 34:18); 'The sacrifices of God are a broken spirit; a broken and contrite heart, O God, you will not despise' (Psalm 51:17); 'Taste and see that the Lord is good; blessed is the man who takes refuge in him' (Psalm 34:8). Commenting on the second of these promises, the nineteenth-century American scholar W S Plummer wrote, 'No man can prove that God is better pleased with innocence in an angel than he is with penitence in a sinner.'

God's promise to the Old Testament Jews remains for every Christian today: 'Rend your heart and not your garments. Return to the Lord your God, for he is gracious and compassionate, slow to anger and abounding in love' (Joel 2:13). Some of the New Testament promises most widely used in evangelistic preaching were in their original context given to Christians. These include John's assurance, 'If we confess our sins, he is faithful and just and will forgive us our sins and purify us from all unrighteousness' (1 John 1:9) and Christ's gracious word to the lukewarm church members in Laodicea: 'Behold, I stand at the door and knock; if anyone hears my voice and opens the door, I will come in to him, and will dine with him, and he with me' (Revelation 3:20, NASB). What wonderful incentives these are to grieve over our divided affections and to cry out with David: 'Create in me a pure heart, O God, and renew a steadfast spirit within me ... Restore to me the joy of your salvation and grant me a willing spirit, to sustain me' (Psalm 51:10,12).

## BLEMISHES IN THE BODY

A sure mark of growing Christian maturity in a believer is his concern for the body of Christ and, just as the Bible calls him to grieve over his own sins, so it calls him to grieve over sin within the church at large. The Holy Communion Service in the 1662 **Book of Common Prayer** includes the confession, 'We acknowledge and bewail our manifold sins and wickedness', and it is difficult to imagine how any spiritually-minded Christian can survey the church scene today and not mourn for what he sees.

Careful, earnest exposition of the Scriptures is in serious decline. Theological compromise is widespread and growing. Biblical authority is being questioned or flouted; a friend of mine recently attended a 'megachurch' in the United States where the preacher's text was taken from the children's book **Adam the Racoon**. Seminary professors deny the inerrancy of Scripture, the deity of Christ and the reality of his atonement. While preaching in Australia, I heard of one professor who told his students that the Bible 'had no more authority than a daily newspaper ...' Mysticism is rampant; professing Christians are often more interested in angels and demons than in the person and work of Christ. Public worship is increasingly being geared to the worshippers rather than to the One being worshipped. Biblical ethics are compromised or abolished. In some charismatic circles epidemic hysteria is masquerading as a mighty work of the Holy Spirit. In others, miraculous healing is being promised on a 'name it and claim it' basis. Rodney Howard-Browne, prime mover in the so-called 'Toronto Blessing' movement which burst on the church scene in the nineteen-nineties, cheerfully announces himself as a bartender for the Holy Spirit. Pseudo-prophets dispense pseudo-prophecy with scant regard to biblical criteria. In some circles, entertainment evangelism has become the norm, and at times is carried to the point of absurdity; on one visit to the United States I was given a leaflet advertising the services of 'Skipper, the Gospel Monkey'. Serious literature is being neglected;

many Christian bookshops are almost a contradiction in terms, with a heavy emphasis on music, games, trinkets and 'Jesus junk'. Moral standards are crumbling, while dishonesty, immorality, greed, pride, sharp practice and self-serving are often tolerated, even among local church leaders, without any semblance of biblical discipline.

What is our reaction to these things, and to other sins that defile the church? Some shrug their shoulders and say, 'It is none of my business'. Others do nothing but criticize. Others gather the robes of their respectability around them and say with the Pharisee, 'God, I thank you that I am not like other men' (Luke 18:11). Some even gloat over the failures of others in the church and get some kind of perverted pleasure in seeing them stumble. Needless to say, there is no blessing associated with any of these reactions. The man who is blessed is the one who is broken-hearted and grieves over the flaws and failures within the Christian church.

The New Testament provides a moving role model. After an encouraging start, the church at Corinth got into serious difficulties, with false doctrine leading to unbiblical practices of one kind and another. The Apostle Paul had a special interest in this particular church, having preached there for some eighteen months, and his subsequent letters to its members show the depth and spirituality of his concern. At one stage he says: 'I am afraid that when I come again my God will humble me before you, and I will be grieved over many who have sinned earlier and have not repented of the impurity, sexual sin and debauchery in which they have indulged' (2 Corinthians 12:21) - and his word 'grieved' is identical to the one used in the Beatitude we are studying. Here is a man with a loving, pastoral concern for the well-being of the church telling its members that he will be heart-broken if he reaches Corinth and finds that sinful behaviour is being tolerated. He mourned that there were so few mourners. He used the same kind of expression in an earlier letter to the same church, when, after casti-gating them for arrogantly sweeping sexual immorality under the carpet, he added, 'Shouldn't you rather have been filled with grief and have put out of your fellowship the man who did this?' (1 Corinthians 5:2). This heartfelt concern for the spiritual well-being of God's people comes across again and again in Paul's writing. In the early part of his second letter to the church at Corinth he said that his earlier letter had been written 'out of great distress and anguish of heart' (2 Corinthians 2:4). He reminded the elders of the church at Ephesus that during his time there he had 'served the Lord with great humility and with tears' (Acts 20:19). Warning them of impending danger that would follow if false doctrine was embraced, he told them: 'So be on your guard! Remember that for three years I never stopped warning each of you night and day with tears' (Acts 20:31). To the church at Philippi he wrote expressing his distress over many professing Christians whose lives were a disgrace to the gospel: 'For, as I have often told you before and now say again even with tears, many live as enemies of the cross of Christ' (Philippians 3:18). Paul was a great weeper, and in his tears we sense something of the heartbeat of biblical mourning, a genuine, loving concern for the spiritual well-being of God's people.

We find the same concern in his Old Testament predecessors. At a time when the first signs of a spiritual reformation were being compromised, Ezra the priest shut himself away in the room of a friend and 'ate no food and drank no water because he continued to mourn over the unfaithfulness of the exiles' (Ezra 10:6). When he heard of the impending doom facing the holy city of Jerusalem, the prophet Daniel 'turned to the Lord God and pleaded with him in prayer and petition, in fasting, and in sackcloth and ashes' (Daniel 9:3).

These and other spiritual leaders were reflecting something of God's jealous concern for the purity of his people. This comes across in an amazing vision in which the prophet Ezekiel saw the holy city of Jerusalem defiled by the practice of idolatry in the temple. In the vision, God sent a messenger through the city with alarming instructions: 'Go throughout the city of Jerusalem and put a mark on the foreheads of those who grieve and lament over all the detestable things that are done in it'. Immediately this had been done, six divinely-appointed executioners were told to go through the city, beginning at the temple, and to carry out an apocalyptic search and destroy mission of divine judgment: 'Slaughter old men, young men and maidens, women and children, but do not touch anyone who has the mark' (Ezekiel 9:4,6).

The only ones spared were those who were concerned over the city's apostasy and the abominations taking place in the house of God. If God were to execute such summary judgment today, who would be exempt from his wrath? How many bear the marks of mourners?

## SATAN ON THE LOOSE

Yet the Christian's concern must go beyond the church and reach out to the world at large. Surely there is scope for mourning there? John tells his fellow Christians: 'We know that we are children of God, and that the whole world is under the control of the evil one' (1 John 5:19) and the evidence for that statement has been piling up for another 2,000 years since those words were written. The whole world order outside of Christ is corrupted and defiled and stinks of sin. Everywhere we look we see signs of Satan's power and sin's pollution. Brian Edwards is not exaggerating when he says that this world has Satan's graffiti all over it. What is our reaction to the injustice, the cruelty, the violence, the self-ishness, the greed, the immorality and the degredation of humanity that we see all around us? Abraham's grandson Lot was hardly a paragon of virtue, but the bible says that he was 'distressed by the filthy lives of lawless man' and was 'tormented in his righteous soul by the lawless deeds he saw and heard' (2 Peter 2:7-8). Peter uses strong language here. Lot's heart ached as he saw what sin was doing to the lives of those among whom he lived day by day. Can the same be said about us?

The bible tells us that when Jesus went to the tomb of his friend Lazarus and saw people weeping, 'he was deeply moved in spirit and troubled' (John 11:33). The English translation hides almost as much as it reveals, because the opening part of the phrase would be better translated 'he was enraged in his spirit'. He was angry - not at the mourners, but at coming into close personal contact not merely with death but with the one who had the power of death. When Jesus came to that tomb he was seething with fury at what Satan was doing. Should we not have the same holy anger when we see the devastation that the devil is wreaking in the lives of our fellow human beings?

When Paul visited Athens 'he was greatly distressed to see that the city was full of idols' (Acts 17:16). How many Christians today are moved to tears by the idolatry, the blasphemy, the sheer godlessness that characterizes our society? When Jesus looked at the city of Jerusalem 'he wept over it' (Luke 19:41). How many Christians today weep over their city, their town, their village, their neighbours? Have our consciences become slowly anaesthetized to the point where we shrug our shoulders when we should be falling to our knees? Many professing Christians happily watch on television things they would never have dreamed of going to see in a cinema 20 years ago or, with even finer hypocrisy, things they would not like to be seen viewing in a cinema today. Profanity, adultery, drunkenness and blasphemy are common ingredients in their daily entertainment. They cackle at the world's crudity without turning a hair, let alone an 'Off' switch. Things that crucified the Son of God are now used by some of those who profess to be his followers to help them relax and unwind at the end of a busy day. Can we seriously expect God to bless that kind of behaviour?

One other dimension must be added. The Christian's mourning for the sin of the world should be driven not mainly by existential consider-ations but by his understanding of God's law and holiness and his knowledge that God's eternal justice cannot be avoided. As W S Plummer puts it, 'The grief of a pious soul for sins is not only or chiefly for the misery thus brought on, but chiefly because sin is exceeding sinful and greatly dishonours God.'

When Moses discovered the Israelites committing idolatry it broke his heart: 'Then once again I fell prostrate before the Lord for forty days and forty nights; I ate no bread and drank no water, because of the sin you had committed, doing what was evil in the Lord's sight and so provoking him to anger' (Deuteronomy 9:18). When the Psalmist saw the society of his day steeped in sin he cried out, 'Streams of tears flow from my eyes, for your law is not obeyed' (Psalm 119:136). Commenting on this verse, the seventeenth-century Scottish preacher David Dickson wrote, 'Two things in sin chiefly move the godly to mourn for it. One is the dishonour it brings on God. The other is the perdition it brings on the sinner.' Do we see the world in that light? Frederick and Arthur Wood, founders of the National Young Life

Campaign in the early part of this century, were walking through a town when they were engulfed by a crowd of young people coming in the opposite direction. When they emerged on the other side, Arthur asked his brother why he was crying. Frederick hung his head and replied: 'They don't know my Saviour.' He was not passing judgment on those young people, but something about their language and behaviour convinced him that they were lost. Do we have that kind of concern? When did you last shed a tear, or pray with genuine concern, for the spiritual welfare of those who live in open defiance of God and are eternally doomed unless he graciously intervenes? R A Jarvie's hymn makes the point well:

With a soul blood-bought, and a heart aglow,
Redeemed of the Lord and free;
I ask, as I pass down the busy street,
Is it only a crowd I see?
Do I lift my eyes with a careless gaze,
That pierces no deep-down woe?
Have I nought to give to the teeming throng
Of the wealth of the love I know?

Let me look at the crowd as my Saviour did,
Till my eyes with tears grow dim;
Let me look till I pity the wandering sheep,
And love them, for love of him.

## THE CHRISTIAN'S COMFORT

Earlier in this chapter we saw something of the outworking of this Beatitude in God blessing the penitent sinner by releasing him from the guilt and grip of sin and granting him a place of eternal security in his kingdom. We also saw God comforting the Christian who grieves over his surviving sin by assuring him of forgiveness and restoring the joy and assurance of his salvation. We can now flesh out the fuller dimension of Jesus' pledge that all true, spiritual mourners will be comforted.

When studying the word 'blessed' we saw that it always includes the Christian's contemporary experience, and we know from the rest of his teaching that blessings mentioned in the Beatitudes - such as mercy, spiritual fullness and the status and privilege of being children of God - were promised by Jesus as an experience to be enjoyed here on earth. As John Stott rightly says, 'It is plain from the rest of Jesus' teaching that the kingdom of God is a present reality which we can "receive", "inherit" or "enter" now. Similarly, we can obtain mercy and comfort now, can become God's children now, and in this life can have our hunger satisfied and our thirst quenched. Jesus promised all these blessings to his followers in the here and now.'

Then what of the specific pledge 'they will be comforted'? The root of the word 'comforted' is **parakaleo,** which means 'to call to one's side', and there are many New Testament illustrations of its use. When Jesus was at Capernaum, 'a centurion came to him **asking** for help' (Matthew 8:5). In a remarkable incident, a high-ranking Ethiopian official returning home in his chariot **'invited** Philip to come up and sit with him' (Acts 8:31). On one of his missionary journeys Paul had a vision of a man from Macedonia 'standing and **begging** him, "Come over to Macedonia and help us"' (Acts 16:9). These instances help us to see that 'comfort' is much more than a consoling pat on the shoulder. It has a dynamic dimension; it speaks of being strengthened by outside resources that are brought alongside to help. What are these resources on which God's mourning people can rely? Keeping to those which are specifically built around the use of **parakaleo** and its cognates, we can end this chapter by looking briefly at seven of them.

The first is **God the Father.** Having warned his readers of the pressures they would be under as Christians, Paul speaks of 'the God who gives endurance and encouragement' **(paraklesis)** (Romans 15:5). Commenting on this statement, W S Plumer wrote, 'All excellencies of moral character ... are never effectually wrought in us but by the power of the Most High. His grace can transform the worst moral character into the image of the heavenly Adam ... Nor is it any kindness, but real cruelty, on the part of preachers to call on the people to work the works of God in their own strength. In doing so they act like the Egyptian taskmasters, who required brick but gave no straw.'

The second is **God the Son.** The Bible urges us to remember that, when we sin 'we have one who speaks to the Father in our defence **(parakletos)** - Jesus Christ the Righteous One. He is the atoning sacrifice for our sins' (1 John 2:1,2). In this translation the phrase 'one who speaks ... in our defence' is unhelpful, and even 'Advocate' (AV, NKJV, NASB) is somewhat misleading, not because the sense of someone coming alongside to help is inaccurate, but because it brings in the picture of a law court, which is not in John's mind. In a court of law, an advocate or lawyer makes out the best case he can for his client, playing down his weak points, playing up his strong ones, and hoping that he can persuade the judge and jury to come to a favourable verdict. But that is not what Jesus does on our behalf, because our case does not have any strong points. There is not one good thing to be seen in us and not a good word to be said for us. We are guilty, depraved, corrupt, helpless and hopeless. What Jesus does on our behalf is not to plead **our** merits, but **his,** not **our** obedience, but **his.** He presents before God's throne all the merits of his atoning sacrifice on behalf of those for whom he died. It is exactly here that the person who mourns over his sin can find the unspeakable encouragement of knowing that, in terms of his eternal relationship with God, all of his sin has been completely and finally dealt with, so that he can sing with the hymnwriter Charitie Lees De Chenez:

> Because the sinless Saviour died,
> My sinful soul is counted free;
> For God, the Just, is satisfied
> To look on him and pardon me

The third is **God the Holy Spirit.** Shortly before his own death, Jesus promised his troubled disciples, 'I will ask the Father, and he will give you another Counsellor **(parakletos)** to be with you for ever - the Spirit of truth' (John 14:16-17). Part of the Holy Spirit's ministry is to come alongside God's people and to strengthen them in their distress. Writing of the Holy Spirit dwelling in the Christian's heart, the nineteenth-century American preacher C R Vaughan expresses something of what this means: 'He is there to impart holiness, to give grace according to the day, to bestow wisdom, patience and courage, to sanctify and comfort in affliction, to erase the image of Satan, to impress the image of God, to conquer the unholy passions, and to fill the soul with all the fruits of the Spirit.'

The fourth is the **Word of God**. In a passage from which we quoted earlier, Paul refers to the Old Testament writings and says, 'For everything that was written in the past was written to teach us, so that through endurance and the encouragement **(paraklesis)** of the Scriptures we might have hope' (Romans 15:4). There are echoes of this in his final word to the Ephesian elders: 'Now I commit you to God and to the word of his grace, which can build you up and give you an inheritance among all those who are sanctified' (Acts 20:32). Countless millions of God's people have found the Bible to be an inexhaustible source of comfort, strength, spiritual insight, encouragement, restoration and hope. In American preacher A T Pierson's words, 'While other books inform, and some few reform, this one book transforms'. We may confidently turn to it in our mourning and ask its Author to speak to us through its sacred pages.

The fifth is **the faithful preaching of the Word of God.** Paul says that 'everyone who prophesies speaks to men for their strengthening, encouragement **(paraklesis)** and comfort' (1 Corinthians 14:3). It is my long-held conviction that one of the reasons why the counselling load in today's church is so heavy is that our preaching is so light. So much preaching today is superficial, empty and profitless. It panders to people's wants rather than to their needs and massages the emotions rather than piercing the heart. But where preaching is sound in its exegesis, accurate in its exposition and passionate in its application, God's people will continue to be strengthened, encouraged and comforted.

The sixth is **the fellowship of other Christians.** In a moving personal comment on their relationship, Paul assures his friend Philemon, 'Your love has given me great joy and encouragement **(paraklesis)**, because you, brother, have refreshed the hearts of the saints' (Philemon 7).

Elsewhere, having impressed upon his readers the need to be self-controlled and vigilant in their spiritual warfare, he adds: 'Therefore encourage **(parakaleo)** one another and build each other up' (1 Thessalonians 5:11). There is a great strength to be found in genuine Christian fellowship in which believers honestly and openly share their burdens and concerns and are 'mutually encouraged by each others faith" (Romans 1:12).

The seventh is **the certainty of Christ's return**. After a magnificent passage on the Second coming of Christ, Paul urges the Christians at Thessalonica, 'Therefore encourage **(parakaleo)** each other with these words' (1 Thessalonians 4:18). The certainty of our Saviour's return should be a source of great comfort to us at every level of our mourning for sin. With regard to our own sin, we have God's promise that 'when he appears, we shall be like him' (1 John 3:2). As far as the church at large is concerned, the Lord's return will usher in the day when it will be 'a radiant church, without stain or wrinkle or any other blemish, but holy and blameless' (Ephesians 5:27). As for the world, we are promised that 'the earth will be filled with the knowledge of the glory of the Lord, as the waters cover the sea' (Habakkuk 2:14) and that there will be 'a new heaven and a new earth, the home of righteousness' (2 Peter 3:13). How can a Christian be other than comforted as he meditates gratefully on these assurances?

### AND FINALLY...

In an Old Testament passage that in its original setting referred to the return of God's people to the promised land after many years in captivity, we read, ' ... and the ransomed of the Lord will return. They will enter Zion with singing; everlasting joy will crown their heads. Gladness and joy will overtake them, and sorrow and sighing will flee away' (Isaiah 35:10). Years later, when God's people looked back on the fulfilment of that prophecy, they were able to say, 'Our mouths were filled with laughter, our tongues with songs of joy' (Psalm 126:2). Yet even when they were restored to their homeland they had to face new problems and pressures and endure other pains and sorrows. In the final fulfilment of Isaiah's prophecy there will be no such qualifications, for God's people will be in his glorious, blissful presence. In the Bible's wonderful words, 'They will be his people, and God himself will be with them and be their God. He will wipe away every tear from their eyes. There will be no more death or mourning or crying or pain, for the old order of things has passed away' (Revelation 21:3-4). Here on earth, the Christian's life is characterized by mourning; in heaven, his life is characterized by its absence, for every cause of mourning will have been finally removed. Hallelujah!

# Chapter 8

# Gentle Giants

'Blessed are the meek, for they will inherit the earth' (Matthew 5:5).

When grappling with the meaning of the Beatitudes we need to constantly remind ourselves that in making these astonishing statements Jesus is not describing what it takes to become a Christian but showing the character and behaviour expected from the person who has become one. The Beatitudes reveal something of what life is like when lived under the authority of the King of kings - and it is radically different from the lifestyle regarded by most people as normal, acceptable and successful.

Thus far, we have seen that the first hallmark of genuine Christianity is poverty of spirit, the sober realization we are spiritually bankrupt, guilty, lost and helpless apart from the saving grace of God. We have also seen that genuine believers grasp something of the true nature of sin and that when they do they mourn over it. They never treat sin lightly or flippantly, but grieve over every sense of its presence and every sign of its power. Yet these qualities are not held in watertight compartments. They flow into each other, there is an inner logic about the order in which they are placed. Nor is that the end of the progression, because those who truly mourn over sin learn to be meek. But what does 'meek' mean?

## DISTORTIONS

Meekness is the third kingdom characteristic listed in the Beatitudes, and one that is difficult to define. This becomes obvious as soon as we see how differently our English Bibles have translated the Greek adjective **praus**. While several (including AV, NKJV and NIV) use the word 'meek', the NASB has 'gentle', the New English Bible 'of a gentle spirit' and the Good News Bible 'humble', while the Amplified Bible explains 'meek' as 'mild, patient, long-suffering'. There are obvious similarities in some of these words, but they are not identical. The Scottish New Testament scholar William Barclay (who must always be read with care but can often be read with profit) is not far wide of the mark when he calls meekness 'the untranslateable word'. It clearly takes more than one English word to convey its meaning.

One dictionary gives the primary meaning as 'patient, mild, not inclined to anger or resentment', but that takes us no farther. However, the same dictionary's secondary definition - 'too submissive, spineless, spiritless' - is not so much a definition as a distortion. If we can clear this distortion out of the way we will be in a better position to see the truth.

**Meekness does not mean being too submissive.** The story is told of a domineeering wife who once shouted at her henpecked husband, 'Are you a man or a mouse? Come on, squeak up!' This was obviously a situation in which the head of the house was allowing himself to be trodden underfoot and in which the woman was riding roughshod over the biblical directive, 'Wives, submit to your husbands, as is fitting in the Lord' (Colossians 3:18). A home with no head is a disaster; one with two heads is a monstrosity. God's pattern calls for home in which the husband exerts loving, biblical leadership and in which wives live in humble submission to their husbands within the parameters of Scripture and conscience.

**Meekness does not mean being spineless.** Some people seem to have a wishbone where they should have a backbone. They are never prepared to attack evil or to defend truth. They are congenital compromisers, unwilling to do anything that might rock the boat, buck the trend, upset the establishment or show themselves to be in the minority. Yet history is full of illustrations of the truth of the eighteenth-century British politician Edmund Burke's famous phrase, 'The only thing necessary for the triumph of evil is that good men do nothing.' The heroes found on the pages of Scripture were anything but spineless, and God rewarded them for their courage. Far from knowing God's favour and blessing, the complacent and the compromisers experienced exactly the opposite. There are few more devastating words in Scripture than God's judgment on the lukewarm Laodiceans: 'I am about to spit you out of my mouth' (Revelation 3:16).

**Meekness does not mean being spiritless.** Meekness must never be confused with weakness. As Don Carson says, 'A meek person is not necessarily indecisive or timid. He is not so unsure of himself that he could be pushed over by a hard slap from a wet noodle'! When we come to look at some biblical examples of meekness we will see that the people concerned were powerhouses, not pushovers.

We can add a fourth important negative to those suggested by the distortions, which is that **meekness is not the same as natural niceness.** We often speak of someone as being 'a nice person', and what we mean is that he or she is naturally affable, agreeable, pleasant, easy-going. Yet, as Martyn Lloyd-Jones rightly observes, 'That is something purely biological, the kind of thing you get in animals. One dog is nicer than another, one cat is nicer than another. That is not meekness.'

Meekness is a matter of grace, not genetics. A person may be naturally submissive, spineless, spiritless or 'nice' by nature, but nobody is meek by nature. Meekness is not part of the human mix. The crucial clue to its meaning is to be found in the fact that the Bible includes meekness (the NIV translating **praotes** as 'gentleness') as part of the 'fruit of the Spirit' (Galatians 5:22-23). This makes it clear that only the new birth can lead to new life and only by the power of the indwelling Holy Spirit can a person be genuinely meek. It is sometimes possible to give a superficial appearance of having one or other of the qualities mentioned in the Beatitudes - but the Beatitudes are not about superficial appearances, they are about the heart. The fact that meekness is part of the fruit of the Spirit also confirms that meekness is not one of the qualifications for entering the kingdom of God, but one of the indications that the person concerned has already entered.

## WINDOWS ON THE WORD

Another way to get at the meaning of 'meekness' is to see how it was used in the ancient secular world. The Bible's writers did not invent their own dictionaries, but used the common language, syntax and idioms of their respective cultures, and three particular uses of the word we translate 'meekness' will help us to unravel what it means.

**Firstly, it spoke of balance.** The Greek philosopher Aristotle taught that meekness was the mean between two extremes, such as that between unjustified anger and the total lack of anger at anything. A few years ago a cosmetics company used to advertise its best-selling shaving cream with the slogan, 'Not too much, not too little. Just right if it's Erasmic'. Meekness always gets the balance right. It is firm but not assertive, principled but not petty, tender but not touchy.

**Secondly, it spoke of control.** Specifically, the Greeks used it of domesticated animals which were trained to obey their masters' voices, or a gesture from their hands. There is a brilliant illustration of this in Scripture where David lays down a vital principle for discovering God's will: 'Do not be like the horse or the mule, which have no understanding but must be controlled by bit or bridle or they will not come to you' (Psalm 32:9). The horse illustrates someone who is wilful and head-strong; the Bible says that this kind of person 'pursues his own course like a horse charging into battle' (Jeremiah 8:6). The mule, on the other hand, illustrates someone who is rigid and stubborn. The only way to control such animals is by bringing painful pressure to bear on them, yet even when they have been brought into line they could hardly be described as being meek. We have all known times when God has had to correct our wilfulness or stubbornness by bringing painful pressures to bear on us, but the more we learn to restrain our self-motivated impulses to act like horses or mules the more we will discover the truth of God's promises: 'The meek he will guide in judgement, and the meek he will teach his way' (Psalm 25:9, AV). The person who is truly meek is genuinely content to follow God's leading and to accept God's providential dealings with him.

**Thirdly, it spoke of the opposite of pride.** One particular Greek word for 'pride' was **hypselokardia**, which we could literally translate 'lofty-heartedness'. Although it does not occur in Scripture, we can get very close to it in one version's narrative of Uzziah, who became King of Judah when he was a teenager and enjoyed almost unbroken success for about 50 years - 'But when he was strong, his heart was lifted up to his destruction' (2 Chronicles 26:16, AV). Specifically, Uzziah began to get such delusions of grandeur that he thought he had a divine right to ignore biblical directions about the public worship of God and to exercise a ministry specifically reserved for priests. When the nation's spiritual leaders courageously confronted him he swept them aside, but within minutes of his arrogant action he was miraculously stricken with terminal leprosy and his reign was over.

Uzziah's story helps us to focus more clearly on the meaning of meekness, because in Greek culture **praotes** was the exact opposite of **hypselokardia**. It meant 'lowly-heartedness', the genuine acceptance of one's own unworthiness and weakness. When we give this technical definition a biblical context we can see it in its right setting, because true meekness is rooted in a proper understanding of God and of ourselves. John Brown is exactly right: 'An enlightened conviction of the infinite greatness and excellence, the sovereignty, and wisdom, and holiness, and righteousness, and condescension and kindness of God, and of our own insignificance as creatures, and demerit as sinners, lies at the foundation of that meekness which forms an essential part of the character of a genuine Christian.' Two minutes' thought about the sublime attributes of God and the soiled attributes of man should be enough to convince us that **hypselokardia** is not merely laughable but lunatic.

### SURVIVAL OF THE MEEKEST?

The best way to flesh out the full meaning of meekness will be to look at examples and principles laid down in the Bible, but before doing so it is worth stepping aside to notice why, as with the previous two statements in the Beatitudes, this one would have sounded not merely improbable but revolutionary. Two background factors would have contributed to this.

The first was the Jewish nation's history. Anybody listening to Jesus and who had a good grasp of the Old Testament might have remembered this prophetic statement: 'A little while, and the wicked will be no more; though you look for them, they will not be found. But the meek will inherit the land and enjoy great peace' (Psalm 37:10-11).

Yet a thousand years had passed since then and to some people 'a little while' may have developed a decidedly hollow ring because the nation's subsequent history seemed to contradict what had been promised. Less than a century after David had penned the prophecy, a clash of wills in the higher reaches of government led to the division of the land and people into the northern kingdom of Israel and the southern kingdom of Judah, in both of which domineering rulers had more than their share of power and there seemed little sign of meekness paying off.

For about 200 years Israel was ruled by a succession of 19 kings, most of them callous and corrupt, until in 722 BC, it was savagely attacked by the Assyrians under the leadership of King Shalmaneser, who deported virtually the entire population. Judah struggled on for about another 140 years under a mixture of good and bad rulers until 587 BC when it was devastated by the notorious king Nebuchadnezzar and his ruthless Babylonian troops, who swept the cream of the population into exile. In both cases victory (and territory) went not to the meek but to those who were exactly the opposite.

By an extraordinary providence, many of the Jews were allowed to return to their homeland in 537 BC, but the fulfilment of David's prophecy remained elusively out of reach. There was nothing meek about the Persian rulers who controlled Judah from 450-330 BC; nor about Alexander the Great, who overcame the Persians, nor about the Egyptian and Syrian rulers who dominated the scene in turn until 166 BC. There followed about 100 years of the Hasmonean dynasty, again marked by ruthless leadership and bitter revolt until 63 BC when the Roman general Pompey captured Jerusalem and the provinces of Palestine became subject to Rome, with local government largely in the hands of kings, procurators and governors appointed by the Emperor. As Jesus spoke, the ruler of Galilee was Herod the Tetrarch, and the procurator of Judea was Pontius Pilate. We know from the New Testament that they could be ruthless, cunning, self-serving and compromising, and there was certainly not a trace of meekness to be found in either of them, nor in the Emperor and state apparatus they represented. Ten centuries of history seemed to contradict Jesus' words about the meek inheriting the earth.

The second background factor was the contemporary Jewish scene, which was dominated by four religious parties, the Pharisees, the Sadducees, the Zealots and the Essenes. The Pharisees were religious conservatives who longed to see Rome overthrown and hoped that this would happen when God raised up a mighty Messiah who would stage a spectacular revolution. The Sadducees, much fewer in number than the Pharisees, were well-educated and, though nearly all of them were priests, they were also highly political. Drawn from the wealthy classes, they looked for an economic solution to the nation's problems. The Zealots were fiercely patriotic and hated the Roman overlords, not least because they believed that paying taxes to a pagan emperor was treason against God. The Zealots looked for a military solution and spawned groups of **sicarii** (literally 'dagger-men') who would clinically assassinate those they believed to be enemies of the Jewish state. The Essenes, on the other hand, opted out of all social responsibility and withdrew from contact with the outside world, largely into desert communities. They wanted nothing to do with financial, social or military enterprises, and believed that the key to future greatness lay in their reclusive lifestyle. To paraphrase John MacArthur's neat summary of the situation: in their search for a restoration of the country's fortunes the Pharisees sought a miraculous answer, the Sadducees sought a materialistic answer, the Zealots sought a military answer and the Essenes sought a monastic answer. Yet Jesus cut right across all four philosophies and taught that 'the **meek** ... will inherit the earth'.

This was truly revolutionary and, as we now turn to examine some biblical examples of meekness, we will see that it governs a person's response not only to God's dealings with him but also to the words and actions of others. We will attempt a fuller definition later in this chapter, but for the moment we will look at some biblical examples through the lens of A W Pink's summarized definition of meekness as 'the opposite of self-will toward God and of ill-will toward men'.

## EARLY GIANTS

Many heroes of faith in Old Testament times displayed notable meekness at critical stages of their lives. Abraham, the ancestor and founder of the Jewish nation, had a chequered career, and was not without his weaknesses and sins, yet when pleading with God for the deliverance of the righteous from the terrible judgment that was about to fall on the vile city of Sodom he did so in the context of one over-riding principle: 'Will not the Judge of all the earth do right?' (Genesis 18:25). Whatever he himself might have desired or done, Abraham humbly submitted himself to the over-ruling providence of God, resting in what Paul was later to call God's 'good, pleasing and perfect will' (Romans 12:2). Do we always pray like that, or are our prayers stained with self-will?

Job provides another example of 'the opposite of self-will toward God'. Although outstanding in his moral and spiritual qualities, someone who 'feared God and shunned evil'(Job 1:1), he was exposed to more concentrated trauma than anyone else on the pages of the Old Testament. In one catastrophic day he heard that he had lost 7,000 sheep, 3,000 camels, 1,000 oxen and 500 donkeys and, while trying to come to terms with this multiple disaster, was told that his seven sons and three daughters had been killed in a tornado. His response has remained a model of meekness for over 3,000 years: 'At this, Job got up and tore his robe and shaved his head. Then he fell to the ground in worship and said: "Naked I came from my mother's womb, and naked I shall depart. The Lord gave and the Lord has taken away; may the name of the Lord be praised"' (Job 1:20-21). The torn robe and shaved head were common outward expressions of personal grief, yet Job was given grace to look beyond his personal catastrophe to the One under whose sovereign direction and control it had taken place and to worship him in what has been called 'one of the most beautiful expressions of submission to the will of God in the fragrant story of faith'.

The prophet Jeremiah illustrates the other element in biblical meekness, what A W Pink calls 'the opposite of ill-will toward men'. When he had fearlessly prophesied God's coming judgment on Judah and was arrested and threatened with summary execution, his concern was for the welfare of others but not for his own welfare: 'Then Jeremiah said to all the officials and all the people: "The Lord sent me to prophesy against this house and this city all the things you have heard. Now reform your ways and your actions and obey the Lord your God. Then the Lord will relent and not bring the disaster he has pronounced against you. As for me, I am in your hands; do with me whatever you think is good and right"' (Jeremiah 26:12-14). He was more concerned to preserve his integrity than to preserve his life and so responded to his threatened execution not with malice but with meekness.

David provides us with a similar example in the context of his stormy relationship with Saul. In spite of everything the unbalanced and irrational king threw at him, David remained a model of meekness. He repaid hatred with love and anger with mildness. At one point Saul had determined to kill David and set out to find him with 3,000 carefully chosen men. One night, David came across Saul fast asleep out in the Desert of Ziph. His companion offered to kill him, but David contented himself with taking away the king's spear and water jug. When the two men met a few hours later, and Saul had realized that his life had been spared, David told him, 'The Lord rewards every man for his righteousness and faithfulness. The Lord delivered you into my hands today, but I would not lay a hand on the Lord's anointed' (1 Samuel 26:23). Presented with this further opportunity to assassinate his venomous enemy (there had been a previous one) David refused to exact self-motivated revenge and meekly submitted his cause into God's over-ruling providence.

On another occasion, when David was in conflict with his son Absalom and one of Saul's former followers cursed him to his face, the same soldier who had volunteered to kill Saul asked for David's permission to cut off his enemy's head, but once more David's meekness was the controlling factor: 'Leave him alone ... It may be that the Lord will see my distress and repay me with good for the cursing I am receiving today' (2 Samuel 16:11-12).

Yet the most notable Old Testament example of meekness is the great Hebrew leader Moses. We are specifically told that Moses was 'more humble (AV "meek") than anyone else on the face of the earth' (Numbers 12:3). When he was 40 years old and living in Egypt, he killed an Egyptian who was attacking one of his fellow Hebrews and then buried his victim in the sand. There were no signs of meekness in Moses at that time. After fleeing the country to save his own life, he stayed away from Egypt for a total of 40 years, working as a shepherd in the isolation of the desert. There is no record of what Moses went through during that time, but we can be sure that those lonely years were also learning and maturing years because, when God commissioned him to deliver the Hebrews from their captivity in Egypt, he was ready for one of the most daunting tasks anyone in history has ever been asked to undertake. He remained flawed in some areas, but the man who led his fellow-countrymen out of their Egyptian slavery was very different from the man who left them there 40 years earlier.

He needed to be. In spite of their miraculous deliverance and God's promise of 'a land flowing with milk and honey' (Exodus 3:8) the Hebrews (perhaps as many as two million of them) proved a recalcitrant and rebellious lot. Moses had constantly to discern the fine line between defending God's honour and his own; and he did it well. When the people grumbled - as they frequently did - he prayed for them; when they quarrelled with him, he prayed for them again. As Thomas Watson says, 'Though they were in a storm, he was in a calm.' Under the most terrible provocation, he kept his cool. His over-riding concern was for God's honour and glory. In the words of the eighteenth-century Bible expositor Matthew Henry, 'He was as bold as a lion in the cause of God, but as mild as a lamb in his own.'

## THE MARTYRS

Turning to the New Testament we find Stephen, the first Christian martyr, exhibiting amazing meekness on the very brink of death. Asked whether the charges against him were true, he took the opportunity of reciting to the Sanhedrin the stunning saga of God's dealings with his people over the centuries, highlighting events involving Abraham and Moses. He then went on to say that his tormentors were the successors of those who had consistently persecuted the prophets, even killing 'those who predicted the coming of the Righteous One'. To make his point even clearer, he went on: 'And now you have betrayed and murdered him - you who have received the law that was put into effect through angels but have not obeyed it' (Acts 7:52-53). His enemies were furious, dragged him out of the city and began stoning him to death, but while lethal missiles were thudding into his body Stephen prayed, 'Lord Jesus, receive my spirit ... Lord, do not hold this sin against them' (Acts 7:59-60). His God-honouring denunciation of his enemies' sin, coupled with his calm acceptance of his own wrongful murder, confirms that we must never confuse meekness with lack of power. Meekness is not weakness, nor is it impotence. It is power under control, a by-product of that brokenness of spirit which leaves no room for self-pity, has no time for defending or promoting one's own reputation, and sees no point in turning all one's rights into claims.

Nobody can match the martyrs for meekness. Read their compelling stories and see for yourself. Many moving examples are found in **Fair Sunshine**, a remarkable little book in which Jock Purves writes about thirteen of the seventeenth-century Covenanters in Scotland. One of these was David Hackston, in whose story there is a parallel with that of David and Saul. Leading a band of fugitives one day, Hackston came across James Sharp, Archbishop of St Andrew's, a vicious killer of the Covenanters and whose record was so vile that one contemporary wondered if a more evil man had lived since Judas Iscariot. Presented with what some of his followers thought to be a God-given opportunity to slay him, Hackston would have none of it, saying that he had no call to kill the cleric. Soon afterwards, Hackston was captured and dragged before his merciless persecutors. Given permission to state his cause, this is what he said: 'I now stand here before you as a prisoner of Jesus Christ for adhering to his cause and interest, which has been sealed with the blood of many worthies who have suffered in these lands and have witnessed to the truths of Christ these few years bygone. And I do own all the testimonies given by them, and desire to put in my mite among theirs, and am not only willing to seal it with my blood, but also to seal it with the sharpest torture that you can imagine.'

They took him at his word and passed the following sentence: 'That his body be drawn backward on a hurdle to the cross of Edinburgh; that there be a high scaffold erected a little above the Cross, where in the first place his right hand is to be struck off, and after some time his left hand; that he is to be hanged up and cut down alive, his bowels to be taken out, and his heart to be showed by the hangman to the people; then his heart and his bowels to be burned in a fire prepared for that purpose on the scaffold; that afterward his head be cut off, and his body divided into four quarters, his head to be fixed on the Netherbrow, one of his quarters with both his hands to be affixed at St Andrew's, another quarter at Glasgow, a third at Leith, a fourth at Burntisland, that none presume to be mourning for him, nor any coffin brought ...'

What must his thoughts have been as he heard those vicious words being recited? Already dying from terrible wounds suffered before being arrested, he was led to the place of execution where the hangman not only carried out the Council's instructions to the letter but inflicted even worse barbarities on his godly prisoner's body. Yet the only record we have of anything he said during his terminal torture is his request that as the hangman had taken so long to hack off his right hand he might take his left hand off at the joint. What amazing meekness! No wonder Jock Purves says that 'the free grace of God was glorified in David Hackston'.


## 'GENTLE JESUS...'

Yet for all that can be said about Abraham, Moses, Job, Jeremiah, David, Stephen and others, the supreme example of meekness is to be found in Jesus himself. We may tend to shy away from Charles Wesley's famous words, 'Gentle Jesus, meek and mild', because of the popular idea that the description sounds somewhat effeminate, but the hymn-writer was accurately reflecting the Saviour's own statement: 'I am meek and lowly in heart' (Matthew 11:29, AV). As Sinclair Ferguson notes, meekness is virtually the only personal quality about himself to which Jesus drew specific attention - and we can therefore be sure that it is of special significance.

The first area in which Jesus exhibited meekness was in his position within the Godhead. In one of the most magnificent passages in Scripture we are told that his very coming into the world involved meekness. Although he was 'in very nature God' he 'did not consider equality with God something to be grasped', but emptied himself, 'taking the very nature of a servant, being made in human likeness' (Philippians 2:6-7). Here is the perfect pattern of meekness. Although he had every right to it, Jesus did not consider the uninterrupted enjoyment of the glory that was rightly his throughout eternity something to be held on to at all costs. In the interests of others (hell-deserving sinners like the writer and the readers of this book) he laid that glory aside and accepted all the limitations of life on earth, surrounded by the loathsomeness of sin in every shape and form. C S Lewis described this as being 'comparable to a man becoming a slug', but even this fails to measure the meekness involved.

Throughout his earthly life he was entirely submissive to his Father in heaven. When he said that 'the Son can do nothing by himself' (John 5:19) he was not admitting to any lack of power, but indicating that there was what William Hendriksen calls 'flawless correspondence between his own will and that of his Father'. His will had always been perfectly in tune with that of his Father; the difference now was that every word, thought and deed was a matter of deliberate, voluntary submission and obedience - in other words, of meekness. That meekness shone out with dazzling brightness against the dark background of his own suffering and death. As the day approached he told his disciples, 'Now my heart is troubled, and what shall I say? "Father, save me from this hour? No, it was for this very reason I came to this hour. Father, glorify your name!"' (John 12:27-28). In the Garden of Gethsemane he prayed, 'Father, if you are willing, take this cup from me; yet not my will, but yours be done' (Luke 22:42). While hanging on the cross in indescribable agony he cried: 'Father, into your hands I commit my spirit' (Luke 23:46). What shines through all these statements is his whole-hearted and unqualified acceptance of the divine will. They also provide us with matchless examples of that meekness which J C Ryle calls 'one of the brightest graces which can adorn the Christian character'.

The second area in which Jesus showed meekness was even more amazing, in that it was in response to the words and actions of men. At no time did he show any lack of concern for God's honour and glory - when he threw the black marketeers and other crooks out of the temple his disciples immediately linked his resolute action with the Old Testament prophecy, 'Zeal for your house will consume me' (John 2:17) - but what a difference we see when men's offensive words and actions were directed against him personally!

Accused of being demon-possessed when driving demons out of others, he courteously appealed to logic: 'If Satan drives out Satan, he is divided against himself. How then can his kingdom stand?' (Matthew 12:26). When accused of being a glutton and a drunkard, he invited his critics to weigh up the effects of his life and ministry and to see that 'wisdom is proved right by her actions' (Matthew 11:19). When accused of blasphemy for assuring a paralytic, 'Son, your sins are forgiven' (Mark 2:5) there was not a trace of pique in his response. When accused of breaking the Sabbath by performing miracles on that day, he quietly identified himself with God's ongoing purposes: 'My Father is always at his work to this very day, and I, too, am working (John 5:17). When hectored by the obnoxious King Herod and given the opportunity of displaying his miraculous powers, 'Jesus gave him no answer' (Luke 23:9). When mocked, stripped, flogged, spat upon and led out to die there was not a word of protest, not a solitary gesture of defiance or defence. In amazing fulfilment of Old Testament prophecy, 'He was oppressed and afflicted, yet he did not open his mouth; he was led like a lamb to the slaughter, and as a sheep before her shearers is silent, so he did not open his mouth' (Isaiah 53:7). In retrospect, Peter's assessment was equally emphatic: 'When they hurled their insults at him, he did not retaliate; when he suffered, he made no threats. Instead, he entrusted himself to him who judges justly' (1 Peter 2:23).

Nothing more vividly illustrates the meekness of Jesus as being power under control than what happened when an armed mob of soldiers and others went to arrest him in Gethsemane. When one of his companions drew his sword and attacked one of the high priest's servants Jesus told him to put his weapon away and added, 'Do you think I cannot call on my Father, and he will at once put at my disposal more than twelve legions of angels?' (Matthew 26:53). A legion of soldiers consisted of about 6,000 men, and there were only about four legions of Roman troops in Palestine at that time. Even on a one-to-one basis twelve legions of angels could have wiped out the entire occupying forces in very short order, but two other factors take Jesus' words far beyond simple mathematics. The first is the awesome power with which God can invest angels: on one occasion, recorded in 2 Kings 19:35, a single angel killed 185,000 pagan soldiers in one night. The second factor is that Jesus' mention of '**more than** twelve legions of angels' points to the fact that all the myriads of angels in heaven - and the Bible says there are 'thousands upon thousands, and ten thousand times ten thousand' (Revelation 5:11) - were at his immediate disposal, yet he deliberately waived their help in order that Scripture might be fulfilled and the will of God accomplished.

## LEARNING THE LESSON

In commenting on this particular quality in Jesus' life A W Pink calls him 'the very King of meekness', yet we must never forget that his example is intended not merely for admiration but for imitation: 'Take my yoke upon you **and learn of me,** for I am gentle (AV 'meek') and humble in heart, and you will find rest for your souls' (Matthew 11:29). As Augustine pointed out, Jesus did not ask us to learn how to perform miracles, open the eyes of the blind, or raise the dead, but he did tell us to learn to be meek. How can we do this? We must begin by looking long and often at the life of Christ and by diligent study of those other parts of Scripture in which we find examples, directions, encouragement and other teaching on this particular subject. Indeed, we must exercise meekness even in our reading of Scripture: we are to 'receive with meekness the implanted word, which is able to save your souls' (James 1:21, NKJV). We must come to the Bible without any preconceived ideas or prejudices and submit ourselves without reservation to its royal authority. We have no more right to tamper with Scripture than a postman has to alter our mail. As J I Packer reminds us, 'To defer to God's Word is an act of faith; any querying and editing of it on our own initiative is an exhibition of unbelief.' When we do submit to the Bible's teaching we will begin to get a grasp of the true meaning of meekness in our response both to God's dealings with us and to the actions and attitudes of others.

In relation to God's dealings with us, meekness acknowledges God as the Supreme Disposer, the One who has the right to do to us or through us whatever he chooses and to act whenever he chooses for whatever purpose he chooses. Meekness defers to the will of God as the supreme good in every situation and says, 'Your will be done on earth as it is in heaven' (Matthew 6:10).

In particular, meekness accepts adversity as being included in God's sovereign purposes. It is easy to speak blithely about accepting God's will when everything is going well, but favourable circumstances are not the best test of meekness. Meekness acknowledges the perfection of God's ways at the worst of times. Meekness says with Job, 'Shall we accept good from God, and not trouble?' (Job 2:10), and with Jeremiah, 'Is it not from the mouth of the Most High that both calamities and good things come?' (Lamentations 3:38). Meekness takes the rough with the smooth - and sees God's hand in both. When the Bohemian Reformer Jan Hus lay in prison shortly before his execution in 1415 he wrote to a friend, 'God deigns kindly to look upon us and to endow us with wondrous gifts; a narrow prison, hard bed, plain food, cruel boards, toothache, vomiting and fever.' That is meekness!

## OTHERS

The Bible has a great deal to say about the way meekness shows itself in response to the words and actions of others, and a brief glance at some of these will help us to get a fuller picture of its meaning.

Firstly, **meekness commits its cause into God's hands**. This can be seen in the Old Testament and New Testament examples we noted earlier. We could have added the Apostle Paul, who meekly accepted his persecution without being ashamed of his ministry, 'because I know whom I have believed, and am convinced that he is able to guard what I have entrusted to him for that day' (2 Timothy 1:12). Meekness does not ask for special privileges, nor does it turn legitimate rights into claims. Instead, meekness removes self from the picture altogether and is solely concerned with God's glory. When someone asked him the secret of his amazingly fruitful service, especially his work among orphans, the nineteenth-century Christian philanthropist George Múller replied, 'There was a day when I died, utterly died; died to George Múller, his opinions, preferences, tastes and will - died to the world, its approval or censure - died to the approval or blame even of my brethren and friends - and since then I have studied only to show myself approved unto God.' This may be slightly overstated, as Scripture makes it clear that dying to self is a continuous process rather than something that is done once for all, but Múller's over-riding concern remains clear.

Secondly, **meekness remains unprovoked by criticism**. The supreme example of this was Jesus, who 'endured such hostility from sinners against himself' (Hebrews 12:3, NKJV). He was openly and bitterly criticized for the words he spoke, the company he kept, the teaching he gave, the claims he made and even the miracles he performed - and the criticism came from 'sinners', a word commonly used in the New Testament for those who were impudent and obstinate in their sins. Yet in spite of this totally unjustified hostility he never once took personal offence. Any who think that meekness means weakness should ask themselves whether they have the inner spiritual strength to follow his example. Our natural tendency is to defend ourselves against every attack and to find some way, however devious, of justifying everything we do and protecting our 'image', while we piously acknowledge our sinfulness in the sight of God. John Stott makes the point perfectly: 'I myself am quite happy to recite the General Confession in church and call myself a "miserable sinner". It causes me no great problem. I can take it in my stride. But let somebody else come up to me after church and call me a miserable sinner, and I want to punch him on the nose!'

There are few greater tests of our meekness than the way we react when others attack us, and Martyn Lloyd-Jones hits the nail on the head when he says, 'To be truly meek means that we no longer protect ourselves, because we see there is nothing worth defending.' In the same general area, we must resist the temptation to be proved right in everything we say or to insist that our view of things is the only right one, whether it be an issue of doctrine, morality, ethics, the church, business, politics or anything else. Untold thousands of relationships have been wrecked by attitudes that are not so much principled as pig-headed. Writing about the need to heal such wounds, the South African preacher Frank Retief points us in the right direction: 'Take the opportunity of restoring broken relationships. Make whatever apologies are necessary. Be willing to eat humble pie and don't be caught up in the pettiness of who said what and when and who was wrong or right. I have often made the observation that five minutes before I die, it will not matter one whit to me who won the last argument. I will have other things of far greater importance on my mind.'

Thirdly, **meekness accepts personal injury without resentment**. In the course of his correspondence with the church at Corinth, Paul had to deal with those who denied his apostolic authority and suggested that, although he was bold enough when writing to them, he was a pathetic coward when he met them face to face. In reply, he refused to retaliate, but deliberately appealed to them on the basis of 'the meekness and gentleness of Christ' (2 Corinthians 10:1) who submitted to the terrible wrongs inflicted on him without ever complaining. Meekness in the face of personal injury runs counter to our natural inclination, which is to retaliate - sometimes with interest! - but it is just as much a Christian's duty to avoid taking offence as it is to avoid giving offence.

Fourthly, **meekness bears patiently with the unfaithfulness of friends**. Writing to Timothy, the Apostle Paul tells him of the way in which his friends had failed him at a time of great need: 'At my first defence, no-one came to my support, but everyone deserted me. May it not be held against them' (2 Timothy 4:16). This 'defence' was probably at some kind of preliminary hearing as part of an official investigation into Paul's ministry. It must have been a desolating experience for him, yet he graciously forgives his fair-weather friends and prays that they might not suffer for their cowardice. The weakness of friends can sometimes cause more pain than the power of enemies, yet

Paul handled the situation without any resentment. His next words give us an insight into why he was able to do so: 'But the Lord stood at my side and gave me strength' (2 Timothy 4:17). Here again we see meekness rooted in the conviction that God is sovereignly sufficient to meet all the demands made upon his people.

Fifthly, **meekness deals gently with the lost**. Paul makes this point in the letter from which I have just quoted: 'Don't have anything to do with foolish and stupid arguments, because you know they produce quarrels. And the Lord's servant must not quarrel; instead, he must be kind to everyone, able to teach, not resentful. Those who oppose him he must gently (**praotes**; literally, "in meekness") instruct, in the hope that God will grant them repentance leading them to a knowledge of the truth' (2 Timothy 2:23-25). Any Christian with experience in personal evangelism (which ought to mean every Christian) knows that this is not always easy. Faced with an argumentative unbeliever, we can quickly find ourselves adopting the same hostile spirit and getting involved in a verbal brawl, forgetting that even if we won every round and convinced the other person at every point, we might do so in such a way as to leave him even more determined to have nothing to do with a religion that produces people like us.

Sixthly, **meekness deals gently with the failures of others**. Paul touches on this when writing about personal relationships within the church: 'Brothers, if someone is caught in a sin, you who are spiritual should restore him gently (**en pneumati praotitos;** literally "in the spirit of meekness"). But watch yourself, or you also may be tempted' (Galatians 6:1). The word 'restore' literally means 'to put back into joint'. It is the word a surgeon would use about setting a broken or dislocated bone, something that needs to be done firmly but gently, correctly but tenderly. Paul also makes it clear that in seeking to restore those who have fallen we should have a clear sense of our own weakness. There is no room here for superiority, condescension or pride. These things are totally out of place when we realize that at any moment we too may be 'caught in a sin'. An acknowledgement of our own frailty is an essential qualification for dealing with another person's failure.

## THE MEASURE OF MEEKNESS

Having looked at some of the ways in which the Bible illustrates meekness, we are now in a position to attempt a concise outline of its meaning. Meekness is a defining grace, produced by the Holy Spirit in the life of the Christian, which characterizes that person's response towards God and man. Meekness towards God is a spirit of submission to all of God's dealings with us, especially those which cause us sorrow or pain, in the settled conviction that in all of these he is graciously, wisely and sovereignly working 'for the good of those who love him' (Romans 8:28). Meekness towards man means bearing patiently with the hurtful actions of others and dealing gently with their failures, not only in the assurance that all of these are under God's providential control, but in the knowledge that, left to ourselves, we have no claim to be any stronger than the weakest of our friends or any better than the worst of our enemies.

## THE INHERITANCE

The promise attached to meekness is astounding - 'they shall inherit the earth'. Jesus seems to have been quoting from an Old Testament passage in which David, puzzled by the prosperity of the wicked, eventually comes to see that the right attitude to all the apparent anomalies and injustices of life is calm and patient faith in the over-ruling providence of God, and that the final outcome of such faith is that 'the meek will inherit the land' (Psalm 37:11). As we saw earlier in this chapter, those who heard Jesus at the time must have been tempted to look back on the history of God's people and question whether it had ever been fulfilled. David's contemporary reference was to Canaan, the promised land 'flowing with milk and honey' (Exodus 3:8), but Jesus' words give it a wider, spiritual context which points us to the first strand of its meaning for today's believers.

Christians clearly have no guarantee of greater economic wealth than non-Christians, nor are they promised material prosperity or success in any of their worldly pursuits. The so-called 'prosperity gospel' which suggests that Christians seeking material benefit have only to 'name it and claim it' is nothing more than a cruel deception, with no biblical basis. What then does Paul mean when he speaks of 'having nothing, and yet possessing everything' (2 Corinthians 6:10)? The answer lies in something he wrote when thanking Christians at Philippi for their gifts: 'I am not saying this because I am in need, for I have learned the secret of being content in any and every situation, whether well fed or hungry, whether living in plenty or in want. I can do everything through him who gives me strength' (Philippians 4:11-13). This kind of thinking cuts clean across the rampant spirit of materialism that dominates the lives of so many people today. Paul had learned (and the word 'learned' is important - it seems to have been a gradual process) to disengage himself from his economic circumstances, to treat riches and poverty in exactly the same way, and to be satisfied with whatever God brought into his life.

The first reward of meekness is contentment, something of much more value than wealth. The Bible is emphatic about this: 'Better the little that the righteous have than the wealth of many wicked' (Psalm 37:16); 'The righteous eat to their hearts' content, but the stomach of the wicked goes hungry' (Proverbs 13:25); 'Better a little with the fear of the Lord than great wealth with turmoil' (Proverbs 15:16); 'Better one handful with tranquillity than two handfuls with toil and chasing after the wind' (Ecclesiastes 4:6). The one who is meek does not get ulcers worrying about erratic movements on the stock exchange, fluctuations on the money market, or the price of property. They may engage his thinking but they never dominate it. The Christian believer may not possess much real estate, or have a great deal of this world's goods, but as he grows in meekness he will increasingly find more satisfaction in his pittance than the sinner in his plenty. As A W Pink neatly puts it, 'The humble Christian is far happier in a cottage than the wicked in a palace.'

A second strand of meaning is reflected in some extraordinary words written by Paul when warning Christians at Corinth about putting preachers on pedestals and setting store by worldly wisdom: 'So then, no more boasting about men! All things are yours, whether Paul or Apollos or Cephas or the world or life or death or the present or the future - all are yours, and you are of Christ, and Christ is of God' (1 Corinthians 3:21-23). Rather than associating themselves with their favourite preacher and then claiming some kind of wisdom or benefit from doing so, Paul wanted his readers to realize that their possessions were immeasurably greater. Their real riches lay in the fact that they were 'of Christ', the Creator of the world, the Giver of life, the Conqueror of death, the Ruler of the present and the Lord of the future. There is a liberating truth here. Those who humbly and contentedly trust in Christ learn that **every** experience - the painful as well as the enjoyable - is intended for their spiritual and eternal good, tailored by an all-wise God for their particular benefit and blessing. Meekness is not looking back and seeing this in retrospect. It is approaching each day, each new set of circumstances, in the settled conviction that, in David's famous phrase, 'Surely goodness and mercy shall follow me all the days of my life, and I will dwell in the house of the Lord for ever' (Psalm 23:6, NKJV). Isaac Watts makes the point superbly in one of his finest hymns:

How vast the treasure we possess!
How rich thy bounty, King of grace!
This world is ours, and worlds to come;
Earth is our lodge, and heaven our home.

All things are ours, the gift of God,
The purchase of a Saviour's blood;
While the good Spirit shows us how
To use, and to improve them too.

If peace and plenty crown my days.
They help me, Lord, to speak thy praise;
If bread of sorrows be my food,
Those sorrows work my lasting good.

I would not change my blest estate

For all the world calls good or great;
And while my faith can keep her hold,
I envy not the sinner's gold.

Father, I wait thy daily will;
Thou shalt divide my portion still:
Grant me on earth what seems thee best,
Till death and heaven reveal the rest.

That leads us to the third strand in this marvellous promise, one which has an eternal perspective. It is not difficult to see the Old Testament land of Canaan as a prefiguration of the Christian's eternal home, that which Peter has in mind when he says that 'we are looking forward to a new heaven and a new earth, the home of righteousness' (2 Peter 3:13). As 'heirs of God and co-heirs with Christ' (Romans 8:17) Christians will inherit a cosmos from which all sin has been eradicated, one in which the present polluted creation will be 'liberated from its bondage to decay' (Romans 8:21) and where there will be 'no more death or mourning or crying or pain, for the old order of things has passed away' (Revelation 21:4). As Isaac Watts puts it in another hymn:

There is a land of pure delight,
Where saints immortal reign;
Infinite day excludes the night
And pleasures banish pain.

This element of the promise has yet to be fulfilled, but the Christian can rejoice in the certainty that he will one day enter into the fulness of the inheritance lost by Adam but regained by Christ. When George VI died quite suddenly in 1952, I vividly remember one newspaper's headline the next day: 'The Queen Flies Home'. Just for a moment, I thought the editor had made a monumental error. Surely we did not yet have a queen? The king had died only a few hours ago and the coronation of his successor would not be until the following year. But I was wrong; we did have a queen. Although the official, public coronation would not be held until much later., the king's eldest daughter Elizabeth, who was in Africa at the time, became queen the moment her father died. The picture may not be perfect but it helps to illustrate the glorious truth that, although God's people are sometimes despised, ridiculed, persecuted, impoverished or broken in health during their earthly lives, they are nevertheless heirs of an eternal and universal kingdom which will make even this amazing planet on which we presently live seem tiny and trivial.

Soon after the American missionary Adoniram Judson began his ministry in Burma he was captured by natives, strung up by his thumbs and flung into a filthy prison. When asked: 'And now what of your plans to win the heathen to Christ?' Judson calmly replied: 'My future is as bright as the promises of God.' Every Christian can say the same - and one of those promises is this 'Blessed are the meek, for they will inherit the earth.'

# Chapter 9

# Unsatisfied satisfaction

'Blessed are those who hunger and thirst for
righteousness, for they will be filled' (Matthew 5:6)

It is important to pay careful attention to the connection of the
fourth Beatitude with the previous three. The Beatitudes are not a
haphazard collection of titbits from which we can pick and
choose whatever takes our fancy at any given time. They are inextricably linked and there is an irresistible logic about the order in
which they appear.

If we are to know the blessedness of which Jesus speaks in these
verses we must begin by being 'poor in spirit', acknowledging our
spiritual bankruptcy before God. Nor is this merely a clinical
acceptance of the facts; true poverty of spirit causes us to 'mourn', to
feel the weight and guilt of our sins and the corruption of our hearts,
and to grieve over the terrible havoc that evil has brought into the
world. This in turn causes us to be 'meek', humbly submitting, as undeserving sinners, to God's providential dealings with us and responding
graciously to the hurtful attitudes and actions of others.

Now comes a shift of emphasis. Whereas the first three Beatitudes
are passive, this one has an active element to it. In speaking of those
who are 'poor in spirit', 'mourn' and are 'meek', Jesus has been
describing what these people **are**; now he turns to describe what certain
people **do**. This is obvious from the text, nor is it difficult to see how the
logical progression is maintained. Those who have a true sense of their
sinfulness and a holy hatred for sin, and accept that they have no right
to be favourably treated either by God or by other people, have also
come to realize not only that they are spiritually destitute and helpless,
but that they are utterly undeserving of either sympathy or help. It is to
these people that Jesus says, 'Blessed are those who hunger and thirst
for righteousness, for they will be filled.'

Coming as they do at this precise moment, these words make three things very clear. The first is that although self-examination is a widely neglected discipline - and C H Spurgeon was right on target when he said, 'The man who does not like self-examination may be pretty certain that things need examining' - God never intends us to wallow in morbid introspection. Self-examination is not the same as self-pity, which can be as addictive as alcohol (and just as deadly) but this Beatitude points us away from our spiritual sickness to its only solution. Secondly, Jesus' words make it clear that the only way out of our deadly dilemma is by the grace of God. The word 'filled' is in the passive voice, which tells us that the filling concerned is not something achieved but something received. Martyn Lloyd-Jones calls this particular Beatitude 'the outstanding declaration of the Christian gospel to all who are unhappy about themselves and their spiritual state, and who long for an order and quality of life that they have not hitherto enjoyed'. As with all the other Beatitudes, the promise is not made on the basis of human sincerity or merit, but as part of God's gracious provision to meet his people's spiritual need. Thirdly (and here is the active element in this Beatitude) the text speaks of those 'who hunger and thirst' rather than 'those who are hungry and thirsty'. This gives added emphasis to the point that the fulness of which Jesus speaks is promised only to those who make a determined effort to receive it.

## THE NEED

From all that we have seen so far, it is obvious that the key word, around which the whole sentence revolves, is 'righteousness'.Understanding the meaning of this word will unlock the whole of the Beatitude for us, yet it will help if, before examining it, we take a close look at what it means to 'hunger and thirst'. In doing so, it is important to remember that the Bible is an Eastern book and that it was written in a primitive culture. In New Testament times, the average working man in Palestine would eat meat only once a week. Many people lived close to the border line between hunger and starvation. Water was an even more precious commodity; life had to be carefully planned around the availability of enough water to stay alive. In our modern Western culture these conditions are difficult for us to imagine. The closest some of us get to them is watching the plight of Third World refugees while we tuck into another TV meal. We tend to think of hunger and thirst as no more than those pleasant feelings we get three times a day and that are made all the more pleasant by anticipating the food we are about to enjoy. When the Bible speaks about hungering and thirsting it means the raging pangs suffered by those who will starve if they do not eat and die if they do not drink.

These images may be difficult to imagine, but they are easy to understand. Food and drink are the most basic human needs for survival, and Jesus could hardly have used a simpler phrase to illustrate what he meant. The intensity of the words 'hunger and thirst for righteousness' comes across even more powerfully in the unusual grammatical construction of the phrase. Technically, the word 'righteousness' is in the accusative case, whereas the genitive would normally be used after such words as 'hunger' and 'thirst'. To put this in non-technical terms, if a person was longing for bread to eat, the literal translation of the Greek would be 'he is hungry for of bread', that is to say, for part of the loaf. In the same way, a person would be said to be 'thirsty for of water', in other words, for some water. There is a similar construction in French, where the same phrases would end 'du pain' and 'de l'eau' (which would be literally translated 'of the bread' and 'of the water'). But in this Beatitude we have a different construction. Instead of 'hunger and thirst for of righteousness' (in other words, for a measure of righteousness) the literal translation is 'for righteousness', that is to say, not a portion of righteousness, or a limited experience of righteousness, but total righteousness, all the righteousness that it is possible to have.

The language Jesus uses here speaks of a passionate spiritual desire to be right with God and to get rid of sin. This longing is expressed again and again in Scripture, and nowhere more clearly than in the Psalms: 'As the deer pants for streams of water, so my soul pants for you, O God. My soul thirsts for God, for the living God' (Psalm 42:1-2); 'O God, you are my God, earnestly I seek you; my soul thirsts for you, my body longs for you, in a dry and weary land where there is no water' (Psalm 63:1); 'My soul yearns, even faints for the courts of the Lord; my heart and my flesh cry out for the living God' (Psalm 84:2). These are not formal religious phrases, nor do they speak of superficial emotions. They are wholehearted, earnest, urgent cries from one for whom life without a sense of God's presence is the spiritual equivalent of starving to death. How often do we feel like that?

In thinking this through, it is important to realize that there is a difference between hunger and emptiness. You may have shared my experience of driving happily along the road, only to discover that the car's fuel gauge is perilously near 'Empty' and the nearest filling station is several miles away. Sometimes the situation is even worse, and a vehicle that has been purring along without any outward sign of trouble suddenly comes to a juddering halt. Some modern cars have warning lights or metallic voices to alert the driver, but the vehicle itself has no desire or thirst for fuel. The illustration is far from perfect, but is it not a picture of many professing Christians? Outwardly, everything seems fine. They live respectable lives, they attend church regularly, they use religious language, but inwardly and spiritually they are very nearly empty. There is no sense of need, no hungering and thirsting after God. Even worse, they are not aware of it. They are dangerously like members of the New Testament church in Laodicea, to whom God said, 'You say, "I am rich; I have acquired wealth and do not need a thing." But you do not realize that you are wretched, pitiful, poor, blind and naked' (Revelation 3:17).

## VITAL SIGNS

This is such an important point that I want to press it home. Commenting on this particular Beatitude, Martyn Lloyd-Jones writes, 'I do not know of a better test that anyone can apply to himself or herself in this whole matter of the Christian profession than a verse like this. If this verse is to you one of the most blessed statements of the whole of Scripture you can be quite certain that you are a Christian; if it is not, then you had better examine the foundations again.' Let me suggest two reasons why I agree with what he says. Firstly, because hunger is a sign of life. One only has to watch a little baby when feeding time comes around to sense something of the intense desire it has for its mother's breast. Nobody has to teach a baby to be hungry. Its longing for its mother's milk is natural. It is a sign of life. In the same way, there is something supernaturally natural about spiritual hunger. This is precisely what Peter meant when he wrote, 'Like newborn babies, crave pure spiritual milk, so that by it you may grow up in your salvation' (1 Peter 2:2). The person who does not have a hunger for the Word of God as nourishment for his soul should surely 'examine the foundations again' to see if there is any evidence of genuine conversion.

Secondly, hunger is a sign of health. One of the most important questions a doctor can ask a patient in the course of an examination is 'How is your appetite?' because lack of appetite is always a cause for concern and may be symptomatic of a serious disorder. The same principle applies in spiritual terms. When a professing Christian has little or no appetite for the things of God, something is seriously wrong, even if outwardly everything seems perfectly in order. These words by the Scottish preacher Thomas Guthrie remain as challenging today as when they were first written in the last century: 'If you find yourself loving any pleasure better than your prayers, any book better than the Bible, any house better than the house of God, any table better than the Lord's table, any person better than Christ, any indulgence better than the hope of heaven - take alarm!'

One of the greatest signs of sickness in the Christian church today is the widespread lack of hungering and thirsting after God. One can often gauge this by dwindling attendances at evening services. Many churches have dropped an evening service altogether because of a lack of interest. I heard of one church in the United States which had done so even though the normal Sunday attendance was over 1,000. Preaching in Scotland on one occasion, I was told of a local church which debated whether to close down for June, July and August in order to give its members a break. Surely this lack of appetite is a sign of sickness? The same sickness shows itself in the behaviour of some people when they do come to church. They seem restless, fidgety, or listless. They barely sing the hymns, rarely open a Bible in order to follow the reading and often seem to treat the sermon as a lullaby. Others seem more interested in musical presentation or 'drama' than in the preaching of the Word. A pastor friend of mine in the United States once told me, 'For many people in our churches today Christianity has become a spectator sport.' He was speaking of those who attend church not so that their spiritual hunger might be met by the living God, but so that their religious feelings might be massaged, preferably to music. Is that not a sign of sickness? This is how Thomas Watson addressed the issue: 'If a man were invited to a feast, and there being music at the feast, he should so listen to the music that he did not mind his meat, you would say, "Surely he is not hungry." So when men are for jingling words, and like rather gallantry of speech than spirituality of matter, it is a sign that they have surfeited stomachs and itching ears.' The seventeenth-century phrases may sound a little quaint, but they have lost nothing of their relevance.

What a contrast when we listen to Job crying, 'I have treasured the words of his (God's) mouth more than my daily bread' (Job 23:12), and to David, who valued the Word of God as being 'more precious than gold, than much pure gold ... sweeter than honey, than honey from the comb' (Psalm 19:10). A terrible tragedy is being enacted in our churches today. We have never had so many Bibles, versions of the Bible, and books to help in studying the Bible, yet there seems to be distressingly little hunger and thirst for God. Many seem to have a restless search for 'power', exotic spiritual gifts, happiness, peace, emotional 'highs', or some other undefined 'blessing', but comparatively few seem to have a deep desire to master God's Word and to be mastered by it. The Beatitude does not read, 'Righteous are those who hunger and thirst after blessedness.' The pursuit of 'blessing' can never in itself be an indication of righteousness and may in fact be self-centred. God calls us to focus our attention and appetite on **him**, not on the benefits that he may give us.

## RIGHT WITH GOD

The words 'righteousness' and 'salvation' stand very close to each other in biblical theology; there are even times when the words are used almost interchangeably. This comes across very powerfully in the writings of the prophet Isaiah, where time and again God ties the two ideas closely together: 'I am bringing my righteousness near, it is not far away; and my salvation will not be delayed...' (Isaiah 46:13); 'My righteousness draws near speedily, my salvation is on the way...' (Isaiah 51:5); 'Maintain justice and do what is right, for my salvation is close at hand and my righteousness will soon be revealed' (Isaiah 56:1). Later on, Isaiah adds his personal testimony that God's promise has been fulfilled in his own life: 'I delight greatly in the Lord; my soul rejoices in my God. For he has clothed me with garments of salvation and arrayed me in a robe of righteousness...' (Isaiah 61:10). In all of these statements the link between salvation and righteousness is so close that we would not be misinterpreting the Beatitude we are now studying if we read it as saying 'Blessed are those who hunger and thirst for salvation, for they will be filled.'

Righteousness relates to every aspect of salvation, the first of which is the initial experience of becoming a Christian. As we focus on this particular aspect we come across yet another word linked very closely with righteousness: that word is **justification**, one of the greatest in Scripture. The noun 'righteousness' occurs about 100 times in the New Testament, and the adjective 'righteous' about 40 times, while the noun 'justification' and the verb 'to justify' occur about 30 times altogether. The all-important thing to notice is that all of these words are based on the same Greek root - **dikaios** - which means 'to be just, or righteous'. This indicates that the English words concerned are virtually interchangeable.

The simplest way to make this point is by a straightforward illustration from Scripture. At one stage in his letter to the Romans, Paul emphasises the fact that 'Jews and Gentiles alike are all under sin' and that 'There is no-one righteous, not even one; there is no-one who understands, no-one who seeks God' (Romans 3:9-11). He then goes on to say, 'Therefore no-one will be declared righteous in his sight by observing the law; rather, through the law we become conscious of sin' (Romans 3:20). Then comes the good news: 'But now a righteousness from God, apart from law, has been made known, to which the Law and the Prophets testify. This **righteousness from God comes through faith** in Jesus Christ to all who believe' (Romans 3:21-22). Towards the end of the passage Paul writes, 'For we maintain that **a man is justified by faith** apart from observing the law' (Romans 3:28). We hardly need my emphasis to see that when Paul says that 'righteousness from God comes through faith' and later that 'a man is justified by faith' he is not talking about two different subjects, but about one, the way in which guilty, lost and helpless sinners can be made right with God. Here is the glorious gospel of the grace of God in all its wonder and power. Martin Luther called this particular passage in Romans 'the chief point, and the very central place of the Epistle and of the whole Bible'. But what exactly is the meaning of justification, or righteousness in this context? In his **Expository Dictionary of New Testament Words,** W E Vine defines it as 'the character or quality of being right'. The old English spelling of the word was 'rightwiseness' which expresses its meaning very clearly. The first important fact to grasp is that righteousness is one of the attributes of God. The Bible speaks of 'God's righteousness' (Romans 3:5) and of 'the righteousness of our God and Saviour Jesus Christ' (2 Peter 1:1). When it does so, it is referring to the moral and spiritual perfection which results in all of God's actions being morally and spiritually perfect. As the British theologian Alec Motyer says in his superb commentary **The Prophecy of Isaiah,** 'Righteousness infills all that he does because that is what he is.'

Man is exactly the opposite, both in his character and in the actions that flow from it, as Paul makes clear in elaborating his statement about nobody being righteous: 'All have turned away, they have together become worthless; there is no-one who does good, not even one. Their throats are open graves; their tongues practise deceit. The poison of vipers is on their lips. Their mouths are full of cursing and bitterness. Their feet are swift to shed blood; ruin and misery mark their ways, and the way of peace they do not know. There is no fear of God before their eyes' (Romans 3:12-18). As he adds a little later, 'For all have sinned and fall short of the glory of God' (Romans 3:23). Man is corrupt, depraved, sinful, vile and godless; in a word, he is unrighteous at the very core of his being, rotten through and through.

This doctrine (which theologians call 'original sin') has never been popular, and today it is often denied. To give just one example, the American television preacher Robert Schuller, who bases much of his philosophy on the 'positive thinking' model popularised by Norman Vincent Peale, flatly denies the whole idea. In **Self-Esteem: The New Reformation**, he writes, 'The most serious sin is the one that causes me to say, "I am unworthy". For once a person believes he is an "unworthy sinner" it is doubtful if he can really honestly accept the saving grace God offers in Jesus Christ.' It would be difficult to concoct a sentence containing the words 'sinner', 'God', 'grace' and Christ', and purporting to be a statement of biblical truth, which would be more heretical than that. On this issue at least, Scripture and Schuller are not even on speaking terms.

The Bible presents us with a situation in which, because God is perfect and 'righteous in all his ways' (Psalm 145:17), he justly condemns sinners and sentences them to spiritual death, both here on earth and for all eternity. As Paul writes earlier in his letter to the Romans, 'The wrath of God is being revealed from heaven against all the godlessness and wickedness of men ...' (Romans 1:18). Here, then, is man's greatest and overwhelming problem: he needs to get right with God, to be justified. But how can he be justified in the sight of a holy God of whom the Bible says, 'Your eyes are too pure to look on evil; you cannot tolerate wrong' (Habakkuk 1:13)? How can anyone who is sinful by nature, and proves it by his life, ever reach heaven when the Bible makes it clear that 'nothing unclean and no one who practises abomination and lying, shall ever come into it' (Revelation 21:27, NASB)? Theoretically, the only way is by perfect obedience to God's law. Paul says very clearly that 'it is not those who hear the law who are righteous in God's sight, but it is those who obey the law who will be declared righteous' (Romans 2:13). Earlier in the letter he says much the same thing: 'To those who by persistence in doing good seek glory, honour and immortality, he (God) will give eternal life' (Romans 2:7). But the theory collapses in practice because no such person exists. Whether we think of God's law In terms of the Ten Commandments, the Old Testament as a whole, the entire Bible, or men's consciences - the law 'written on their hearts' (Romans 2:15) - the fact is that everyone stands condemned for having failed to live up to the light they have received, the standard they have known. Elsewhere, Paul drives the point home by emphasizing that the obedience required of anyone hoping to get right with God by their own efforts is **perfect** obedience: 'All who rely on observing the law are under a curse, for it is written: "Cursed is everyone who does not continue to do **everything** written in the Book of the Law"' (Galatians 3:10). This is the death-blow to good works as a means of justification. Nor can the blow be avoided by religious observance, because 'all our righteous acts are like filthy rags' (Isaiah 64:6).

## THE SUBSTITUTE

It is against the background of this hopeless and horrifying situation, with man as a guilty, corrupt, godless and helpless sinner standing under the terrible and eternal judgement of a just and holy God, that the gospel shines in all of its brilliance. **God has intervened** by sending his Son Jesus Christ into the world on a rescue mission, in which he took the place of sinners and acted on their behalf. Jesus is 'the Righteous One' (1 John 2:1) and his perfect nature explains the fact that, although he was 'tempted in every way, just as we are', he was 'without sin' (Hebrews 4:15). He kept the law of God in every part, down to the last detail. He was able to say of his heavenly Father, 'I always do what pleases him' (John 8:29). Then, having kept the law in every part, he voluntarily paid sin's penalty as if he himself had broken it in every part. As Alec Motyer rightly says, 'The saving work satisfies every standard of the Lord's righteous nature, meets every legal claim and discharges every debt before the eternal law.' Peter's words to a group of early believers could not have been clearer: 'For Christ died for sins once for all, **the righteous for the unrighteous**, to bring you to God' (1 Peter 3:18).

The words I have emphasized are crucially important. Theologians used to speak of Jesus as a 'public person', meaning that everything he did was on behalf of others. They were spelling out the Bible's teaching that he came into the world on behalf of others, lived on behalf of others, resisted temptation on behalf of others and died on behalf of others. In all of these actions, Jesus was a substitute for sinners, doing for them what they could not do for themselves. He lived the life they could not live and died the death they should have died. As Paul put it, 'For you know the grace of our Lord Jesus Christ, that though he was rich, yet for your sakes he became poor, so that you through his poverty might become rich' (2 Corinthians 8:9). When a sinner comes to faith in Christ, all that Christ did on his behalf is applied to him. The theological word for this is 'imputation', which means ascribing, reckoning or accounting. When he puts his trust in Christ, all the sinner's sin is debited to Christ and all of Christ's righteousness is credited to him, with the result that God 'justifies the man who has faith in Jesus' (Romans 3:26).

This does not mean God announcing that the guilty sinner has not sinned (which would be a contradiction in terms and make God a liar). Rather, the sinner who trusts in Christ is declared by God to be righteous because he is united by faith to the One who as the sinner's Representative fully discharged the claims of God's law. God's law makes a double demand on sinners, absolute obedience to its precepts and the death penalty for disobedience. In his righteous life and substitutionary death Christ met both demands in full. In the Bible's words, 'Christ Jesus ... has become for us ... our righteousness' (1 Corinthians 1:30) and 'Therefore, there is now no more condemnation for those who are in Christ Jesus' (Romans 8:1). Justification means more than being forgiven; it means being brought into favour with God. Whereas to be pardoned by an earthly judge would not bring any rewards, justification brings with it eternal benefits. The Christian is not only spared the punishment of his sins, he is treated as if he had always been perfectly holy. The Christian is not only pardoned, he is promoted, brought into living and eternal fellowship with his Creator. When a man's bank account is overdrawn, his best option is to work hard, spend less, and do everything he can to get his account back in credit. In salvation, an amazing transaction takes place, in which all the sinner's debt is cancelled and all of the perfect righteousness of Christ is placed to the credit of his account. No wonder David speaks of 'the blessedness of the man to whom God credits righteousness apart from works' (Romans 4:6). In an amazing 'credit transfer' the sinner's overdraft is eliminated for ever, the penitent pauper becomes a spiritual millionaire, and from that moment onwards his account remains permanently and inexhaustibly in credit.

## INVITATION TO LIVE

When Jesus spoke of the blessings offered in the gospel he sometimes used language which fits in exactly with the words of the Beatitude we are presently studying. To the crowds at Capernaum, he said, 'I am the bread of life. He who comes to me will never go hungry, and he who believes in me will never be thirsty' (John 6:35). A little later, on the last day of the great Feast of Tabernacles in Jerusalem, 'Jesus stood and said in a loud voice, "If anyone is thirsty, let him come to me and drink. Whoever believes in me, as the Scripture has said, streams of living water will flow from within him"' (John 7:37-38).

Hundreds of years earlier, God had said the same kind of thing through the prophet Isaiah: 'Come, all you who are thirsty, come to the waters; and you who have no money, come, buy and eat! Come, buy wine and milk without money and without cost' (Isaiah 55:1). These gospel invitations are perfectly reflected in the words of our Beatitude, which speak of the needy soul being 'filled'. The guilty sinner who comes to Christ is filled with all the fulness of righteousness that there is in God's sinless Son. The penniless penitent is given 'fulness in Christ, who is the Head over every power and authority' (Colossians 2:10).

Yet, as all three of these invitations make clear, the needy sinner must come if he is to be fed and filled. He must hunger and thirst for salvation if he is to be saved. Commenting on Isaiah 55:1, Thomas Watson wrote, 'If a friend invites guests to his table he does not expect that they should bring money for their dinner, only come with an appetite.' God's promise to his Old Testament people remains true for every sinner in the world today: 'You will seek me and find me **when you seek me with**

**all your heart'** (Jeremiah 29:13). There is no promise here for the browser, the person who is 'just looking', or the one who is content with religious forms and ceremonies. There must be a hunger and thirst, a passionate longing to get right with God, to be forgiven, to be cleansed from sin and set free from self. The tragic reason why so many well-meaning churchgoers are still outside of the kingdom of heaven is that they are seeking God formally rather than fervently, vaguely rather than vehemently. Jesus made it clear that while entering the kingdom of heaven was not a reward for merit, it did call for effort. He said that 'forceful men lay hold of it' (Matthew 11:12). Elsewhere, he defused a question about how many people might eventually be saved by urging his questioner, 'Make every effort to enter through the narrow door' (Luke 13:24).

Nobody drifts into the kingdom of heaven. As the American preacher Bob Brown has helpfully put it, 'God never saves a spectator.' On the other hand, those who come to God crying, 'I will not let you go unless you bless me' (Genesis 32:26) will receive the salvation they seek. The negative and positive sides of this truth are reflected in Mary's song of praise: 'He has filled the hungry with good things but has sent the rich away empty' (Luke 1:53). God grants salvation to beggars, not to boasters or bargainers. God has nothing to give to the person who imagines that his own sincerity, morality or religion is sufficient to earn his salvation, or even to make a contribution to it. But, as Thomas Watson delightfully puts it, 'God keeps open house for hungry sinners.' Let someone plead his emptiness with God as a starving sinner and God will fill him with 'good things' - justification, a new heart, eternal life, the presence of the Holy Spirit, and 'everything we need for life and godliness' (2 Peter 1:3).

## SIAMESE TWINS

The second aspect of salvation in which the words of this Beatitude can be seen to operate is that of sanctification, or holiness of life. Justification and sanctification are closely connected, but they are not identical. To put the difference at its simplest, justification is an act of

God in which he graciously and sovereignly declares the believing sinner to be just and righteous in his sight, while sanctification is an ongoing process in which the believer, enabled by the indwelling power of the Holy Spirit, grows in holiness and therefore in conformity to the will, character and purposes of God.

What cannot be emphasized too strongly is that, although they are different, justification and sanctification are inextricably linked in the sense that the one never exists without the other. They are Siamese twins. Nobody can know any measure of sanctification unless he has first experienced the miracle of justification, and nobody is justified without beginning the process of sanctification. God never does a saving work in the heart without doing a changing work in the life. Christ saves the Christian not only from the guilt and penalty of sin but from its power: 'Therefore, if any man is in Christ, he is a new creature; the old things passed away; behold new things have come' (2 Corinthians 5:17, NASB).

This is a powerful argument against antinomianism, which teaches that God's moral law is not binding upon Christians as a way of life, and against what has been called 'cheap grace', the idea that in salvation Jesus changes the sinner's destination but not necessarily his disposition, in other words that one can trust him as Saviour without submitting to him as Lord. To say that a person can be converted without being changed is not merely bad theology, it is gobbledygook. In a book on personal evangelism C H Spurgeon wrote, 'Another proof of the conquest of a soul for Christ will be found in a real change of life. If the man does not live differently from what he did before, both at home and abroad, his repentance needs to be repented of, and his conversion is a fiction.'

When someone confronted Martin Luther after he had come to an understanding of the biblical doctrine of justification with the comment, 'If this is true, a person could simply live as he pleased!', the Reformer answered, 'Indeed! Now, what **pleases** you?' David's answer to that question (and the one that every Christian ought to be able to give) would have been, 'I desire to do your will, O my God; your law is within my heart' (Psalm 40:8). When God's law is written on the

Christian's heart, obedience is not seen as a drudgery or a duty, but as a delight.

Another difference concerns the 'mechanics' of justification and sanctification. Whereas justification is imputed, sanctification is imparted. In justification the believer is 'in Christ' (Ephesians 1:3); in sanctification, Christ is 'in him' (John 6:56). In justification, the sinner is passive, in the sense that he makes no contribution to it: 'For it is by grace you have been saved, through faith - and this not from yourselves, it is the gift of God - not by works, so that no-one can boast' (Ephesians 2:8-9). In sanctification, the sinner, saved by grace, is active: 'For we are God's workmanship, created in Christ Jesus to do good works, which God prepared in advance for us to do' (Ephesians 2:10). Those who hunger and thirst after righteousness are those who long to see God's eventual and eternal triumph over evil and who recognize that by doing what is right and just themselves they play an important part in bringing this about.

Yet a biblical longing for righteousness will go far beyond one's own personal experience. Biblical righteousness has a social dimension. It is impossible to read the Bible (and especially the Old Testament) without realizing that righteousness is something that God requires throughout society. As John Stott says so clearly, social righteousness 'is concerned with seeking man's liberation from oppression, together with the promotion of civil rights, justice in the law courts, integrity in business dealings and honour in home and family affairs. Thus Christians are committed to hunger for righteousness in the whole human community as something pleasing to a righteous God.' The fact that no amount of effort, even by all who profess and call themselves Christians, will ever succeed in transforming the whole of human society is no excuse for opting out of the struggle against evil. In Martin Luther's words, 'If you cannot make the world completely pious, then do what you can.'

## NUMBER ONE PRIORITY

There seems little doubt that when Jesus speaks of righteousness in the Beatitudes his main concern is with sanctification. The immediate context demands it because, as we have already seen, Jesus has been developing a theme. He begins with those who recognize that they are spiritual bankrupts; then he says that they are genuinely broken-hearted over their sin; then that in acknowledging their own unworthiness they submit without complaint to the disciplines of God and ill-treatment by their fellow men - and now, that they long to be holy.

This longing for holiness is not intended to be a spiritual 'extra', something that relates only to those in full-time Christian service or to some kind of Christian elite. Godliness should be the aim of every one of God's people. The new nature he has given them was 'created to be like God in true righteousness and holiness' (Ephesians 4:24). The Bible says, 'It is God's will that you should be holy' (1 Thessalonians 4:3). Nor is God satisfied with holiness being buried somewhere in the middle of the Christian's agenda. Later in the Sermon on the Mount, after warning his hearers about being preoccupied with things like food and clothing, Jesus urged them, 'Seek first (God's) kingdom and his righteousness' (Matthew 6:33). The number one priority of God's people is that he should reign in men's hearts - theirs included. Paul told his young friend Timothy (again in the context of the pursuit of worldly possessions), 'But you, man of God, flee from all of this, and pursue righteousness' (1 Timothy 6:11). The word 'pursue' is particularly intensive, as we can see in two extracts from Paul's testimony. He confessed to the Corinthians that before his conversion he 'persecuted (**dioko**) the church of God' (1 Corinthians 15:9), and we can sense something of what that meant when we read that he 'began to destroy the church ... dragged off men and women and put them in prison' and was 'breathing out murderous threats against the Lord's disciples' (Acts 8:3; 9:1). He had been consumed by a passionate crusade to wipe out what he believed to be a blasphemous cult. Yet he told the Philippians that as a Christian, 'I press on (**dioko**) to take hold of that for which Christ Jesus took hold of me ... I press on (**dioko**) towards the goal to win the prize for which God has called me heavenward in Christ Jesus' (Philippians 3:12,14). Before his conversion, his passionate priority was the destruction of Christ's church; after his conversion, it was the imitation of Christ's life.

Elsewhere in the New Testament an exhortation to pursue holiness of life is linked to a solemn warning: 'Make every effort (**dioko)** to live in peace with all men and to be holy; without holiness no-one will see the Lord' (Hebrews 12:14). Someone has said that holiness is 'the preparation for the presence of God'. That being the case, the Christian should seek to cultivate personal and practical holiness with relentless determination, commitment and perseverance. Holiness is not something we can 'claim' or 'take by faith'. As J I Packer finely puts it, 'Holiness is no more by faith without effort than it is by effort without faith.'

Almost immediately after teaching the Beatitudes, Jesus also warned that God would not be fobbed off with something that merely gave the outward appearance of holiness: 'For I tell you that unless your righteousness surpasses that of the Pharisees and the teachers of the law, you will certainly not enter the kingdom of heaven' (Matthew 5:20). The Pharisees went in for high-profile religion, but their 'righteousness' was flawed in at least three ways. It was superficial: they were meticulous in the ceremonial washing of cups and plates, but in their own hearts they were 'full of greed and self-indulgence' (Matthew 23:25). It was selective: they scrupulously observed Old Testament teaching about tithing (and even went 'over the top' by giving a tenth of things like spicy herbs that grew in their gardens) yet 'neglected the more important matters of the law - justice, mercy and faithfulness' (Matthew 23:23). It was self-centred: even their public prayers, in the synagogue or on street corners, were offered 'in order to be seen by men' (Matthew 6:5, NASB).

The righteousness which God requires and rewards must be exactly the opposite. It must be genuine, whole-hearted and God-centred. For the Christian who is hungering and thirsting for righteousness, the written law of God is not the limit of obedience, but what Michael Green calls 'the kerbstone on the road of love'. Hungering and thirsting for righteousness is not a matter of averages or percentages. It is commitment to being conformed to the will of God in every way, a constant longing to be 'filled to the measure of all the fulness of God' (Ephesians 3:19). Such a person is spiritually focused. As Don Carson comments, 'He is not drifting aimlessly in a sea of empty religiosity; still less is he puttering about distracted by inconsequential trivia.'

## TRAINING FOR TRIUMPH

The Christian who is hungering and thirsting after righteousness will never be satisfied with anything less. He knows that true righteousness is not a matter of externals and that however active he may be in Christian service, his activity is no substitute for growth in godliness. However much he reads and studies, he knows that mere knowledge is no substitute for grace. He will nevertheless do everything he can to 'grow in the grace and knowledge of our Lord and Saviour Jesus Christ' (2 Peter 3:18). He will regularly and eagerly attend the public ministry of God's Word, and make sure that he spends quality time in personal Bible study and prayer. He will avoid unnecessary involvement in godless company and seek to develop his closest relationships with those who share a concern for personal godliness. He will read the biographies (and especially the autobiographies, which can be much more telling) of those whose godly lives have left a significant impression. He will constantly search his heart for tell-tale signs of complacency, indifference or coldness. He will carefully try to avoid getting caught up in today's fatal preoccupation with 'things'. In a word, he will seek to lead a disciplined life. In his deeply challenging book **Spiritual Disciplines for the Christian Life**, my friend Don Whitney quotes Paul's words, 'Discipline yourself for the purpose of godliness' (1 Timothy 4:7, NASB) and testifies, 'In my own personal and pastoral experience, I can say I have never known a man or woman who came to spiritual maturity except through discipline.'

Paul's word for 'discipline' is **gumnaze**, from which we get words such as 'gymnasium' and 'gymnastics'. This makes it crystal clear that just as nobody drifts into justification so nobody drifts into sanctification. Christians are called to a constant, life-long, self-denying, costly, painful struggle, but just as the reward of an Olympic medal drives athletes to almost unbelievable lengths in terms of training and self-discipline, so the promised reward of godliness ought to draw the

Christian on to do whatever it takes to bring it about. This does not mean that biblical Christianity is terminal drudgery. As Don Whitney rightly says, 'If your picture of a disciplined Christian is one of a grim-faced, joyless half-robot, then you've missed the point. Jesus was the most disciplined man who ever lived and yet the most joyful and passionately alive.'

It should be clear by now that hungering and thirsting for righteousness is not an intellectual exercise, nor is it what Sinclair Ferguson calls 'a hard-nosed pursuit'. It is not an option but an obsession. It arises from a deep sense of personal failure and a heart-felt concern to glorify God in every part of one's life.

These are the kind of questions that a Christian who is concerned to know whether he is hungering and thirsting for righteousness will ask: Am I longing not merely to be good, but to be godly? Do I really want to get rid of my sins - every single one of them? Do I long to be holy in my thoughts as well as in my speech? Do I want to be purified from 'everything that contaminates body and spirit' (2 Corinthians 7:1)? Am I willing to die to my own comforts and ambitions? Am I prepared to put to death everything that belongs to my earthly nature? Am I determined to resist the devil? Do I really want to have done with self-pity, self-interest, self-protection, self-justification, self-concern and self-assertion? Do I long for purity of heart? Do I want to see the fruit of the Spirit developing in my life? Do I truly want to be like Christ in his humility, kindness, compassion and love, and in his perfect obedience to God's law? If you are genuinely in tune with questions like these and can honestly join the nineteenth-century Scottish preacher Robert Murray McCheyne in praying, 'Lord, make me as holy as it is possible for a redeemed sinner to be', you have reason to believe that you are hungry and thirsty for righteousness; and if not, what good reason can you give for not beginning now?

## ONE OF THE BLACKBERRIES

The promise Jesus makes in this Beatitude is that the people to whom it applies 'will be filled'. But this immediately brings us face to face with what seems a very strange situation, because the words 'hunger and thirst' are in the form of a present active participle. Literally, the phrase reads 'the hungering ones'. In non-technical terms this means that those who are filled continue to be hungry. In the physical realm, this is obviously not the case. The person who eats a meal and leaves the table with his hunger satisfied is no longer hungry. If he were to continue eating he would become bloated, uncomfortable, or even sick. Here, the Christian who hungers and thirsts for righteousness is graciously granted the desires of his heart, yet goes on hungering and thirsting. What we have here is a paradox, but that should be neither a surprise nor a stumbling-block. As C H Spurgeon commented, 'You say that is strange. Yes, it is; but everything is wonderful in the kingdom of God. Paradoxes, in spiritual things, are as plentiful as blackberries; in fact, if you cannot believe a paradox, you cannot believe in Christ himself, for he is God and man in one person, and that is a paradoxical mystery.' A W Pink makes much the same kind of point: 'Our text presents such a paradox that it is evident that no carnal mind ever invented it.'

This particular paradox can be expressed in a number of ways, none of which will make sense to unbelievers or to those who have no interest in making serious, godly progress, but all of which will resonate in the hearts of those who have. Hunger for righteousness demands to be satisfied, and satisfaction will increase the hunger. The more earnestly a Christian pursues holiness, the greater the progress he will make; and the greater the progress he makes the greater the progress he will want to make. To change the analogy for the moment (though it will fit in well with what we saw earlier about the need for spiritual discipline) the Christian is rather like a high jumper who with every successful leap asks for the bar to be set even higher - then longs to clear it again. In a way beyond our understanding, but not beyond our experience, the spiritual hungering and thirsting of which Jesus speaks in this Beatitude increases in the very act of being satisfied. The more the Christian is filled, the more he hungers and thirsts. The normal Christian life is one in which believers, 'beholding as in a mirror the glory of the Lord, are being transformed into the same image from glory to glory' (2 Corinthians 3:18, NASB) and every stage of transformation brings with it an unsatisfied satisfaction, the longing to be more like Christ in word, thought and deed.

The American missionary Jim Elliot, who was to be murdered in Ecuador eight years later by Auca Indians whom he was trying to reach with the gospel, wrote these words in his Journal in 1948: 'All I have asked has not been given, and the Father's withholding has only served to intensify my desires. He knows that the "hungrier" one is, the more appreciative he becomes of food, and if I have gotten nothing else from this year's experience he has given me a hunger for himself I never experienced before. He only promises water to the thirsty, satiation to the unsatisfied (I do not say **dis**satisfied), filling to those famished for righteousness.' God, and God alone, can fill the hungry soul with the righteousness it craves. Those who seek him are unanimous in their testimony that he does.

The third aspect of salvation in which this fourth Beatitude is seen to operate takes us beyond time and into eternity, what Jesus called 'the age to come' (Matthew 12:32). The vital clue here is that, as we saw in the last chapter, one of the Bible's descriptions of the future and eternal state of God's people is that they will live in 'a new heaven and a new earth, the home of righteousness (**dikaiosune**)' (2 Peter 3:13). Peter's choice of words is particularly interesting because in an earlier letter he warned his readers that as long as they lived in the present world they faced the likelihood of misunderstanding, opposition and persecution: 'Who is going to harm you if you are eager to do good? But even if you should suffer for what is right (**dikaiosune**), you are blessed' (1 Peter 3:13-14). The world has no valid reason for mistreating those whose only concern is to do good, but such is the corruption of humanity that the best of people sometimes receive the worst of treatment, and Christians who faithfully try to maintain godly standards are often prime targets for the world's abuse. The German theologian Richard Lenski pinpoints the reason for this: 'The unrighteous world cannot stand righteousness. The very presence of true righteousness irritates it, for this righteousness silently condemns its own unrighteousness.'

The Christian determined to pursue a life of righteousness can expect no favours from an unrighteous world - 'In fact, everyone who wants to live a godly life in Christ Jesus will be persecuted' (2 Timothy 3:12). But things are going to change, and God's people are 'longing for a better country - a heavenly one' (Hebrews 11:16). The day is coming when they will live in a society from which every vestige of unright-eousness has been permanently removed and in which, perfected by grace, they will know the joy of living for ever in a state of glory. As the nineteenth-century American preacher Albert Barnes wrote, 'It is for this that the Christian desires to dwell in that world, and waits for the coming of his Saviour. It is not primarily that he may be happy, desirable as that is, but that he may be in a world where he himself will be perfectly pure, and where all around him will be pure; where every being that he meets shall be "holy as God is holy", and every place on which his eye rests, or his foot treads, shall be uncontaminated by sin.' C H Spurgeon once preached that if a thief ever got to heaven, the first thing he would do would be to pick the angels' pockets. Soon afterwards, he was taken to task by a member of his congregation who suggested to him that angels did not have pockets. 'In that case', Spurgeon replied, 'he would pluck the feathers from their wings!' This was his typically teasing way of saying that heaven was hermetically sealed against sin, so that 'nothing unclean and no one who practises abomination and lying shall ever come into it, but only those whose names are written in the Lamb's book of life' (Revelation 21:27, NASB).

Although there are glimpses of this 'better country' in Scripture, it is impossible for us to imagine such an environment. Ever since man first sinned, humanity has lived in a fallen world, with the result that there has never been a truly godly country, city, society or community. With the exception of Jesus and an occasional angel, no holy being has ever set foot on our planet. The world in which we live is the home of unrighteousness. What a contrast there will be in the age to come, when God's people will live in 'the Holy City, the new Jerusalem' (Revelation 21:2), in an environment utterly uncontaminated by sin and in which they themselves will be perfectly holy and permanently happy. Those who go through life hungering and thirsting for righteousness without interruption or end will have their hearts' desires fully met.

One of the things the Bible tells us about God's people in their future state is this: 'Never again will they hunger; never again will they thirst' (Revelation 7:16). The primary reference is to physical hunger and thirst; there will be no more struggling to survive, no more battling against the elements, no more rationing of resources, no more drought or flooding, no more parched earth, no more failed crops. This must have come as wonderful news to those living in the harsh conditions of the primitive Middle East, but we know that its meaning goes far beyond the physical because the very next words tell us: 'For the Lamb at the centre of the throne will be their shepherd; he will lead them to springs of living water' (Revelation 7:17). This tells us that in the age to come the Christian will have no needs. As the British preacher Richard Brooks says, 'We shall have everything we desire and desire everything we have. Our bodies will be glorified and perfected. Our sin will be stamped out for ever, our hearts will be fixed upon him in whose heaven we dwell.'

What a prospect! 'There will be no more death or mourning or crying or pain, for the old order of things has passed away' (Revelation 21:4). Never again will we have cause to repent over a besetting sin or grieve over even the smallest failure. Never again will we feel the blush of shame, the pain of a wounded conscience, or the sorrow brought by disappointment. Every desire of our perfected hearts will be met to the full and, as we join in the endless worship of our God and Saviour, 'we shall be like him, for we shall see him, as he is' (1 John 3:2). Many centuries before, David had written in joyful anticipation of what this would mean: 'And I - in righteousness I shall see your face; when I awake, I shall be satisfied with seeing your likeness' (Psalm 17:15). Here, surely, is the perfect and final fulfilment of the promise: 'Blessed are those who hunger and thirst for righteousness, for they will be filled.'

# Chapter 10

# God's overflow

'Blessed are the merciful, for they will be shown mercy'
(Matthew 5:7)

None of the Beatitudes is shorter than the one to which we now turn. Yet with just six words in its original written form it has such a wealth of meaning that it is virtually impossible to give a satisfactory exposition of its teaching in a book of this size. In trying to do so, I am reminded of the story (probably apocryphal, but entirely feasible) of the man sentenced to 99 years' imprisonment. As he was already 76 years old, he told the judge, 'But your Honour, I will never be able to do it all'. 'Never mind,' the judge replied, 'just do as much as you can.'

The best way to begin is by reminding ourselves of two essential facts. The first is that the Beatitudes are not a map showing us the way to be saved, but a mirror reflecting the character of those who are already saved. This becomes clear when we realize that the only imperative in the whole of the Beatitudes comes right at the end, when Jesus says, 'Rejoice and be glad, because great is your reward in heaven' (Matthew 5:12). Nowhere in the Beatitudes are we told to do anything in order to become something. The Beatitudes are not a series of exhortations, they are an exhibition, a portrait gallery of what a genuine Christian is like.

## CHARACTER BEFORE CONDUCT

This point is emphasized by the fact that the Beatitudes come at the very beginning of the Sermon on the Mount, and constitute an essential introduction to the remainder of the discourse. If we bypass the introduction the rest of the sermon makes no sense. It is foolish and futile to thumb through the Sermon on the Mount, select a few of its instructions and then hope that by trying to obey them one will please God and earn one's own salvation. Many people, however, make precisely this mistake.

A favourite choice of those who make this mistake is, 'Do not judge, or you too will be judged' (Matthew 7:1). Many people take this to mean that there is great virtue in being easy-going, indulgent and uncritical, and that if they are endlessly tolerant they will avoid the terrors of God's final judgment at the end of life. But this flabby interpretation flies in the face of the Bible's clear teaching that we are to exercise firm discernment in all matters of doctrine and practice and, in Jesus' own words, to 'make a right judgment' (John 7:24). In matters of doctrine, for example, the Bible warns against being dazzled by claims about spiritual phenomena and says that instead of uncritically accepting them as genuine we are to 'test the spirits to see whether they are from God, because many false prophets have gone out into the world' (1 John 4:1). John Stott's comments on this verse are particularly relevant in today's climate: 'There is an urgent need for discernment among Christians. We are often too gullible, and exhibit a naive readiness to credit messages and teachings which purport to come from the spirit-world. There is such a thing, however, as a misguided charity and tolerance towards false doctrine.'

The same discernment is needed in the matter of people's behaviour. There is not the slightest suggestion in Scripture that we are to take people at what we might call their 'voice value' and assume their good character regardless of their conduct. Instead, Jesus made it clear that 'by their fruit you will recognize them' (Matthew 7:20). But how can we recognize the source and significance of corrupt fruit unless we exercise our critical faculties? Nor is it enough merely to recognize evil. Paul gave the Corinthians directions which take matters much farther: 'But now I am writing to you that you must not associate with anyone who calls himself a brother but is sexually immoral or greedy, an idolater or a slanderer ... With such a man do not even eat' (1 Corinthians 5:11). This statement is particularly relevant to the point I am making here, because taken out of context it might seem not only harsh but hopelessly unrealistic. The key, however, is that Paul is writing to Christians and the prohibition is limited to 'anyone who calls himself a brother'. He confirms this by saying that in order to avoid intimate contact with all 'the people of this world who are immoral, or the greedy and swindlers, or idolaters' his readers 'would have to leave this world' (1 Corinthians 5:9-10). Paul is not telling everyone in the world that they must have nothing to do with anyone whose life does not conform to biblical standards. He is telling Christians that they must not recognize as fellow believers those who live flagrantly sinful lives.

This underlines the principle which needs to be established at this point in our study. The idea that anyone can pluck Matthew 7:1 out of the Sermon on the Mount and assume that by adopting a laid-back attitude to everything he is obeying God, gaining his approval and avoiding his judgment misses the whole point that the Beatitudes set the scene for everything that follows. In them, Jesus gives us what A W Pink calls 'the birthmarks by which the true subjects of his kingdom may be identified'. Only then does he go on to give detailed instructions on subjects such as spiritual standards, personal relationships, marriage and divorce, prayer and fasting. Jesus puts character before conduct, because the first dictates the second. As he told his disciples, 'The good man brings good things out of the good stored up in his heart, and the evil man brings evil things out of the evil stored up in his heart. For out of the overflow of his heart his mouth speaks' (Luke 6:45). This ties in exactly with what we are told elsewhere in Scripture: 'Above all else, guard your heart, for it is the wellspring of life' (Proverbs 4:23).

This is precisely the pattern we see in the Sermon on the Mount. Only those who possess the truly Christian character reflected in the Beatitudes can be expected to obey its instructions - and the Beatitudes are true, at least in some measure, of all of those who are in the kingdom of God.

## THE LADDER OF LIGHT

The second important thing to underline before we can begin to understand what Jesus meant by the saying, 'Blessed are the merciful, for they will be shown mercy' is that the Beatitudes are deliberately connected and in logical sequence. They are not like a collection of pearls thrown together so that those touching each other are only doing so by accident. Instead, they are separate yet inseparable. C H Spurgeon called them a 'ladder of light', with each rung leading further upwards.

Jesus begins by defining those in the kingdom of God as being 'poor in spirit'. They realize that in the sight of a holy God they are morally and spiritually defiled and depraved, and cannot contribute in any way to their salvation. He then says that such poverty of spirit goes far beyond a bare acknowledgement of their sinfulness; God's people 'mourn' over it. Sin grieves and hurts them. This in turn leads them to become 'meek'. Their egos have been fatally wounded. They make no claims for themselves, nor do they resent it when God disciplines them or other people denounce them. They know perfectly well that the worst things which happen to them are better than they deserve. But that is not the whole picture. God's people do not slink away into a corner and wallow in self-pity. They 'hunger and thirst for righteousness'. They long to be holy and to live holy lives, and do everything they can to use the means of grace which God has provided to bring about the holiness for which they long.

But the clear progression in the Beatitudes does not stop there. The promise given to those who hunger and thirst for righteousness is that 'they will be filled'. In the normal course of events, something continually being filled would overflow, and that is precisely the picture we have when Jesus goes on to say 'Blessed are the merciful, for they will be shown mercy'. To put this in another way: having concentrated almost exclusively on the believer's inner spiritual condition, Jesus now goes on to speak of one of the ways in which this will be expressed outwardly. Poverty of spirit, mourning over sin, meekness and a longing for righteousness are essentially matters of the heart and are largely concerned with a person's relationship to God. But although genuine Christianity begins there, it goes beyond that and finds expression in the Christian's relationships with others. Specifically, the person filled with righteousness finds that this righteousness overflows to others in what Jesus defined as 'mercy'.

As with so much of what Jesus taught in the Sermon on the Mount, this would have sounded particularly revolutionary at the time. One Roman philosopher called mercy 'the disease of the soul'. The Romans glorified justice, courage, discipline and power; mercy was despised as a contemptible sign of weakness. The received wisdom of the day among the Jews was that those most likely to make it big in Messiah's reign were the hard-nosed conservatives, those who, when the tide finally turned, would wreak vengeance on their nation's enemies and then be rewarded by Messiah for showing no mercy on those who had opposed his people. Yet once again Jesus turned conventional, worldly wisdom on its head and said that those assured of God's favour were 'the merciful'. What did he mean by merciful?

## WINDOWS ON WORDS

A glance at any secular dictionary will begin to suggest the general idea - words like 'kindness', 'clemency' and 'forbearance' are among those we will find. However, secular dictionaries are not the best source for scriptural definitions and I want to focus on three particular New Testament words which relate to our subject.

The first is **oiktirmos**, which speaks of the pity of compassion which one has for the needs or sufferings of others. The Bible uses it of God when it calls him 'the Father of compassion (**oiktirmos**) and the God of all comfort' (2 Corinthians 1:3). We might have expected a phrase such as 'the compassion of the Father', but 'the God of compassion' says much more. It gives added emphasis to the fact that compassion (the word in the original is in the plural, and the AV, NKJV and NASB all render it 'mercies') is one of God's inherent characteristics. The essential meaning of **oiktirmos** lies in the area of feeling. It speaks of being moved by the misery of others. It is the word Paul used when he wrote to Christians of his day, 'Therefore, as God's chosen people, holy and dearly loved, clothe yourselves with compassion (**oiktirmos**), kindness, humility, gentleness and patience' (Colossians 3:12). Just as God sees humanity in the self-inflicted misery which sin has brought upon it, so we are to be moved at the plight of our fellow men and women. The modern author Guy Appéré writes, 'The Christian is conscious more than anyone else of the plight of the world in which, behind men's physical and moral troubles, he sees their spiritual ruin.'

The second relevant New Testament word is **splagchnizomai** The root of this particular word is **splagchnon,** which in classical Greek was chiefly used of the upper viscera of animals, such as the heart, lungs and liver. Figuratively, it came to mean deep, inner feelings of affection, compassion, pity and love. We are told that when Jesus saw the crowds, 'he had compassion (**splagchnizomai**) on them, because they were harassed and helpless, like sheep without a shepherd' (Matthew 9:36). As a young boy during World War II, I was evacuated from my native Guernsey to the Hebridean island of Islay, where I lived on a remote farm, and I can still picture occasions when I came across the carcases of sheep that had become separated from the shepherd and fallen into a ditch or bog from which they had not been able to escape. In New Testament times, when shepherds went ahead of their flocks, a sheep becoming detached from the others would soon perish in the burning heat, a fact which gives Matthew's words an added impact.

Thirdly, we come to the word **eleeo,** the one used by Jesus in this Beatitude. **Eleeo** is a stronger word than the other two in that it speaks not only of feelings but of action. In its adjectival form it describes those who take active steps to help others by whose misery they have been moved. The merciful will certainly feel pity and compassion towards those in need, but they will express these emotions by taking practical steps to relieve the misery that triggered their concern. The difference between emotions and actions can be seen in something the Apostle John wrote: 'Let us not love with words or tongue but with actions and in truth' (1 John 3:18). Telling people we are sorry for them is no substitute for giving whatever help we can. John Wesley used to say that if we felt for people in need we ought to feel in our pockets!

As we work our way through Scripture we see that mercy operates in two general areas, the practical and the spiritual. Practically, mercy operates in giving help to the needy; spiritually, it operates in granting forgiveness to the guilty. The rest of our study will flow in and out of these two areas, but before we go any further we need to remind ourselves yet again that the Beatitudes are not laws, or commandments, or conditions of membership in the kingdom of God. They are characteristics of true Christians, while containing an inescapable challenge to believers. The writer to the Hebrews tells us that the Word of God 'judges the thoughts and attitudes of the heart' (Hebrews 4:12). The Beatitude we are now studying certainly does, in at least two obvious ways.

Firstly, **the absence of mercy is a bad sign**. As John asks, 'If anyone has material possessions and sees his brother in need but has no pity on him, how can the love of God be in him?' (1 John 3:17). Later, he drops the rhetorical approach: 'For anyone who does not love his brother, whom he has seen, cannot love God, whom he has not seen' (1 John 4:20). Pious phrases about one's concern for others are not only worthless in meeting anyone else's need but, unless they are joined to positive, practical action, they are equally worthless as evidence of saving faith. An exposition of Christianity is no substitute for an exhibition of it.

No New Testament writer is more insistent on this than James, who makes the point with a typically terse illustration: 'What good is it, my brothers, if a man claims to have faith but has no deeds? Can such faith save him? Suppose a brother or sister is without clothes and daily food. If one of you says to him, "Go, I wish you well; keep warm and well fed," but does nothing about his physical needs, what good is it? In the same way, faith by itself, if it is not accompanied by action, is dead' (James 2:14-17). James is condemning what Alec Motyer calls the 'armchair philanthropist', the kind of person who is long on theology but short on charity, strong on the nouns of the Christian faith, but weak on the verbs. The Scottish preacher Alexander Maclaren hit the nail on the head when he wrote, 'The people who least live their creeds are not seldom the people who shout loudest about them. The paralysis which affects the arms does not, in these cases, interfere with the tongue.' We dare not miss the lesson. The absence of mercy is a bad sign. It shows that, however loud his profession of faith, the person who shows no mercy (spiritually and practically) to others is not a Christian.

Secondly, **the presence of mercy is a good sign.** One of the clearest biblical indications of this comes in a simple Old Testament maxim:

'The wicked borrow and do not repay, but the righteous give generously' (Psalm 37:21). This tells us that open-handed giving to those in need is characteristic of the righteous; it is one of their traits. As Sinclair Ferguson rightly says, 'Showing mercy to the poor and needy is a touchstone and hallmark of a true conversion to Christ.' This underlines something we have seen throughout these studies in the Beatitudes, namely that what the writer of Hebrews calls 'the thoughts and attitudes of the heart' govern a person's life. This means that only a truly godly person can act in a truly godly way. As Martyn Lloyd-Jones puts it: 'A Christian **is** something before he does anything; and we have to **be** Christian before we can act as Christians.' This is just another way of saying that nobody except the Christian can live the Christian life. One sometimes hears people say such things as, 'He lives a good Christian life, though I know he wouldn't call himself a Christian'; or 'They do a lot of good, Christian things'; or 'She makes no profession of faith, but she certainly lives a Christian life.' What people mean when they say such things is that those concerned **do** some of the things commended or commanded in the Bible - but equating that with genuine Christianity is light years away from the truth. A Christian is a person whose heart has been radically changed, someone who has been transformed by the grace of God at the very core of his being. As a result, his whole attitude to God, to man, to sin, to life, to death and to everything else has been permanently revolutionized and brought under the authority of the Word of God.

## FINE, BUT FLAWED

This opens up a very important area which we dare not overlook, namely that unconverted people do sometimes show commendable mercy to those in need. We can see this in Scripture and elsewhere. In a well-known parable, Jesus told of two orthodox Jews who ignored the needs of a wounded traveller. The only person who 'had mercy (**eleos**) on him' was a despised Samaritan (Luke 10:37). Luke tells us that when he, Paul and others were shipwrecked on Malta, 'The islanders showed us unusual kindness. They built a fire and welcomed us all, because it was raining and cold' (Acts 28:2).

Contemporary illustrations are all around us, sometimes filling our newspapers and television screens. One will be sufficient to make the point. When a terrorist bomb demolished the Federal Building in Oklahoma City in April 1995, killing over 200 men, women and children and wounding hundreds of others, there was an overwhelming response to the emergency. This came not only from official agencies, such as the Police, the Fire Department and the medical services, but from countless people who queued to give blood or to help in any other way they could. Here was genuine, commendable, practical mercy, with no hidden agenda. But where does it fit in to Jesus' promise that 'the merciful ... will receive mercy'?

One should obviously have nothing but admiration for the dedication, skill and sacrificial efforts of those who rendered such great service in the Oklahoma City incident, or of those who are professionally committed to works of mercy on a daily basis, but there is not necessarily any spiritual dimension to what they do. As a general principle (I am obviously not commenting on what may or may not be true in regard to any particular individual) their actions are humanitarian and commendable, but they are nevertheless flawed if they are not biblically motivated. People may be motivated by natural affection, a love for humanity, or a conviction about the solidarity of the human species. Many people engage in worthwhile professional or voluntary work with no reference whatever to God. Some of those with impressive records of service may not even believe that God exists. That being the case, their work cannot possibly come within the orbit of the Beatitude we are presently studying.

The flaw in the otherwise commendable actions of many people is that the mercy they show is incomplete. It is directed to the body or the mind, but not to the soul. There is great care and concern to provide such needs as food, clothing, accommodation, healing, counselling or comfort, but no concern for the souls of those being helped. John Brown put it like this: 'The good-natured, generous man of the world pities and relieves the temporal wants of his fellow-creatures; but he thinks not of their spiritual state, their everlasting prospects. He feels tender compassion for naked, starving, diseased bodies ... but he feels no pity for souls perishing in ignorance of God, and under the condemning sentence of his holy law. This cannot indeed be expected; for how should he feel for others, when, in reference to such subjects, he has no feeling for himself? - though there is something monstrously absurd in men's being so exceedingly concerned about the removal of the sufferings of a few years, and altogether careless about the prevention of the intolerable miseries of eternity.'

Brown is right - but we must dare to go one step further. While the kind of mercy that is humanitarian or 'horizontal' in its motivation and its objectives may be of great benefit to those who receive it, it is not acceptable to God as something that will contribute to the salvation of those who show it. Even at their most sacrificial, such actions are spiritually worthless and are included in the Bible's blunt statement that 'all our righteous acts are like filthy rags' (Isaiah 64:6). As Alec Motyer writes in commenting on this phrase, 'Even what we might consider to be in our favour, **our righteous acts**, flow from a fallen nature and partake of its fallenness.' This kind of statement will seem shocking to many people, but is it surely true? If not, we must say that all acts of mercy are not only satisfying to God but make a decisive contribution to the salvation of those who perform them. But that takes us straight into the heresy of justification by works which says that there are two ways of getting right with God, one through faith in Christ and the other through the merits of our own humanitarian service. Quite apart from going against the grain of everything the Bible teaches, this would produce the absurd scenario in which, for example, a doctor who was an atheist would be brought into a right relationship with a God in whom he did not even believe. Nothing could make it clearer that the Beatitudes are not to be seen as keys for unlocking the door of the kingdom of heaven.

## THE WHOLE MAN

Biblically-based mercy has an altogether different dimension to it. It sees man both in his mortality and in his immortality. It seeks to care not only for physical and mental needs but also for spiritual needs, which it recognizes as the most important of all. Yet biblical mercy never seeks to meet one need at the expense of another. In **Walk in His Shoes**, John Stott says, 'Naturally if we had to choose between evangelism and compassionate service, we would have to agree that the spiritual and the eternal have a higher priority than the material and the temporal. But we don't have to choose, or very seldom.'

This balance is clearly reflected in the New Testament, in which Jesus showed mercy to the whole man. In setting the scene for the Sermon on the Mount, we saw that 'Jesus went throughout Galilee, teaching in their synagogues, preaching the good news of the kingdom, and healing every sickness and disease among the people' (Matthew 4:23). The same kind of thing is repeated a little later: 'Jesus went through all the towns and villages, teaching in their synagogues, preaching the good news of the kingdom and healing every disease and sickness' (Matthew 9:35). Luke paints the same picture in telling us that when crowds flocked after Jesus he 'spoke to them about the kingdom of God, and healed those who needed healing' (Luke 9:11). When he commissioned the twelve disciples 'he sent them out to preach the kingdom of God and to heal the sick' (Luke 9:2) and we are then told that they 'went from village to village, preaching the gospel and healing people everywhere' (Luke 9:6). Preaching **and** healing are mentioned, to show that both are important, yet in each case preaching is mentioned first, as if to show that this is of primary importance because of the eternal dimension of the message.

The history of the Christian church not only reflects the same balance but, as the historian F J Foakes-Jackson writes, the message has motivated the mercy: 'History shows that the thought of Christ on the cross has been more potent than anything else in arousing a compassion for suffering and indignation at injustice ... The later evangelicalism, which saw in the death of Christ the means of salvation for fallen humanity, caused its adherents to take the front rank as champions of the weak: prison reform, the prohibition of the slave trade, the abolition of slavery, the Factory Acts, the protection of children, the crusade against cruelty to animals, are all the outcome of the great

Evangelical revival of the 18th Century.' We can put names to some of the crusades involved: the Seventh Earl of Shaftesbury, Elizabeth Fry, William Wilberforce, Thomas Barnardo and Jean Henri Dunant, the founding father of the Red Cross, are among those who showed the reality of their faith by the passion and compassion of their works.

In none of these cases did the concern to meet physical and material needs eliminate the concern to meet spiritual need. Mercy that ignores spiritual need is not the full-orbed mercy shown by Jesus. Christian mercy includes gospel mercy, and this can be shown only by those who have received God's mercy and long that others should receive it too. This stands as a constant challenge to all who profess and call themselves Christians. Do we have what used to be called 'a passion for souls' (how old-fashioned it sounds in these trendy days!)? Do we have a sense of urgency about men's spiritual condition? What is our response to the Bible's standing orders on this: 'Be merciful to those who doubt; snatch others from the fire and save them; to others show mercy, mixed with fear - hating even the clothing stained by corrupted flesh' (Jude 22)? Are we doing anything to show mercy to those on skid row, to alcoholics, to those affected by drug abuse or stricken by AIDS? Or do we gather up our self-righteous robes and let them 'stew in their own juice'? Not that these are the only ones who need the gospel of God's mercy and grace. People at every level of society, from the richest to the poorest, are outside of God's kingdom, exposed to his righteous anger and in desperate danger of spending eternity in hell. Should that not move those who have received God's mercy to do everything we can to warn them of their plight and to point them to the only way of salvation? Thomas Watson asks, 'When we see others sleeping the sleep of death and the fire of God's wrath ready to burn about their ears, and we are silent, is not this to be accessory to their death?' There is no escaping the impact of his question, nor can we avoid the challenge of those asked by his great contemporary Richard Baxter: 'If you have the hearts of Christians and of men, let them yearn towards your poor, ignorant, ungodly neighbours. Alas, there is but a step between them and death and hell ... Have you hearts of rock, that you cannot pity men in such a case as this? If you believe not the Word of God, and the dangers of sinners, why are you Christians yourselves? If you do believe it, why do you not bestir yourselves to the helping of others? Do you not care who is damned, so long as you are saved?'

## MOTIVATION FOR MERCY

This leads us to ask an obvious question: What is the Christian's motivation for showing mercy to others? To answer the question negatively, it is **not** in order to receive mercy in return. As we will see at the end of this chapter, that is not the meaning of the words ' ... for they will be shown mercy'. One writer paraphrased this particular Beatitude to read, 'This is the great truth of life; if people see us care, they will care', but that makes a mockery of its meaning. The Christian is never to show mercy in the hope that he will be shown mercy in return. Biblical mercy is not speculating in order to accumulate. It is not a sprat to catch a mackerel. It never has an eye to reciprocal benefit of any kind. The straightforward answer to the question is this: **God's people are motivated to show mercy by the mercy they have themselves been shown by God.**

Earlier in this chapter, we touched on the fact that mercy is one of God's attributes, and Scripture teems with this particular truth. In one of the most moving passages in the Old Testament we are told of an occasion when the Israelites assembled before God, read Scripture for a quarter of the day and spent another quarter in confession of sin and in worship. As their spiritual leaders acknowledged God's providential dealings with his people, going all the way back to creation, they returned again and again to emphasize his mercy: 'But you are a forgiving God, gracious and **compassionate**, slow to anger and abounding in love' (Nehemiah 9:17); 'Because of your great **compassion** you did not abandon them in the desert' (Nehemiah 9:19); 'From heaven you heard them, and in your great **compassion** you gave them deliverers, who rescued them from the hand of their enemies' (Nehemiah 9:27); 'And when they cried out to you again, you heard from heaven, and in your **compassion** you delivered them time after time' (Nehemiah 9:28); 'But in your great **mercy** you did not put an end to them or abandon them, for you are a gracious and **merciful** God' (Nehemiah 9:31). It is important to notice that, in every case, God is seen not merely as One who has sympathetic thoughts over the plight of his people, but as One who takes decisive action to help them. Yet these statements do no more than highlight a truth that runs all the way through Scripture and is summed up perfectly by James when he reminds his readers of God's dealings with Job: 'The Lord is full of compassion and mercy' (James 5:11). The Christian's incentive to be compassionate and merciful to others is that God has been compassionate and merciful to him - in two ways.

**The first is in the area of common mercy**, or what theologians often call 'common grace' (the words 'mercy' and 'grace' are often synonymous in Scripture), namely the provision of man's basic needs for survival. This is what Paul had in mind when he told the Athenians, 'The God who made the world and everything in it ... gives all men life and breath and everything else' (Acts 17:24-25) and quoted the pagan poets' statement that 'For in him we live and move and have our being' (Acts 17:28). It is God alone who enables human life to be sustained on the face of this planet. Every atom and element that contributes to man's survival is granted to us by a merciful and gracious God. God is not an 'absentee landlord'.

The Bible makes it clear that everything included in what we call 'the natural order', such as the movement of sun, moon and stars, changes in the weather and the life cycles of every living creature (man included), is directly related to the work of God. In a superbly succinct statement the Bible tells us that the eternal Son of God is 'sustaining all things by his powerful word' (Hebrews 1:3). As Bruce Milne states, 'If God were to withdraw his withholding word, then all being, spiritual and material, would instantly tumble back into nothing and cease to exist.'

At a time of intense personal trauma, which unbelievers might have used as a reason for rejecting the very existence of God, one of the Old Testament writers affirmed, 'Because of the Lord's great love we are not consumed, for his compassions never fail. They are new every morning;

great is your faithfulness' (Lamentations 3:22-23). As the Scottish writer Robert Louis Stevenson put it, 'There is nothing but God's grace. We walk upon it; we breathe it; we live and die by it; it makes the nails and axles of the universe.' God owes us nothing; we owe God everything. In Thomas Watson's phrase, 'Every time you draw in your breath you suck in mercy.' The fact that I am alive to write these words and that you are alive to read them is evidence of God's common mercy. This is the Christian's first incentive to show mercy to others.

**The second is in the area of saving mercy.** God's common mercy or grace is received by unbelievers as well as believers, by God's enemies as well as his friends. Jesus made it clear that God 'causes his sun to rise on the evil and the good, and sends rain on the righteous and the unrighteous' (Matthew 5:45). God's people recognize this and constantly thank him for his life-sustaining mercy. But this points them to an even greater expression of God's mercy - that which has brought about their salvation. Contrasting believers with those who are not, Paul writes, 'Like the rest, we were by nature objects of wrath. But because of his great love for us, God, who is rich in mercy (**eleos**), made us alive with Christ even when we were dead in transgressions - it is by grace you have been saved' (Ephesians 2:3-5). Sharing his personal testimony with a friend, he testifies, 'Even though I was once a blasphemer and a persecutor and a violent man, I was shown mercy (**eleeo)'** (1 Timothy 1:13).

Here again, we can see that God's mercy is not passive, but active. God's mercy is not a divine disposition to overlook sin but an active intervention to deal with it. To say that God is 'rich in mercy' does not mean that he has a spineless, **laissez-faire,** or complacent attitude as far as sin is concerned, nor that he lacks the capacity to be angry over sin. God's eyes are 'too pure to look on evil'; he 'cannot tolerate wrong' (Habakkuk 1:13). David cries, 'You are not a God who takes pleasure in evil; with you the wicked cannot dwell. The arrogant cannot stand in your presence; you hate all who do wrong' (Psalm 5:4-5). What is more, the Bible makes it clear that he 'will not leave the guilty unpunished' (Nahum 1:3). It is precisely in this context that God's mercy comes into effect. God saw mankind in its rebellion and sin and in the self-inflicted misery that sin had brought to the whole of the human race, and was moved in his heart to take action to relieve guilty and undeserving sinners from their miserable condition. The action he took defies human imagination and understanding: 'The Father sent the Son to be the Saviour of the world' (1 John 4:14). The sinless Son of God left the glory of heaven, took upon himself human form and nature, and then, in his death on the cross, bore the full, horrifying brunt of God's wrath which others deserved. As Peter told his fellow believers, 'He himself bore our sins in his body on the tree' (1 Peter 2:24).

Here is God's mercy in all its magnificence. There was nothing in humanity which deserved God's mercy. In the Bible's blunt verdict, 'There is no one righteous, not even one; there is no one who understands, no one who seeks God. All have turned away, they have together become worthless; there is no one who does good, not even one' (Romans 3:10-12). Yet God was moved to act in mercy, and the Christian rejoices in the amazing fact that he has become the undeserving beneficiary. When a godly preacher lay dying and a friend tried to comfort him with the assurance that he would soon receive the reward which his faithful labours deserved, he replied, 'I deserve to go to hell, but God interfered.' Every believer's testimony is the same. If you are reading these words as a Christian, it is because God interfered in your life. By nature you were an enemy of God and paving your own way to hell, but God interfered by sending the Second Person in the Godhead to die for you and the Third Person to tell you that he had done so and to draw you to Christ in repentance and faith. The American hymnwriter Philip Bliss expressed his own response in words that have been gratefully sung by millions ever since he wrote them:

> Bearing shame and scoffing rude,
> In my place condemned he stood;
> Sealed my pardon with his blood:
> Hallelujah! What a Saviour!

Why should Christians be merciful? Because they have been shown mercy. Why should Christians love others? Because God first loved them. Why should Christians seek to help those in need? Because God has reached down to help them. Why should Christians be willing to give unsparingly to the needs of others? Because God 'did not spare his own Son, but gave him up for us all' (Romans 8:32). When we grasp this, we begin to see the close link between mercy received and mercy given. Being merciful to others is the natural result of receiving the mercy of God - and provides evidence that we have received it. In the Sermon on the Plain Jesus told his disciples, 'But love your enemies, do good to them, and lend to them without expecting to get anything back. Then your reward will be great, and you will be sons of the Most High' (Luke 6:35). Jesus did not say 'you will **become** sons of the Most High', suggesting that this might somehow be as a reward for doing good to others. The phrase he used means that as believers show mercy to their fellow men and women they will be identified as the children of God by reflecting his mercy to them. As Albert Barnes writes, 'Nowhere do we imitate God more than in showing mercy.'

## GIVING TO GOD

Although the major, over-ruling motive for believers to act mercifully is that God has acted mercifully to them, the Bible does indicate another, which is that in giving to the poor it is as if one were giving to God. In the Old Testament we are told, 'He who oppresses the poor shows contempt for their Maker, but whoever is kind to the needy honours God' (Proverbs 14:31). Jesus brought this principle into even clearer focus when he said that on the day of judgment he would remind those welcomed into the heavenly kingdom of their acts of mercy in helping the needy and tell them that 'whatever you did for one of the least of these brothers of mine, you did for me' (Matthew 25:40). Whatever the precise meaning of these words, they surely provide a powerful incentive to show mercy to those in need. As Thomas Watson comments, 'The poor man's hand is Christ's treasury, and there is nothing lost that is put there.'

One of the most impressive images in Scripture is God's identification with the needs of the poor and his concern that those needs should be met. William Temple, Archbishop of Canterbury from 1942-1944, once said, 'It is a mistake to think that God is interested only in religion' and the Bible is full of statements that press upon God's people the duty of showing mercy to the disadvantaged. In the Old Testament we are told, 'Defend the cause of the weak and fatherless; maintain the rights of the poor and oppressed' (Psalm 82:3). Paul reminded the Ephesian elders that they must 'help the weak, remembering the words the Lord Jesus himself said: "It is more blessed to give than to receive"' (Acts 20:35). Writing to the Galatians, he urged, 'Therefore, as we have opportunity, let us do good to all people, especially those who belong to the family of believers' (Galatians 6:10). Earlier in the same letter there is another very telling phrase. Paul told of the time when he attended a meeting of church leaders in Jerusalem at which it was agreed that, whereas James, Peter and John should concentrate their ministry on the Jews, Paul had a special ministry to the Gentiles. He then added, 'All they asked was that we should continue to remember the poor, the very thing I was eager to do' (Galatians 2:10).

Do we see that same eagerness in the Christian church today? In his book **Rich Christians in an Age of Hunger**, American author Ronald Sider writes, 'If at this moment in history a few million Christians in affluent nations dare to join hands with the poor around the world, we will decisively influence the course of history.' Is he overstating the case? Will we ever have the opportunity of finding out? Earlier he says, 'The gulf between what affluent Christians give and what they could give is a terrifying tragedy.' In his Foreword to the book, the British preacher David Watson is just as trenchant: 'We have accepted a largely middle-class culture, with its worldly values and selfish ambitions, and have conveniently ignored the utterly radical teaching of Jesus concerning money, possessions and social standing within the kingdom of God. Most serious of all, perhaps, our lifestyle, both individual and corporate, is astonishingly different from the lifestyle of our Master whom we profess to follow and serve. We know (and preach) all about the grace of our Lord Jesus who, though he was rich, for our sakes became poor, really and extremely poor; but we do not demonstrate the same grace in our own lives. We have not become poor so that others might become rich. We have not even chosen to live simply that others may simply live.' One of the articles in the Lausanne Covenant, issued following an international conference of church leaders held in Switzerland in 1974, reads as follows: 'Those of us who live in affluent circumstances accept our duty to develop a simple lifestyle in order to contribute more to both relief and evangelism.' Notice the blending of two important facets of mercy - practical relief and the preaching of the gospel. It is much easier to discuss doctrine than to reflect these important principles in our lives.

Two brief points should be added about the manner in which Christians should show mercy. In the first place **we should give gladly.** Paul writes, 'Each man should give what he has decided in his heart to give, not reluctantly or under compulsion, for God loves a cheerful giver' (2 Corinthians 9:7). Elsewhere, writing of the particular gifts a believer might have, he says, ' ... if it is showing mercy, let him do it cheerfully' (Romans 12:8). The root of the words 'cheerful' and 'cheerfully' is the Greek **hilaros**, from which we get the words 'hilarious' and 'hilarity'. Giving to others is not to be thought of as a fine or a tax. Our benevolence should not have to be prised out of our hands. The Scottish theologian James Denney puts it well: 'What we spend in piety and charity is not tribute paid to a tyrant, but the response of gratitude to our Redeemer.'

In the second place, **we should give humbly.** Jesus laid down this principle in the Sermon on the Mount: 'Be careful not to do your "acts of righteousness" before men, to be seen by them. If you do, you will have reward from your Father in heaven. So when you give to the needy, do not announce it with trumpets, as the hypocrites do in the synagogues and on the streets, to be honoured by men. I tell you the truth, they have received their reward in full. But when you give to the needy, do not let your left hand know what your right hand is doing, so that your giving may be in secret. Then your Father, who sees what is done in secret, will reward you' (Matthew 6:1-4). There should be a delightful amnesia about our benevolence. We should not forget to give, but forget that we have given. There are times when works of mercy have a somewhat high profile, but they should never be done with that in mind. We may at times be seen to do good works, but they must never be done in order to be seen. We need to remember that when we have done all we can we remain no more than 'unprofitable servants' (Luke 17:10).

## BURYING THE MAD DOG

I have touched very little on the mercy of forgiveness, though again the Bible is very clear about both our motivation and our model: 'Be kind and compassionate to one another, forgiving each other, just as in Christ God forgave you' (Ephesians 4:32); and again, 'Bear with each other and forgive whatever grievances you may have against one another. Forgive as the Lord forgave you' (Colossians 3:13). On one occasion, Peter asked Jesus, 'Lord, how many times shall I forgive my brother when he sins against me? Up to seven times?' (Matthew 18:21). Contemporary rabbinical teaching said that one should forgive three times, but that that was the limit. Peter took the current yardstick, doubled it, and added one more for good measure, presumably thinking that this would demonstrate impressive tolerance. Jesus replied, 'I tell you, not seven times, but seventy times seven' (Matthew 18:22). In this stunning answer, Jesus was not setting a new limit of 490 times. He was more concerned with mercy than with mathematics. He was not telling Peter to keep count but to lose count. Forgiveness was not to be dispensed with the first century equivalent of a calculator in his hand. We cannot claim to have repented of our sins if we disobediently refuse to forgive the sins of others.

The questions are inescapable. Do you have a forgiving spirit? Are you prepared to turn the other cheek, go the extra mile? Are you prepared to be wronged, insulted or unfairly treated without retaliating? C H Spurgeon used to say, 'Forgive and forget. When you bury a mad dog, don't leave his tail above the ground.' Much as I enjoy quoting Spurgeon, he may in this case have been just slightly unrealistic, because it is not always possible to forget - but by the grace of God it is not impossible to forgive. In all the media attention given to the aftermath of the Poppy Day Massacre in Enniskillen, Northern Ireland in

1987, when eleven people were blasted to death by a terrorist bomb, nothing made a greater impact than the statement by Gordon Wilson, the father of one of the victims, who said that as a Christian he completely forgave the killers and that he would pray every day for God to have mercy on them. In one interview he told a BBC reporter, 'I bear no ill will. I bear no grudge. It's part of God's greater plan and God is good. Only a Christian could possibly react like that. In author Corrie Ten Boom's words, 'You never so touch the ocean of God's love as when you forgive and love your enemies.

On the other hand, failure to forgive has horrific consequences. Jesus once told a parable about a king to whom a servant owed a huge amount (something in excess of £1,000,000) but as the servant was penniless the king graciously 'took pity on him, cancelled the debt and let him go' (Matthew 18:27). The servant later met a man who owed him a few pounds. Grabbing him by the throat, he demanded instant repayment, and when the debtor pleaded for mercy he had him thrown into prison until the last penny was paid.

When the king heard about this he called the servant in: '"You wicked servant," he said, "I cancelled all that debt of yours because you begged me to. Shouldn't you have had mercy on your fellow servant just as I had on you?"' (Matthew 18:32-33). He then had him jailed until he had repaid the debt in full. When he had finished telling the parable, Jesus left no doubt as to its meaning: 'This is how my heavenly Father will treat each of you unless you forgive your brother from your heart' (Matthew 18:35).

## MULTI-FACETED MERCY

Although a great deal of our study has concentrated on giving to the poor and the forgiveness of those who wrong us, these by no means exhaust the manifestations of mercy. Mercy means giving help regardless of the attitude of the person in need. As American author D Edmond Hiebert says, 'Mercy prefers to deal with the needy in terms of what is needed rather than what is deserved.' Mercy does not insist on its rights, but is prepared to forfeit them for the sake of the greater good.

Mercy does not demand everything that is legally due, but is willing to make concessions on the basis of love and concern. Mercy does not retaliate in the face of criticism. Mercy has defective hearing when rumours are flying around, and refuses to join in condemnation without cause. C H Spurgeon used to say, 'My blind eye is the best eye I have, and my deaf ear is the best ear I have.' Mercy seeks to understand situations that at times seem beyond understanding. Some years ago my wife went through a time of deep depression, and in attending to her needs over a long period of time I discovered to my shame how much I needed to learn about patience, compassion, gentleness and mercy. Mercy is always prepared to give the benefit of the doubt. Finally, mercy extends beyond the human race to all of God's creatures. The Bible says, 'A righteous man cares for the needs of his animal, but the kindest acts of the wicked are cruel' (Proverbs 12:10). Whatever the irrational statements of some of those crusading for 'animal rights', a Christian should not cause unnecessary pain to so much as a fly. The nineteenth-century preacher Rowland Hill once said, 'I would not give anything for that man's religion whose very dog and cat are not the better for it.' Mercy to dumb animals sometimes speaks volumes.

## COVENANT IN KIND

The promise to those who are merciful is that 'they will be shown mercy', a phrase which may over the years have been more misunderstood and misinterpreted than any other in the Beatitudes. At first glance it seems to say that the person who shows mercy will receive mercy as a reward, but this cannot possibly be the case as it would undermine the pervasive biblical doctrine of the unmerited grace of God. None of the characteristics in the lives of those who are blessed are natural or the result of human effort. To become poor in spirit is a mercy from God, delivering the person concerned from the deadly disease of pride which would otherwise have shut him out of the kingdom of heaven. It is of God's mercy that the sinner is brought to mourn over sin, to loathe what he once loved, and to know God's comfort. It is of God's mercy that the mourning sinner becomes meek, humbly acknowledging that he has no right to favours from God or man and yet inherits the earth. It is of God's mercy that the meek sinner is moved to hunger and thirst for righteousness and to have the growing joy of being filled. And it is of God's mercy that his hard and unforgiving heart has been made merciful. It would therefore shatter the whole grace-controlled picture if the mercy promised to the merciful was something they had earned. As A W Pink points out, the Beatitude would then read 'Blessed are the merciful, for they shall obtain justice.'

Yet some interpretations fall into this very error. In Roman Catholic moral theology certain actions are called 'works of supererogation'. The Latin word **supererogare** means 'to pay out more than is necessary' and its use goes back to the story of the Good Samaritan who told the innkeeper 'I will reimburse you for any extra expense you may have' (Luke 10:35). The Roman Catholic doctrine concerned was not formulated until the Middle Ages, and eventually it taught that through such things as regular attendance at church, masses, rosary prayers, fastings, and the wearing of medals, crucifixes and the like the 'saints' can store up an excess of merit in heaven beyond the requirements of duty. Mary and the 'saints' are said to have accumulated vast treasures of such merit, from which the Pope can draw and which he can then dispense to those who meet whatever terms the church lays down.

But the whole idea of mercy by merit is an unbiblical sham. It makes a mockery of the death of Christ, in which the Bible says 'he offered for all time one sacrifice for sins' (Hebrews 10:12) and it ignores the fact that even Mary and the greatest of the so-called saints are included in the Bible's verdict that 'all have sinned and fall short of the glory of God' (Romans 3:23). As God's people are called to be perfect, it is difficult to see how any excess of merit can be left over and made available to others. Those who interpret the Beatitude in this strictly legal way are condemning themselves in the process. It is impossible for a Christian to do more than his biblical duty, and when he has done it God owes him nothing. Our mercy to others is not the cause of God's mercy to us, but rather the reverse. That is why John says, in referring to a parallel virtue in God's people, 'We love because he first loved us' (1 John 4:19). In the same way, God's mercy is free, and J C Ryle is perfectly right in saying that 'to talk of merit or claim to God's favour is absurd and preposterous'. If God's mercy had to be entered on your Tax Return it would go under 'Unearned Income'! Man has no more right to mercy than a murderer has to go free.

Then in what ways is it true that the merciful will receive mercy? As with all the promises in the Beatitudes, the answer is two-dimensional, temporal and eternal. As far as the temporal promise is concerned, the first thing to be said is that there is therapeutic value to the person showing mercy. The Bible tells us: 'A kind man benefits himself' (Proverbs 11:17) and 'It is more blessed to give than to receive' (Acts 20:35). Only those who give can understand the truth of these statements. There is genuine happiness in serving and caring. When I was a young Christian I was told that the spelling of the word 'joy' was a reminder as to how it was attained - Jesus first; others second; yourself last. That may sound sentimental and simplistic - but it has the merit of being scriptural. Simon Kistemaker comments, God's greatest desire is to give. When man follows God's example, he receives a divine blessing because he demonstrates that he is one of God's children.'

There are times when this blessing is in the form of material things. The Old Testament tells us, 'One man gives freely, yet gains even more' (Proverbs 11:24), and again, 'He who gives to the poor will lack nothing' (Proverbs 28:27). Jesus promised much the same thing: 'Give, and it will be given to you. A good measure, pressed down, shaken together and running over, will be poured into your lap. For with the measure you use, it will be measured to you' (Luke 6:38). Countless Christians over the centuries have proved that you cannot outgive God. One prosperous businessman, asked how he could afford to give so much to Christian service, replied: 'I shovel it out, and God shovels it back - and God uses a bigger shovel!' Who has ever come across a Christian who gave so much away to those in genuine need that he himself was reduced to ruin? Yet the principle goes beyond material things, and the promise of God through Isaiah knows no limits: 'If you do away with the yoke of oppression, with the pointing finger and malicious talk, and if you spend yourselves on behalf of the hungry and satisfy the needs of the oppressed, then your light will rise in the darkness and your night will become like the noonday' (Isaiah 58:9-10). What is more, we can be sure that the promise also relates to the mercy of granting forgiveness, because God always blesses those who obey him. As the nineteenth-century writer and philanthropist Hannah More testified, 'A Christian will find it cheaper to pardon than to resent. Forgiveness saves us the expense of anger, the cost of hatred, and the waste of spirits.' What is more, there are all kinds of 'hidden extras'. The more we try to reflect in our dealings with others the mercy God has shown to us, the more of God's mercy we will experience.

Finally, the promise of mercy has an eternal dimension. Jude urges believers, 'Keep yourselves in God's love as you wait for the mercy of our Lord Jesus Christ to bring you to eternal life' (Jude 21). Writing to Timothy of the way in which he had appreciated the fellowship and help of his friend Onesiphorus, Paul says, 'May the Lord grant that he will find mercy from the Lord on that day!' (2 Timothy 1:18). James combines the negative and positive aspects of the same truth: 'Speak and act as those who are going to be judged by the law that gives freedom, because judgment without mercy will be shown to anyone who has not been merciful. Mercy triumphs over judgment!' (James 2:12,13).

Negatively, those who show no mercy; and those whose hearts are cold, crusty and unforgiving, have clearly never received God's mercy and been brought into the kingdom of heaven. Those who never enjoy a foretaste of the kingdom in this life will never enter into its fulness in the life to come. For such people, there will not be judgment without justice, but there will be judgment without mercy. Their merciless, unforgiving lifestyle will boomerang on them with terrible force. As someone has solemnly said, 'What we weave in time we wear in eternity.'

Positively, those who know in their hearts that they have been changed from self-centred, self-serving sinners, who find themselves instinctively reaching out in mercy to those in need, and who know that by the grace of God they have become tolerant, gracious and forgiving, have cause to rejoice. One day they will discover that even the greatest of blessings they have received here on earth from 'the Father of mercies' (2 Corinthians 1:3, NKJV) will be surpassed by those they will enjoy for ever in his glorious presence. God's mercy to them will overflow into eternity. The Puritan divine Thomas Manton comments on this with his usual quaintness: 'It is no small thing that we may expect from infinite mercy an infinite mercy. Would an emperor give brass farthings?' Those who are merciful in this life show that God has been merciful to them, and will enter into the infinite enjoyment of the truth that 'his mercy endures for ever' (Psalm 118:1). The contemporary Welsh preacher and hymnwriter Vernon Higham has exactly the right words with which to finish our study of this particular Beatitude:

> For yonder a light shines eternal,
> Which spreads through the valley of gloom;
> Lord Jesus, resplendent and regal,
> Drives fear far away from the tomb.
> Our God is the end of the journey,
> His pleasant and glorious domain;
> For there are the children of mercy,
> Who praise him for Calvary's pain.

# Chapter 11

# Seeing in the dark

'Blessed are the pure in heart, for they will see God'
(Matthew 5:8)

The Beatitudes have been analysed by some 50 generations of theologians, teachers and preachers, many of whom have sought not only to understand their meaning but to fit them into a symmetrical pattern. As we have already seen, the first four Beatitudes flow naturally into each other - the poor in spirit mourn over sin, meekly accept life's difficulties and disciplines as being no more than they deserve, and long to be filled with righteousness. Put another way, the first Beatitude leads onward and upward to the second, the second to the third, and the third to the fourth. But what happens next? Martyn Lloyd-Jones suggests that in the first three Beatitudes we are going up one side of a mountain, reaching the summit in the fourth, and that in the next three we are coming down the other side of the mountain. He even suggests that the 'downhill' Beatitudes correspond to the 'uphill' ones, in the sense that the 'uphill' Beatitudes are perfectly reflected in the 'downhill' ones. In this model, poverty of spirit leads Christians to be merciful, those who mourn seek purity of heart, and (anticipating our next chapter) only the meek can truly be peacemakers. This is beautifully tidy, but marrying each of the 'ascending' Beatitudes into one in the 'descending' group runs the risk of blurring the important truth that all Christians are meant to display all of the characteristics Jesus mentions. Christians are not given the liberty of specializing in a chosen area of grace, but are called upon to 'grow up in all aspects' (Ephesians 4:15).

It might be better to see the first four Beatitudes as emphasizing the Christian's right relationship to God and the remainder as emphasizing his relationship to other people. This would obviously be true of the Beatitude we studied in the last chapter, where we saw that being filled with righteousness resulted in an overflow of mercy to others. A good case can be made for seeing this same picture in the remaining three Beatitudes, beginning with the astounding statement, 'Blessed are the pure in heart, for they will see God.'

As with each of the Beatitudes we have studied so far, this one is packed with truth which has an impact out of all proportion to its length. Martyn Lloyd-Jones says of these eleven words (ten in the original language) that they are 'undoubtedly one of the greatest utterances to be found anywhere in the whole realm of Holy Scripture' and that anyone who realizes even something of their meaning 'can approach them only with a sense of awe and complete inadequacy'. John MacArthur agrees: 'To attempt to deal with such an incredible statement in one brief chapter is almost an insult to God and to the power and depth and insight of his Word. This is one of the greatest utterances in all the Bible. It stretches over everything else in Scripture. The theme of purity of heart being necessary to see God is vast and infinite and draws in almost every biblical thread.'

If these assessments are even close to being right, the Beatitude now before us presents a daunting challenge to any would-be expositor. Nevertheless, its astonishing brevity at least suggests that the most straightforward and obvious way of discovering something of what Jesus meant is to take each of the key words - 'pure', 'heart' and 'see', put them under a biblically-controlled microscope one at a time, and examine them with great care. For reasons which will become obvious, let us take the middle word first.

## UNCOVERING THE WELL

The word 'heart' is used hundreds of times in our English Bible, almost always translating the Hebrew words **leb** and **lebab** or the Greek word **kardia** (the root of 'cardiac', 'cardiology' and the like). Sometimes, it simply means the centre or middle of something. For example, in a wonderful song of praise, Moses and the Israelites remembered how, when crossing the Red Sea in the course of their escape from Egypt, 'the deep waters congealed in the heart of the sea' (Exodus 15:8). At other times, it means the physical organ in the human body. When King David's rebellious son Absalom was accidentally trapped in a large oak tree while riding his mule, he was assassinated by Joab, one of the king's loyal army officers, who 'took three javelins in his hand and plunged them into Absalom's heart while Absalom was still alive in the oak tree' (2 Samuel 18:14). But in almost every other case, the word 'heart' means something very different. Whatever the particular emphasis (and the context will decide this) a person's 'heart' is much more than the muscular organ which circulates blood around the body. One New Testament use of the word will be particularly helpful in pinpointing its true meaning. In one of his letters, Peter writes about marriage relationships and in the course of a passage addressed to wives says, 'Your beauty should not come from outward adornment, such as braided hair and the wearing of gold jewellery and fine clothes. Instead, it should be that of your inner self, the unfading beauty of a gentle and quiet spirit, which is of great worth in God's sight' (1 Peter 3:3-4). The words 'inner self' translate the Greek **kruptos tes kardias anthropos**, and the New American Standard Bible comes as close to its literal meaning as any English version in rendering it 'the hidden person of the heart'. Reading the Bible with that filter on the lens of our microscope, we soon begin to see something of what the 'heart' means in a person's life and experience.

In the first place, **the heart is the seat of the emotions**. David expressed his faith in God by saying that when his enemies attack him, 'my heart will not fear' (Psalm 27:3). Elsewhere, he wrote, 'My heart leaps for joy' (Psalm 28:7). Confessing his initial reaction to the prosperity of the wicked, another Psalmist said, 'My heart was grieved' (Psalm 73:21). Jesus emphasised this emotional dimension in his matchless summary of the first four Commandments: 'Love the Lord your God with all your heart and with all your soul and with all your mind and with all your strength' (Mark 12:30). Matthew Henry called this love 'the commanding principle of the soul' and said that when this is in place 'there is a disposition to every other duty'.

**The heart is the seat of the understanding**. At one point, Jesus said of those who refused to be convinced by his miracles that they had become spiritually deadened and could not 'understand with their hearts' (John 12:40). Paul lamented that when his fellow Jews read the Old Testament, 'a veil covers their hearts' (2 Corinthians 3:15). There was a deep-rooted mental blockage, a stubborn resistance to the truth, which prevented their acceptance of Jesus as Messiah.

**The heart is also the seat of reason.** When Jesus knew that certain religious teachers thought it blasphemous of him to say that he could forgive sins, he asked them, 'Why do you entertain evil thoughts in your hearts?' (Matthew 9:4). Their corrupt reasoning was rooted in their sinful natures.

**The heart is associated with the conscience.** When the crowds heard Peter declare on the Day of Pentecost that, as a nation, the Jews had been guilty of crucifying the One whom God had made 'both Lord and Christ' they were 'cut to the heart' (Acts 2:36,37). This was no mere flicker of emotion; they were devastated with a sense of corporate and personal guilt.

**The heart is involved with human motive and intention.** One of the New Testament writers tells us that God's Word 'judges the thoughts and intentions of the heart' (Hebrews 4:12, NASB), reaching into the depths of the human psyche, where issues are weighed and purposes settled.

**The heart is at the root of our desires.** Later in the Sermon on the Mount Jesus said that 'anyone who looks at a woman lustfully has already committed adultery with her in his heart' (Matthew 5:28). The Pharisees taught that the seventh commandment - 'You shall not commit adultery' (Exodus 20:14) - referred only to the physical act, but Jesus made it clear that it is just as sinful for a man to give rein to immoral imagination and desire.

**The heart is closely associated with our decision-making.** When laying down basic guidelines for charitable giving, Paul told the Christians at Corinth, 'Each man should give whatever he has decided in his heart to give, not reluctantly or under compulsion' (2 Corinthians 9:7). The two negatives used here underline the significance of a person's heart when choosing what to do in a given situation.

Finally, **the heart is the seat of faith.** Positively, the Bible tells us, 'For it is with your heart that you believe and are justified' (Romans 10:10); negatively, it warns us, 'See to it, brothers, that none of you has a sinful, unbelieving heart that turns away from the living God' (Hebrews 3:12). The Bible's writers are unanimous in saying that saving faith is not superficial emotion, nor merely mental assent to propositional truth, but unqualified commitment which is rooted in the heart of the believer.

When we pull all of this data together we begin to get an impressive picture of what the Bible means when it uses the word 'heart' in a symbolic sense. It is that which radically governs not only our emotions but our thoughts, desires, motives, ambitions, affections, will, words and actions. The heart stands for the entire personality, the whole man. It is that which makes a person what he is. As Thomas Manton explains: 'There is nothing in the life but what was first in the heart.' Nobody in Scripture states this particular truth more succinctly than Solomon, who calls the heart 'the wellspring of life' (Proverbs 4:23). This biblical principle is reflected in our current symbolic use of the word 'heart'. When we speak of someone as 'stout-hearted' or 'big-hearted' we are referring to his bravery or benevolence. To call a person 'cold-hearted' is to comment on his temperament. The fact that we use many such phrases helps to underline the point that outward characteristics are determined by inner character.

Jesus was constantly at pains to make this clear, especially when confronting the Pharisees. When they complained that some of his disciples were eating food without going through the rigmarole of ceremonial hand-washing which had been traditionally imposed on the Jews, he told them, 'Listen and understand. What goes into a man's mouth does not make him "unclean", but what comes out of his mouth, that is what makes him "unclean"' (Matthew 15:10-11). Later, he elaborated to his disciples: 'Don't you see that whatever enters the mouth goes into the stomach and then out of the body? But the things that come out of the mouth come from the heart, and these make a man "unclean". For out of the heart come evil thoughts, murder, adultery, sexual immorality, theft, false testimony, slander. These are what make a man "unclean"; but eating with unwashed hands does not make him "unclean"' (Matthew 15:17-20). Jesus was clearly not belittling the importance of personal hygiene, but driving home the point that outward ceremony was no substitute for inner purity, and that the heart of the human problem was the problem of the human heart. It is there, at the very core of life, that the real problem lies, and where the real solution must be sought.

Paul brings this into focus by seeing the Christian life as an unrelenting conflict in which 'the sinful nature desires what is contrary to the Spirit, and the Spirit what is contrary to the sinful nature' (Galatians 5:17). The sinful nature (that is, the sinful heart) produces 'sexual immorality, impurity and debauchery; idolatry and witchcraft; hatred, discord, jealousy, fits of rage, selfish ambition, dissensions, factions and envy; drunkenness, orgies and the like', and Paul warns his readers that 'those who live like this will not inherit the kingdom of God' (Galatians 5:19-21). The person whose life is characterized by things like these has no right to call himself a Christian, because this kind of behaviour betrays the fact that his sinful nature remains in control of his life. By contrast, Paul goes on to say that when the Holy Spirit is the controlling influence the result is 'love, joy, peace, patience, kindness, goodness, faithfulness, gentleness and self-control' (Galatians 5:22).

This is why the critical questions for anyone to ask are not 'Do I have enough religion?', 'Do I belong to the right church?' or even 'Am I doing the right kind of things?', but 'Has God changed my heart?' 'Has he radically changed my motives and affections?' 'Do I love what I once loathed, and loathe what I once loved?' 'Are my moral and spiritual endeavours driven by a passionate love for God and his ways, or by a lingering belief that they contribute something to my salvation?' 'Do I have a genuine longing to be obedient to God in every area of my life?' 'Can I truthfully say with David, "I desire to do your will, O my God; your law is within my heart"?' (Psalm 40:8). Christian conversion is not an external rearrangement of certain actions, but a radical transformation of the heart which inevitably results in an equally radical transformation of the life.

## THE DIVINE CARDIOLOGIST

Because of a chronic condition which has persisted for over 20 years, the first thing my doctor does when I go for my two-yearly medical examination is to take a careful electrocardiogram so that he can monitor the state of my heart. Whatever else he checks, this is always the crucial test, the one which most affects my life and lifestyle. What Jesus is telling us in the Beatitudes is that God is a spiritual cardiologist, and the Bible confirms this in a number of ways.

Firstly, it tells us that **God looks at the heart**. When King Saul fell from grace the prophet Samuel was sent to Bethlehem to anoint his successor, with the prior knowledge that he would come from among the sons of Jesse. Initially, he was impressed with Eliab and felt sure that he should be chosen, but God intervened and told him, 'Do not consider his appearance or his height, for I have rejected him. The Lord does not look at the things man looks at. Man looks at the outward appearance, but the Lord looks at the heart' (1 Samuel 16:7). Human judgements are often superficial and at best inadequate. We see people as they appear; God sees them as they are.

Secondly, **God searches the heart**. When Solomon was chosen to build a temple which would be the focal point of the nation's worship, his father told him, 'And you, my son Solomon, acknowledge the God of your father, and serve him with wholehearted devotion and with a willing mind, for the Lord searches every heart and understands every motive behind the thoughts' (1 Chronicles 28:9). The New Testament confirms that there is no point in trying to deceive God about our spiritual condition: 'Nothing in all creation is hidden from God's sight. Everything is uncovered and laid bare before the eyes of him to whom we must give account' (Hebrews 4:13).

Thirdly, **God desires the heart**. Speaking through Solomon, he says to the believer, 'My son, give me your heart and let your eyes keep to my ways' (Proverbs 23:26). God is not satisfied with surface religion. Nor is he merely concerned with one facet or another of the believer's life, such as his thoughts, words or actions. God cannot be fobbed off with warm feelings, religious thoughts, ecclesiastical rituals or outward morality. God requires from each one of his people total submission of the heart. He demands allegiance and obedience at every point though, as the eighteenth-century preacher Charles Bridges helpfully adds, 'The command of authority is an invitation of love.'

This divine insistence on the surrender of the heart was radically different from the stern but shallow teaching of the Pharisees and their associates. They concentrated in meticulous detail on the strict observance of hundreds of rules and regulations which they had drawn up as interpretations of the Old Testament law. In a previous chapter we saw something of how ridiculous their position had become, but many other absurdities could be quoted. For example, a new lamp could be moved from one place to another on the Sabbath, but not an old one. Hot food could be kept warm on the Sabbath day by covering with clothes, feathers or dried flax, but not with damp herbs or straw, which might stimulate fresh heat (and therefore 'work'). Someone with a sore throat could swallow liquid to ease the discomfort, but was not allowed to gargle, which would count as 'work'. The same kind of nonsense is still being perpetrated. A few years ago a Jerusalem newspaper carried a kind of 'Dear Rabbi ...' column in which an anxious reader asked whether it was acceptable to open a refrigerator on the Sabbath. The answer given was that it was perfectly proper to do so if the refrigerator was not fitted with a light which came on when the door was opened. If it was fitted with a light this would be an infraction of Sabbath law as it would be causing the electricity suppliers to work on the 'day of rest'.

To make matters worse, the Pharisees not only concentrated all their attention on ceremonial detail, they largely ignored spiritual issues, which is why Jesus rebuked them so frequently and so severely. On one occasion he told them, 'Woe to you, teachers of the law and Pharisees, you hypocrites! You clean the outside of the cup and dish, but inside they are full of greed and self-indulgence. Blind Pharisee! First clean the inside of the cup and dish, and then the outside also will be clean' (Matthew 23:25-26).

The key words in our present context are 'but inside'; that is where God's concern lies. God's primary interest is in the heart, and we dare not miss the lesson. It is right for a professing Christian to read the Bible and to pray, but what about your heart? It is right to meet with God's people in public worship, but what about your heart? What about the hidden springs of affection, motive and ambition? What about spiritual qualities such as love, mercy, faithfulness, humility and justice? These are the issues about which God is primarily concerned. God is more concerned about the state of your heart than he is about your health, your bank balance, your business, your family, your 'Christian work', your church-attendance record, your giving to charitable causes, or anything else. As Martyn Lloyd-Jones rightly says, 'The Christian faith is ultimately not only a matter of doctrine or understanding or of intellect, it is a condition of the heart.' In the light of this, no right thinking person can fail to face up to one all-important question: 'Is my heart right with God?'

## PURE BUT IMPERFECT

The second key word in the Beatitude we are studying is 'pure', which translates the Greek **katharos**. It is the root of our English word 'catharsis', which means the purgation of the digestive system or, in psychiatry, the relieving of fears by bringing them to the surface of a person's consciousness. New Testament writers did not invent their own language, but used that which was common currency in the secular world of their day, and **katharos** was a word used, for example, of soiled clothing which had been washed clean, grain from which all chaff had been removed, metal without any trace of alloy, or a man with all his bills and taxes paid.

We can see examples of some of these in the New Testament. After Jesus had been crucified, Joseph of Arimathea took the body down from the cross and 'wrapped it in a clean **(katharos)** linen cloth' (Matthew 27:59). In his amazing vision of the world to come, John saw the new Jerusalem as 'a city of pure **(katharos)** gold' (Revelation 21:18). Sometimes, it carries what we might call a legal meaning. When Paul was leaving the Ephesian elders for the last time he told them, 'Therefore I declare to you today that I am innocent **(katharos)** of the blood of all men. For I have not hesitated to proclaim to you the whole will of God' (Acts 20:26-27). At other times it carries a ceremonial meaning. Mark records some teaching Jesus gave concerning the right application of ceremonial laws about washing and eating, then adds,

'In saying this, Jesus declared all foods "clean (**katharos**)"' (Mark 7:19). By saying what he did, Jesus not only abolished the ancient ceremonial rules and declared them obsolete, but focused his hearers' attention on the need for inner cleanliness.

What then does it mean to be 'pure in heart'? Before giving some positive answers to the question, one important negative point needs to be made, namely that purity of heart does not mean perfection. If it did, not even the finest believer who has ever lived would have the remotest possibility of embracing the promise that the pure in heart 'will see God'. Over the centuries, a number of 'sinless perfection' movements have taught that at conversion the sinful nature is eradicated and have claimed the possibility of perfect purity in this life, but the Bible gives no warrant for such teaching.

All the Bible's saints were sinners, and remained so when they were at their most saintly. The Bible asks, 'Who can say, "I have kept my heart pure; I am clean and without sin"?' (Proverbs 20:9) - and all of humanity must remain silent. John, who was given that remarkable vision of heaven, bluntly admits, 'If we claim to be without sin, we deceive ourselves and the truth is not in us' (1 John 1:8). Paul, who writes again and again about his joyful certainty of spending eternity in God's presence, nevertheless confesses, 'For what I do is not the good I want to do; no, the evil I do not want to do - this I keep on doing' (Romans 7:19). He was not saying that he never stopped sinning but that, in spite of all the progress he had made, sin kept rearing its ugly head.

There is nothing in the Bible - let alone in this Beatitude - which gives anyone the right to claim sinless perfection on this side of the grave. In fact, as A W Pink rightly says: 'One of the most conclusive evidences that we **do** possess a pure heart is to be conscious of and burdened with the impurity which still indwells us.' Conviction of sin and purity of heart are by no means incompatible. The gospel promises are not to those who think they are perfect, but to those who grieve over their imperfections, and long to be holy. With this negative principle in place, we can now turn to the issues involved in purity of heart.

## 'TO WILL ONE THING'

In the first place, **purity of heart includes sincerity**. The greatest single charge that Jesus levied against the Pharisees was that of hypocrisy. Nothing made him angrier than their self-righteous posturing. He denounced them as being 'like whitewashed tombs, which look beautiful on the outside but on the inside are full of dead men's bones and everything unclean' (Matthew 23:27). On one occasion he confronted 'some who were confident of their own righteousness and looked down on everybody else' (Luke 18:9) by telling them of two men, one a Pharisee and the other a tax collector, who went up to the temple to pray. In his so-called 'prayer', the Pharisee boasted about his religious and moral achievements, while the tax collector was crushed with conviction and could only cry, 'God, have mercy on me, a sinner' (Luke 18:13). There is no question as to which of them would have appeared to have the better religious credentials, yet Jesus told his hearers that it was the penitent sinner and not the proud Pharisee who left the temple 'justified before God' (Luke 18:14).

As we have already seen, the great concern of the Pharisees was **external** purity. The three contemporary expressions of Jewish piety were giving, praying and fasting, and the Pharisees went to extraordinary lengths to present an impressive image in all three areas. When making charitable gifts, they would 'announce it with trumpets ... to be honoured by men'; when they prayed, they would do so 'standing in the synagogues and on the street corners to be seen by men'; and when they fasted they would 'disfigure their faces to show men they are fasting' (Matthew 6:2,5,16). This kind of behaviour would undoubtedly have made a big impression on other people, but it cut no ice with God because it hid moral corruption, spiritual apathy and deadly formalism.

Hypocrisy is nothing better than skin-deep holiness, and nothing is more loathsome in the sight of God. The Bible says of hypocrites, 'They claim to know God, but by their actions they deny him. They are detestable, disobedient and unfit for doing anything good' (Titus 1:16). This is some of the strongest language in Scripture, and it is used of those whose religion is a performance rather than an experience, whose piety is external rather than internal, and who are more show than substance. No professing Christian dare brush this principle aside. What we are in public will never blind God to what we are in private, and we can never be too careful in rooting out every trace of hypocrisy as soon as it is discovered. John Stott has some telling words on this: 'How few of us live one life and live it in the open! We are tempted to wear a different mask and play a different role according to each occasion. This is not reality but play-acting, which is the essence of hypocrisy. Some people weave round themselves such a tissue of lies that they can no longer tell which part of them is real and which is make-believe.'

The task of self-examination is made all the more difficult by the fact that the human heart is 'deceitful above all things and beyond cure. Who can understand it?' (Jeremiah 17:9). The great seventeenth-century theologian John Owen said that at one and the same time the heart could be 'flaming hot and key cold, weak and yet stubborn, obstinate and facile' and added that 'the frame of the heart is ready to contradict itself every moment.' That being the case, we dare not take anything for granted in responding to the impulses or instincts that move us to speak and act in any given situation. This is particularly true in the matter of motive, when there can so often be a fine line between serving God and serving ourselves. Charles Colson, who was special counsel to United States President Richard Nixon during the notorious Watergate scandal and served a prison term for his part in the high-level sleaze that rocked the United States in the nineteen-seventies, provides a telling illustration of this. After his conversion Colson founded Prison Fellowship, which now has an international ministry. In a feature for **Jubilee**, Prison Fellowship's newsletter, he faced up to the following proposition: 'Critics say you were a power broker for Nixon, and now you're a power broker for Jesus - that you've just transferred your loyalties.' This was part of his reply: 'All my life I've been ambitious, hard-driving, a perfectionist desiring to win, very idealistic. So have I just transferred my loyalties? To be absolutely honest, I can't ever be certain what motivates me. Jeremiah tells us that nothing is more deceitful than the human heart - and he's right. I **think** I'm in this ministry because of my love for the Lord and desire to serve, but maybe it's because Chuck Colson has to be in the centre of things and has to be the big organizer and doer.' His transparent testimony suggests that he has safely negotiated a very dangerous hazard - but it should serve as a clear warning about the treachery of the human heart.

Sincerity is exactly the opposite of hypocrisy, and is precisely the quality God requires. In his moving penitential prayer David cried out to God, 'Surely you desire **truth in the inner parts**' (Psalm 51:6). Elsewhere he asks, 'Who may ascend the hill of the Lord? Who may stand in his holy place? He who has clean hands and **a pure heart**, who does not lift up his soul to an idol or swear by what is false' (Psalm 24:3-4). This is the person to whom God has promised his blessing, as David tells us: 'Blessed is the man whose sin the Lord does not count against him and in whose spirit is no deceit' (Psalm 32:2). Another Psalmist agrees: 'Surely God is good ... to those who are **pure in heart**' (Psalm 73:1).

The Danish philosopher Soren Kierkegaard may have come as close as anyone to a precise definition of purity of heart with his famous aphorism that it means 'to will one thing'. The pure in heart are the same on the inside as they are on the outside. As R V G Tasker puts it, they are 'free from the tyranny of a divided self'. They may not be sinless, but they are sincere. They are the same in private as they are in public. Their religious activities are not a cover-up, hiding more than they reveal, as was the case with the Pharisees, of whom Jesus said, 'These people honour me with their lips, but their hearts are far from me' (Mark 7:6). When the pure-hearted man goes to church, his heart is there. He can truthfully say with the Psalmist, 'I rejoiced with those who said to me, "Let us go to the house of the Lord"' (Psalm 122:1). When he prays, his heart is in it. He is among those who 'call on the Lord out of a pure **(katharos)** heart' (2 Timothy 2:22). His religion is not a lifeless performance but a living experience. He worships, prays, gives, serves and witnesses for Christ, and seeks to live in obedience to God's Word, not because these things are expected of him, but because he has no wish to do otherwise.

A friend of mine used to say that a hypocrite was someone who let his light so shine before men that nobody could tell what was going on behind. Not so the pure in heart. There is no hidden agenda, no moral, spiritual or religious sleight of hand. When Brian Johnston, the well-known British broadcaster, died in 1994, friends published a tribute called **Summers will never be the same**. In it, the blind American pianist George Shearing, a close friend for nearly 40 years, wrote, 'To meet Brian Johnston was to know Brian Johnston.' Author and songwriter Tim Rice added, 'The man behind the microphone was the man himself ... it is this aspect of Brian that first and foremost springs to mind.' Cricket correspondent John Woodcock called him 'quite without artifice', and Andrew Johnston, the broadcaster's second son, saw him as 'one who had no hidden side'. According to fellow commentator Peter West, 'He was always totally, irrepressibly and unrepentantly himself: what you saw or heard was exactly what you got.'

These tributes were not paid in a religious or spiritual context, and they need to be assessed with this in mind, but they surely prompt any Christian reading them to ask some probing questions: Is pleasing others sometimes more important to me than pleasing God? Is what I do consistent with what I really think? Do I sometimes put popularity before principle? Am I more concerned about making an impression than about doing what is right? What occupies my mind when I am alone, and have nobody to impress? Am I more concerned about my reputation than I am about my character? As John Calvin reminds us, 'The Lord first of all wants sincerity in his service, simplicity of heart without guile and falsehood.' Every Christian should continually pray with the Psalmist, 'O Lord ... give me an undivided heart' (Psalm 86:11).

## INSTRUMENTS OF RIGHTEOUSNESS

Yet sincerity alone will not ensure that the person concerned will 'see God'. **Purity of heart also includes integrity.** The Buddhist, Muslim, Hindu or atheist may well be sincere in the sense of holding to a position with unqualified commitment, but there is clearly no way in which the promise of the present Beatitude extends to any of these. Purity of heart demands biblical integrity both in belief and behaviour, and the examples I have given fall at the first hurdle. As they grow in grace the pure in heart increasingly recognize the authority, integrity, infallibility and perfection of Scripture, acknowledging it as having been 'God-breathed' (2 Timothy 3:16). They learn to say with David, 'The law of the Lord is perfect, reviving the soul. The statutes of the Lord are trust-worthy, making wise the simple. The precepts of the Lord are right, giving joy to the heart. The commands of the Lord are radiant, giving light to the eyes' (Psalm 19:7-8).

But there must also be integrity in behaviour. Purity of heart is always revealed in the life. 'Purity' sounds a very old-fashioned word today, when relativism, compromise, permissiveness and situational ethics are common currency, but no true believer dare flinch from its challenge. Purity of life goes far beyond common decency, acceptable morality, or a veneer of piety or religion. It means relentlessly seeking to bring every area of life into conformity with God's Word and will. The Bible's instructions are uncompromising and inclusive: 'Therefore do not let sin reign in your mortal body so that you obey its evil desires. Do not offer the parts of your body to sin, as instruments of wickedness, but rather offer yourselves to God, as those who have been brought from death to life; and offer the parts of your body to him as instruments of righteousness' (Romans 6:12-13). The Christian's mind (what he thinks), feet (where he goes), eyes (what he sees) and hands (what he does) are all to be 'instruments of righteousness'. The believer is to have a conscious, continuous concern to live a Christlike life. Nor will this be a burden to the one who is pure in heart. In Thomas Watson's words, 'A pure heart breathes after purity. If God should stretch out the golden sceptre and say to him, "Ask and it shall be given thee, to the half of the kingdom", he would say, "Lord, a pure heart."'

The difference between a pure and an impure heart is well illustrated in the testimony of Augustine. In his **Confessions** he tells how, as a young man struggling with his emerging sexuality, he prayed, 'Give me chastity and continency, only not yet'. He confessed to being afraid that God would answer him immediately, whereas at that time he wanted his lust 'satisfied rather than extinguished'. He was at least being honest in his prayer, but as an unbeliever he was far from pure in heart. Augustine was eventually converted when in his early thirties, and the language of his prayer changed dramatically: 'Power of my soul, enter into it, and fit it for thee, that thou mightest have and hold it without spot or wrinkle.' Augustine was still not perfect, but his heart was pure.

There is no clearer biblical example of this element of purity of heart than that of David. Guilty of adultery with Bathsheba and of complicity in the murder of her husband, he ransacks the dictionary in a confession of his wrongdoing: 'Have mercy on me, O God, according to your unfailing love; according to your great compassion blot out my **transgressions**. Wash away all my **iniquity** and cleanse me from my **sin**' (Psalm 51:1-2). Adultery and murder were not the only burdens crushing David as he pleaded with God for mercy. Discontent, ingratitude, covetousness, hardness of heart, selfishness, pride, worldliness and unbelief were also on the record against him, and he pleads with God for complete forgiveness. But he goes beyond that, and later in the same prayer cries, 'Create in me a pure heart, O God, and renew a steadfast spirit within me' (Psalm 51:10). David was not concerned merely with getting relief from his guilt. He longed to have the wellspring of his thoughts, words and actions purged and sanctified. Merely to pray for forgiveness would have shown an impure heart, one wanting not to get rid of sin but just of sin's consequences. Instead, David longed for that inner purity that would lead to outward probity, and in doing so showed the sincerity and integrity which are the hallmarks of the pure in heart. This comes powerfully across in another of his prayers that should often be on the lips of the contemporary Christian: 'Search me, O God, and know my heart; test me and know my anxious thoughts. See if there is any offensive way in me, and lead me in the way everlasting' (Psalm 139:23-24).

## GROWING IN GRACE

Finally, **purity of heart means fervency**. The pure in heart are never satisfied with purity of doctrine, nor with purity as a philosophy, nor even with acceptable outward behaviour. For the pure in heart, holiness is not a pastime but a passion. They are fervently focused on glorifying God in every part of life. J C Ryle puts it well: 'A zealous man in religion is pre-eminently a man of one thing. He only sees one thing, he cares for one thing, he is swallowed up in one thing; and that one thing is to please God. Whether he lives or whether he dies; whether he has health or whether he has sickness; whether he is rich or whether he is poor; whether he pleases man or gives offence; whether he is thought wise or whether he is thought foolish; whether he gets blame or whether he gets praise; whether he gets honour or whether he gets praise; for all this the zealous man cares nothing all. He burns for one thing ... and that one thing is to please God and to advance God's glory.'

Even though perfect holiness can never be achieved in this life, it should be what Charles Colson calls 'the everyday business of every Christian'. Nobody drifts into holiness, nor can it be 'claimed by faith' or achieved through some climactic spiritual experience. Negatively, it requires a ruthless hatred of evil, coupled with a relentless attack on sin in every way, shape or form. One of the Psalmists testifies, 'I gain understanding from your precepts; therefore I hate every wrong path' (Psalm 119:104), and Paul's instruction is that we should 'abstain from every form of evil' (1 Thessalonians 5:22, NASB). There is to be no place in our lives for what the Puritans used to call 'darling sins'. All sin, every sin is to be hated, loathed, not least in the realization that it was sin that crucified the Son of God. John Owen writes, 'I do not understand how a man can be a true believer unto whom sin is not the greatest burden, sorrow and trouble.'

Positively, holiness requires a relentless pursuit of purity: 'Make every effort ... to be holy; without holiness no-one will see the Lord' (Hebrews 12:14). There is no room here for the devilish deceit of antinominanism, which teaches that the believer is not subject to the moral demands of God's law. To quote John Owen again: 'Let not men deceive themselves. Sanctification is a qualification indispensably necessary unto those who will be under the conduct of the Lord Christ unto salvation. He leads none to heaven but whom he sanctifies on earth.'

The pure in heart are not only conscious of this, but they seek to make diligent use of the means of grace which God has provided for their spiritual growth. The Psalmist asks, 'How can a young man keep his way pure? By taking heed to your word' (Psalm 119:9), and in that conviction he is able to add, 'I have hidden your word in my heart that I might not sin against you' (Psalm 119:11). Loss of appetite for physical food is serious; loss of appetite for spiritual food is disastrous. Anyone who wilfully or habitually neglects reading and studying the Bible has no grounds for claiming to be pure in heart, and no hope of becoming so. As Matthew Henry says, 'We love God as much as we love his Word.'

By the same token, the pure of heart are people of prayer; they 'pray continually' (1 Thessalonians 5:17). Their praying is not restricted to a few minutes at a set time of day, nor to a 'shopping list' of practical requirements. Knowing something of their own weakness and of Satan's strength, they are constantly asking their heavenly Father for 'grace to help...in...time of need' (Hebrews 4:16). There was never a man of purity or spiritual power who was not first a man of prayer. As the eighteenth-century preacher Octavius Winslow put it, 'Prayer is the pulse of the renewed soul and the constancy of its beat is the test and measure of the spiritual life.'

The pure in heart also covet the fellowship of like-minded Christians. Paul urged his young friend Timothy, 'Flee evil desires of youth, and pursue righteousness, faith, love and peace, **along with those who call on the Lord out of a pure heart**' (2 Timothy 2:22). Few things were of greater help to me in the early days of my Christian life than constant, honest, unjudging inter-action with others who had recently come to faith in Christ and longed to grow in grace. Nearly 40 years on, I find it impossible to over-estimate the stimulation and strength I receive from time spent in the company of those whose thoughts seem to gravitate towards spiritual things, and whose sole concern is to 'grow in the grace and knowledge of our Lord and Saviour Jesus Christ' (2 Peter 3:18).

## BELIEVING AND SEEING

The third key word in the Beatitude we are studying in this chapter is 'see', and the all-important question to ask is, 'What does it mean to "see God"?' We can immediately rule out crass literalism as a possibility. The Bible tells us, 'No man has seen God at any time' (John 1:18, NASB), a fundamental truth not essentially contradicted by Old Testament visions experienced by Isaiah, Ezekiel and others. The long-range answer to the question clearly lies in the life to come, but there are a number of ways in which the promise of these words is fulfilled for God's people here on earth. We shall take a brief glance at seven of them.

The pure in heart 'see God' at their conversion, when they lay hold of God's promise: 'You will seek me and find me when you seek me with all your heart' (Jeremiah 29:13). The unconverted are 'without God in the world'. Satan has 'blinded the minds of unbelievers, so that they cannot see the light of the gospel of the glory of Christ, who is the image of God' (2 Corinthians 4:4), but when someone seeks the Lord with sincerity, integrity and intensity, he will find him and in that sense 'see' him, not merely as his Creator and Sustainer, but as his Lord and Saviour. We can take this one step further. Jesus told one of his disciples, 'Anyone who has seen me has seen the Father' (John 14:9), so that to know him is to know God, and in that sense to 'see' him.

The pure in heart 'see God' in creation. When they look at the physical universe they gladly join their Old Testament predecessors in saying to God, 'You alone are the Lord. You made the heavens, even the highest heavens, and all their starry host, the earth and all that is on it, the seas and all that are in them. You give life to everything, and the multitudes of heaven worship you' (Nehemiah 9:6). The minds of those who are pure in heart are not cluttered with confusion as to the origins of matter or life, but are assured that these reflect God's stupendous power, awesome intelligence and marvellous imagination. What a liberating contrast to the brilliant blindness of people like the evolutionary biologist Richard Dawkins who says that we are living in a universe of 'blind physical forces and genetic replication' in which there is 'no design, no purpose, no evil and no good, nothing but blind, pitiless indifference' and who makes the bleak diagnosis that 'Life is just bytes and bytes and bytes of digital information.'

The pure in heart 'see God' in the unfolding of the world's history.

They agree with the seventeenth-century soldier and statesman Oliver Cromwell: 'What are all histories but God manifesting himself?' While others speculate about movements on the stage of international politics and agonize over their implications, the pure in heart rejoice in the assurance that 'dominion belongs to the Lord and he rules over the nations' (Psalm 22:28).

The pure in heart 'see God' in Scripture. They never read the Bible in a hesitant, critical or prejudicial frame of mind. Nor do they edit it to fit in with their own theological presuppositions. Instead, with Augustine, they see the Bible as 'a volume of letters from the heavenly country', in which they hear God's voice, see his face and know his mind. They are fully assured that the Bible is 'the living and enduring word of God' (1 Peter 1:23).

The pure in heart 'see God' in prayer. They 'call on the Lord out of a pure heart' (2 Timothy 2:22), sincerely and wholeheartedly committing their cause to God and firmly believing that 'he hears the prayer of the righteous' (Proverbs 15:29). As a result, they can testify again and again to the truth of the Bible's promise, 'The Lord is near to all who call on him, to all who call on him in truth. He fulfils the desires of those who fear him' (Psalm 145:18-19). George Müller testified, 'I live in the spirit of prayer. I pray as I walk about, when I lie down and when I rise up. And the answers are always coming.' What a contrast to the person whose prayers are described by William Barclay as 'a walking civil war in which trust and distrust of God wage a continual battle against each other' and whose prayers are riddled with double-minded doubts. 'That man,' the Bible says, 'should not think he will receive anything from the Lord' (James 1:7).

The pure in heart 'see God' in their Christian service. They serve God with genuine humility, not seeking in any way to enhance their own reputations, and knowing that even if tangible results are absent or insignificant they can rest in God's promise that 'your labour in the Lord is not in vain' (1 Corinthians 15:58). When God does bless their work, the pure in heart give him all the glory and take none of the credit. They follow the example of The nineteenth century Scottish minister Robert Murray McCheyne who, when he first heard of someone converted through his ministry, cried, 'Lord I thank thee that thou hast shown me this marvellous working, though I was but an adoring spectator, rather than an instrument.' Only the pure in heart can 'see God' as clearly as this.

The pure in heart 'see God' in all of life's circumstances. There is an illustration of this in the Old Testament story of Hannah. After being childless for many years, and being constantly taunted about it, she eventually gave birth to a son, and in a great song of praise cried, 'The Lord brings death and makes alive; he brings down to the grave and raises up. The Lord sends poverty and wealth; he humbles and he exalts' (1 Samuel 2:6-7). To the pure in heart there is no such thing as luck (good or bad), no situations that 'just happen to work out', no 'bad breaks'. There are many things beyond their comprehension, but they know of nothing that is beyond the control of the One who 'in all things works for the good of those who love him' (Romans 8:28). This conviction brings a blessing which they alone can experience. In the words of the British preacher G Campbell Morgan, 'The man who measures things by the circumstances of the hour is filled with fear; the man who sees Jehovah enthroned and governing has no panic.'

In particular, the pure in heart 'see God' in times of trial and adversity. Their vision is not blurred by delusions of dualism, in which the control of events is shared by God and Satan. Instead, they trust God even where they cannot trace him. The Bible tells us that, when faced with the momentous task of leading God's people out of slavery in Egypt and under constant threat from a pagan and powerful Pharaoh, Moses 'persevered because he saw him who is invisible' (Hebrews 11:27). His faith was focused not on the pressures and problems that surrounded him, but on the One who was in control of them all and who intended them for his own glory and for his people's good. As he looked to God in uncluttered faith, Moses was given the courage, strength and determination to overcome every obstacle. The pure in heart have the same experience - and for the same reason. In the words of the Puritan preacher Thomas Brooks, 'A gracious soul may look through the darkest cloud and see God smiling on him.'

## FACE TO FACE

These are some of the secondary ways in which the pure in heart may be said to 'see God'. The ultimate thrust of Jesus' words, however, relates not to time but to eternity. Paul pinpoints the contrast by saying, 'Now we see but a poor reflection ... then we shall see face to face' (1 Corinthians 13:12). Whatever experiences of God the pure in heart may have here on earth they are as nothing compared to the glorious vision which will be theirs in heaven and the Bible sees the Christian life as one of steady progress towards that radiant conclusion: 'The path of the righteous is like the first gleam of dawn, shining ever brighter till the full light of day' (Proverbs 4:18). This exhilarating truth has rejoiced the hearts of God's people for thousands of years and made them long for the time when they would enter God's glorious presence. David provides a perfect example of this: 'And I - in righteousness I will see your face; when I awake, I will be satisfied with seeing your presence' (Psalm 17:15). When that day arrives, the promise of Jesus' words will come to full fruition: 'They will see his face, and his name will be on their foreheads. There will be no more night. They will not need the light of a lamp or the light of the sun, for the Lord God will give them light. And they will reign for ever and ever' (Revelation 22:4-5). The significance of God's name being 'on their foreheads' is that his people will know him in a fuller, deeper sense than ever before. But what of the statement that they will 'see his face'? Generations of theologians have wrestled over the issue of whether this will be with the 'naked eye' of the resurrection body or whether this 'seeing' will be purely spiritual, but all their ponderings have been pointless. Martyn Lloyd-Jones agrees: 'We just do not know. The very Being of God is so transcendent and eternal that all our efforts to arrive at an understanding are doomed at the very outset to failure.' Yet that failure need not stifle our faith or limit our excitement at the prospect. If knowing God here on earth can mean so much, how much more will it mean in heaven? If we sense his presence, power and love so deeply here, how much more must we do so there? If worshipping and serving God can be such a delight now, what must these be like then? If there is 'joy and peace in believing'

(Romans 15:13), how much greater will these be in seeing? In heaven, the blessedness of the pure in heart in seeing God will be utterly beyond anything we can presently imagine or describe.

The Bible sometimes relates the heavenly vision specifically to the person of Christ. In one of the most breathtaking phrases in Scripture, John says that at the Second Coming of Christ 'we shall be like him, for we shall see him as he is' (1 John 3:2), a statement which sometimes helps Christians to concentrate more clearly on the experience that awaits them. My good friend Peter Jackson - pastor, preacher, and gospel pianist extraordinary - was blinded through measles when he was just eighteen months old. He knows that God could restore his sight immediately, and he would no doubt rejoice in the blessings that would follow, but nevertheless delights to say, 'If I remain as I am, the next person I see will be my Saviour.' Could any vision be greater than that?

In this life, God's people are gradually 'being transformed into his likeness with ever-increasing glory' (2 Corinthians 3:18). That transformation will be instantaneously completed when they see their Saviour and in doing so become like him. In seeing their Saviour, the pure in heart will be made perfectly happy by being made perfectly holy. They will have no frustrated ambitions, no unfulfilled longings, no unsatisfied desires. In Thomas Watson's words, 'The saints shall have their heads so full of knowledge and their hearts so full of joy that they shall find no want ... We shall never be weary of seeing God, for, the divine essence being infinite, there shall be every moment new and fresh delights springing forth from God into the glorified soul ... The more the saints behold God the more they will be ravished with desire and delight.' These words from a hymn by Rowland Hill put into verse something of what this experience will mean - and remind us of the only way in which it can be attained:

Lo! round the throne, a glorious band,
The saints in countless myriads stand,
Of every tongue, redeemed to God,
Arrayed in garments washed in blood.

They see their Saviour face to face,
And sing the triumphs of his grace;
Him day and night they ceaseless praise,
To him the loud thanksgiving raise.

So may we tread the sacred road
That saints and holy martyrs trod;
Wage to the end the glorious strife,
And win, like them, the crown of life.

# Chapter 12

# God's peace corps

Blessed are the peacemakers, for they will be called sons of God' (Matthew 5:9).

Of all the Beatitudes, this is the one most likely to meet with the approval of almost everyone who reads it, regardless of whether the reader is a Christian. Nor is it difficult to see why this should be the case. Surely none but the most bitterly militant would object to peacemaking and none but the most blatantly atheistic refuse to be numbered among the 'sons of God'? Superficially, this would seem to be the least controversial and the least revolutionary of the Beatitudes. Any philosophy which advocates peace has emotional and universal appeal, and one of the main reasons why this appeal is so powerful is humanity's horrifying record of armed conflict.

## CATALOGUE OF CONFLICT

It has been estimated that in the past 4,000 years there have been less than 300 without a major war. As John MacArthur wryly comments, 'Peace is merely that brief glorious moment in history when everybody stops to reload.' Humanity made an early start to its grisly career of militancy; as far back as Noah's day 'the earth was corrupt in God's sight and was full of violence' (Genesis 6:11). From then on, the Old Testament echoes to over a thousand years of armed conflict. David wrote of 'violence and strife in the city' (Psalm 55:9), and Asaph of those who 'clothe themselves with violence' (Psalm 73:6). One of the Old Testament prophets spoke of Jerusalem as being 'full of violence' (Ezekiel 7:23). Another writer went so far as to say that 'the unfaithful have a craving for violence' (Proverbs 13:2). In each case the word 'violence' translates the Hebrew **hamas**, which is used nearly 70 times in the Old Testament, often carrying with it a sense of extreme wickedness. In the 400 years between Old and New Testament history there were at least five bloody battles for the possession of Jerusalem, and over one million Jews were massacred when the Roman Emperor Titus invaded the city in AD 70.

The following centuries saw no reduction in humanity's appetite for aggression. One authority states that during the period from 1480 to 1941 Great Britain was involved in 78 major wars, France in 16, Spain in 64, Russia in 61, Austria in 52, Germany in 23, the United States in 13, China in 11 and Japan in 9. The twentieth century was hailed by many as the beginning of a millenium of peace and prosperity, but this claim proved to be nothing more than empty idealism. In World War I (1914-1918), believed by some to be 'the war to end all wars', 30,000,000 people were killed. To help avoid a repetition of this cata-strophe, the League of Nations was founded in 1920, with the main-tenance of international peace as its primary aim. By 1928 some 58 nations had signed its covenant of membership, yet eleven years later almost all of them were embroiled in World War II, which eventually cost over 90,000,000 lives. The Puritan preacher John Trapp was surely not exaggerating when he wrote, 'War is the slaughterhouse of mankind and the hell of this present world.'

The League of Nations was formally wound up in 1946, when its functions were taken over by the newly-founded United Nations, estab-lished with the determination 'to have succeeding generations free from the scourge of war'. But the silenced guns of global conflict were followed by the so-called Cold War, when for nearly half a century the world lived under the real threat of nuclear extinction. At one point the nuclear powers had stockpiled the equivalent of 320,000,000,000 tons of high explosive, over 100 tons for every man, woman and child on earth, and spent the equivalent of one million dollars a minute arming themselves for future battles. The United States had enough aerosol nerve gas to kill all life in an area of 455 million square miles, or eight times the area of the whole surface of the earth. Addressing the United Nations General Assembly in September 1961, United States President John F Kennedy warned, 'Every man, woman and child lives under a nuclear sword of Damocles, hanging by the slenderest of threads, capable of being cut at any moment by accident, miscalculation or madness.' Nor was the threat of nuclear annihilation the only evidence of what the Scottish poet Robert Burns called 'man's inhumanity to man'. In 1967 Britain's Secretary of State for Defence admitted, 'This has been the most violent century in history. There has not been a day since the end of World War II when hundreds have not been killed by military action.' In 1969, the Chairman of the 21st International Congress of the Red Cross confessed, 'If we continue on this road of violence ... our century will figure ... as the most humiliating in the history of the human race.'

His fears were well founded. Untold millions of Chinese lost their lives as the result of atrocities perpetrated during the decade of the so-called Cultural Revolution which began in 1966. Millions of Cambodians were put to death in four years of savagery following the country's takeover by the Marxist-led Kymer Rouge in 1975. As the Cold War eventually thawed and hard-line Soviet Communism began to disintegrate, other threats to national and international stability continued to emerge in Asia, Africa, the Middle East, the Balkans and elsewhere. Sometimes, man's blood-lust explodes within the confines of one small nation. In the six weeks from 7 April 1994 some 500,000 Rwandans, one-fifteenth of the country's population, were killed when civil war broke out between Hutus and Tutsis. In the first month alone, fishermen in neighbouring Uganda reported that as many as 20,000 bodies had floated down the Kagera river into Lake Victoria. At the height of the conflict, over 15,000 men, women and children were shot or hacked to death on church premises in a single day.

These statistics are literally numbing and give credence to the comment by American evangelist Billy Graham that if someone was sent from Mars to report earth's major business, 'he would in all fairness have to say that its chief industry was war'. Yet for all their horror, these statistics represent only part of the story. Even if we narrow our focus to our own nation we can find ample evidence of man's contentious nature.

In spite of legislation which has curbed their worst features, fractious industrial relations continue to cause expensive disruption.

Disputes and unrest within local communities are commonplace. Racial tension simmers in many cities. Current police statistics show that crimes against the person have spiralled in recent years. As has always been the case, many young people rebel against authority in their search for identity, reality and security. The constant clash of high-profile personalities is as manna to the media. Political debate is often acrimonious and sometimes vicious. The breakdown of family life has reached epidemic proportions. One marriage in three now ends in divorce, while thousands of others are semi-detached charades in which love has given way to bitterness or to a cold consensus to live a lie.

## THE ROOT OF THE TROUBLE

What is man's problem? Why the tension, bitterness, strife, conflict, violence, bloodshed and wars? Why is it that while 'peace' is one of the most significant words in man's lexicon, it is one of the most elusive in his experience? Two significant testimonies, coming from vastly different sources, will prepare us to hear what the Bible has to say on the subject. The first is that of the Scottish theologian John Murray, writing in **National Republic Magazine** at the end of 1942 when World War II was at its height: 'It is, no doubt, impossible for us to diagnose all the affections, motives, acts and purposes that have converged upon one another, that have interacted with one another, and that in unison bear the onus of responsibility for the gigantic catastrophe that has now befallen the world. We must recognize that a complex movement having its root far back in history, a complex movement of sinful impulse, ambition and action that only the all-seeing eye of God can fully view and diagnose, lies back of, and comes to fruition in, this present conflict.' The second testimony is that of Albert Einstein, who won the Nobel Prize for physics in 1921 and whose theories of relativity revolutionized man's thinking about the nature of time and space. In the course of a lecture delivered in 1948, he made the following comment on the threat of nuclear warfare: 'It is not a physical problem, but an ethical one. What terrifies us is not the explosive force of the atomic bomb, but the power of the wickedness of the human heart, its explosive power for evil.'

These two statements line up precisely with this blunt verdict from the Bible: 'What causes fights and quarrels among you? Don't they come from your desires that battle within you? You want something but don't get it. You kill and covet, but you cannot have what you want. You quarrel and fight ...' (James 4:1-2). The key phrase here is 'your desires that battle within you'. The word 'desires' translates the Greek **hedonon**, from which we get the word 'hedonism', the doctrine that self-satisfaction is all-important. The word 'battle' translates the Greek **strateumenon**, the same militant word used by Peter when he writes of 'sinful desires, which war against your soul' (1 Peter 2:11). James is saying that the cause of all human conflict is man's deep-rooted determination to get his own way, an attitude which inevitably brings him into contention not only with God but with his fellow men. It would be simplicity itself to show that every conflict in human history, from global war to a broken marriage, has proved the accuracy of James' diagnosis.

Time and again, the Bible traces human conflict to the same core. Isaiah says 'The wicked are like the tossing sea, which cannot rest, whose waves cast up mire and mud' (and significantly adds, '"There is no peace," says my God, "for the wicked"') (Isaiah 57:20-21). Isaiah's words make it clear that the root of man's problem is not external but internal. The 'mire and mud' are stirred up from within. David asks God to protect him from 'men of violence, who devise evil plans in their hearts and stir up war every day' (Psalm 140:1-2). Jesus makes it clear that 'evil thoughts', 'murder', 'malice' and 'envy' are among the evils that come 'from within, out of men's hearts' (Mark 7:20-22). Paul goes into similar detail and specifically says that 'hatred, discord, jealousy, fits of rage, selfish ambition, dissensions, factions and envy' are all 'acts of the sinful nature' (Galatians 5:19-21). It was after Adam had rebelled against God that he had a son 'in his own likeness, in his own image' (Genesis 5:3) and humanity has been a river of rebellion ever since. Man has belligerence in his bones. He is a trouble-maker by nature. In his thought-provoking book **The Dust of Death**, contemporary writer Os Guinness says, 'Man, alienated from God as a sinner, when he acts according to his fallen nature, is not totally free to choose his action but is forced to react according to who he is ... Violence is normal in a fallen world.' This is very different from the romantic view of man which sees him as the innocent victim of circumstances, but is completely in line with what the Bible teaches about the depravity of the human heart. It is in the human heart that the problem lies and where action must be taken if the problem is to be solved.

This is precisely where the Beatitudes come in. The Sermon on the Mount is not a political manifesto, nor would it serve as an agenda for an international peace conference. Pinning the words of the Beatitudes to the walls of the United Nations headquarters in New York or Geneva would be irrelevant. The efforts of many of those involved in the United Nations are no doubt commendable and may spring from honourable motives, but it would be quite wrong to suggest that those involved are what Jesus meant by 'peacemakers' and ridiculous to suggest that, regardless of their spiritual standing, their activities show that they are 'children of God'. Some of them are atheists, others are humanists, none of whom have either a sound moral basis upon which to oppose violence nor any realistic hope of preventing it. All efforts to prevent unjust conflict deserve our support and merit our prayers, but we dare not say that the Beatitude we are presently studying automatically applies to such efforts.

Immediately after listing some of the evils that were 'acts of the sinful nature', Paul goes on to say, 'But the fruit of the Spirit is love, joy, peace, patience, kindness, goodness, gentleness and self-control (Galatians 5:22-23). All of these qualities are in some way related to the issue of peace, and it is important to notice that these are all part of what Paul calls 'the fruit of the Spirit'. They are not natural attributes, nor are they the result of disciplined and unaided self-effort. Instead, they represent the organic development of the new life implanted in the heart by the Holy Spirit, something which can never be present in the life of an unbeliever. As John Calvin warns, 'There have often appeared in unrenewed men remarkable instances of gentleness, integrity, temperance and generosity; but it is certain that they were all specious disguises .

All of this points us back to something we discovered at the very beginning of our studies, and which has become increasingly obvious as we have gone along, namely, that the Beatitudes are not directions on how to become a Christian but a multi-faceted description of what a Christian is and how a Christian behaves when the Holy Spirit governs his thoughts, words and actions. The unbeliever who says 'My religion is the Sermon on the Mount' is talking nonsense, because he is condemned by the very words to which he looks for salvation. As Martyn Lloyd-Jones rightly says, 'There is nothing more fatal than for the natural man to think that he can take the Beatitudes and put them into practice.' The Beatitudes are not a programme but a portrait, not a directive but a description.

## GOD'S WORD OF PEACE

With all of this to establish the context, we can turn to examine the text. We shall do so by answering three questions: What does the Bible mean by 'peace'? What is involved in being peacemakers? In what way are peacemakers said to be 'blessed'?

There are some 400 references to peace in Scripture, the best-known word being the Hebrew **shalom**. In the Septuagint, the first Greek translation of the Old Testament, this was usually translated **eirene**, which in the New Testament is a truly major word, occurring in 26 out of 27 books. It is used of international relations: at one point the people of Tyre and Sidon came to Herod and 'asked for peace' (Acts 12:20). It is also used of conditions within a nation: when prosecuting Paul, Tertullus began by telling Felix, Governor of Judea, 'We have enjoyed a long period of peace under you' (Acts 24:2). Again, it is used to describe a time when the early church prospered: Luke reports a period when 'the church throughout Judea, Galilee and Samaria enjoyed a time of peace' (Acts 9:31). It is used of interpersonal relationships: Jesus urged his hearers to 'be at peace with each other' (Mark 9:50). It is also used of personal serenity: when an old Jewish believer called Simeon, who had been earnestly waiting for Messiah to appear, held the infant Jesus in his arms he praised God by saying, 'Sovereign Lord, as you have promised, you now dismiss your servant in peace. For my eyes have seen your salvation' (Luke 2:29-30).

Yet above all the word is used in the Bible to speak of God and the gospel. God the Father is called 'the God of peace' (1 Thessalonians 5:23). He is, as the **Book of Common Prayer** so beautifully puts it, 'the God of peace and the author of concord'. God the Son is called 'Prince of Peace' (Isaiah 9:6). He came to earth 'to guide our feet into the way of peace' (Luke 1:79) and as he prepared to leave he told his disciples, 'Peace I leave with you; my peace I give you' (John 14:27). The word 'peace' is not directly applied in Scripture to the Holy Spirit, the third Person in the Godhead, but we are told that at Jesus' baptism 'he saw the Spirit of God descending on him like a dove and lighting on him' (Matthew 3:16) and Scripture makes it clear that all three Persons in the Godhead are involved in the greatest peace enterprise the world has ever known.

The need for such peacemaking stems, as we saw earlier in this chapter, from man's unilateral declaration of independence from God, his deliberate revolt against divine authority. In rebelling against God's holy rule, man became God's enemy - and he remains so to this day. Men are born rebels against their Maker and their enmity is by no means formal or superficial. Paul goes so far as to say, 'The sinful mind is hostile (literally, 'hostility') to God' (Romans 8:7). This enmity is so deeply entrenched that, as the great eighteenth-century theologian and preacher Jonathan Edwards put it, 'Unconverted men would kill God if they could get at him.' The other side of the coin is that God has become man's enemy. After man had sinned, God banished him from the Garden of Eden and barred the way against his re-entry. From then on, Scripture gives numerous illustrations of God's enmity against rebellious humanity, and Paul does not hesitate to describe unconverted men and women as 'God's enemies' (Romans 5:10), objects of divine hostility. This is the horrifying impasse which faces unregenerate humanity. Man is sinfully the enemy of God and God is righteously the enemy of man.

The glory of the Christian gospel is that in this otherwise intractable situation, one which man had neither the desire nor the ability to remedy, God, the innocent party, did something which enabled man, the guilty party, to return in peace: 'God was reconciling the world to himself in Christ' (2 Corinthians 5:19). In sending Jesus into the world to take upon himself the sin, guilt and condemnation which men richly deserved, God removed the barrier which separated sinful creatures from their sinless Creator. In his death, Jesus made peace between God and all those for whom he died by removing once and for all the cause of their separation. As Paul reminded a group of fellow Christians, 'Once you were alienated from God and were enemies in your minds because of your evil behaviour. But now he has reconciled you by Christ's physical body through death to present you holy in his sight, without blemish and free from accusation' (Colossians 1:21-22).

Man's reconciliation to God is the very heart of the gospel. God's righteous wrath was turned away from those who deserved it and borne by his own sinless Son, who died in their place and on their behalf. In the Bible's words, 'God made him who had no sin to be sin for us, so that in him we might become the righteousness of God' (2 Corinthians 5:21). Sinners are therefore urged, 'Be reconciled to God' (2 Corinthians 5:20) and those who, through regeneration, are enabled to respond in repentance and faith are brought into a right relationship with God and enabled to join with Paul in saying, 'Therefore, since we have been justified through faith, we have peace with God through our Lord Jesus Christ' (Romans 5:1).

The death of Christ in the place of sinners has broken down not only the barrier between God and man but the barriers which divided men from each other. Writing about the ancient and acrimonious division between Jews and Gentiles, Paul says of Christ, 'For he himself is our peace, who has made the two one and has destroyed the barrier, the dividing wall of hostility, by abolishing in his flesh the law with its commandments and regulations. His purpose was to create in himself one new man out of the two, thus making peace, and in this one body to reconcile both of them to God through the cross, by which he put to death their hostility. He came and preached peace to you who were far away and peace to those who were near. For through him we both have access to one

Father by one Spirit' (Ephesians 2:14-18).

In Old Testament times, God had given the Jews a law, embodied in a series of 'commandments and regulations' which they were called upon to obey in order to approach God, but this God-given law eventually became the flashpoint of a terrible enmity between Jews and Gentiles. The Jews pointed to it as a sign of their superiority over the despised Gentiles, who in turn hated the Jews for their arrogant claims. But in his death Christ put an end to these commandments and regulations. In Paul's words to the Colossians, he 'cancelled the written code, with its regulations, that was against us and stood opposed to us; he took it away, nailing it to the cross' (Colossians 2:14). This 'written code' was a statement of indebtedness, evidence of man's disobedience and guilt through his failure to keep the law. But when Christ satisfied the demands of the law by his perfect obedience and substitutionary death he opened the way for Jews and Gentiles to get right with God on the same basis - his life and death on their behalf.

As a result, there is no place for human distinctions among those who trust in Christ. Paul made this clear when writing to Christians living in Galatia, deep in the heart of Gentile territory: 'You are all sons of God through faith in Christ Jesus, for all of you who were baptized into Christ have clothed yourselves with Christ. There is neither Jew nor Greek, slave nor free, male nor female, for you are all one in Christ Jesus' (Galatians 3:26-28). Paul does not mean that within the Christian community distinctions of race, social standing and sexuality are totally obliterated, but that they have no ultimate significance; they are unimportant in relation to issues of salvation or Christian living.

One further thing can be added. Christians, having been reconciled to God and been made 'all one in Christ Jesus', are also at peace with the world, in the sense that they do not fragment mankind into ethnic or other groupings and treat them on that basis. Instead, they regard all of humanity with what John Brown calls 'sincere benevolence' and long with equal concern for people of every race, colour and creed to know genuine peace with God. Small wonder that the apostles' message was called 'the good news of peace through Jesus Christ, who is Lord of all' (Acts 10:36)!

## CONTRADICTION?

But what of Jesus' statement, 'Do not suppose that I have come to bring peace to the earth. I did not come to bring peace, but a sword' (Matthew 10:34)? Critics of Christianity are quick to pounce on this as a fatal contradiction in the Bible's testimony, but the explanation is perfectly simple. Both the Bible and secular history confirm that the gospel is inevitably divisive. When people's lives are transformed by its power, and their affections, desires and energies become focused on the things of God, they are bound to come into conflict with those who remain 'under the control of the evil one' (1 John 5:19). How could it be otherwise? A sudden change of lifestyle is likely to result in misunderstanding at best and persecution at worst. Indeed, the more closely integrated the unit to which the new convert belongs the greater the potential for conflict. This is precisely why Jesus quoted an Old Testament prophecy and warned, 'For I have come to turn "a man against his father, a daughter against her mother, a daughter-in-law against her mother-in-law - a man's enemies will be the members of his own household"' (Matthew 10:35-36).

There are, of course, countless cases in which there is no traumatic upheaval, but Jesus gave clear warning of what might happen. Whatever else may be true, the Christian should never adopt a confrontational attitude. There may be situations within family and other units that call for great wisdom, patience and tact, and the Christian will constantly need the grace of his peacemaking God to exercise these. One thing is certain; when conflicts arise as a result of the gospel's work in people's hearts, the blame belongs not to the 'Prince of Peace' but to those who refuse to be reconciled to him.

## DOING THE WORK

This brings us to our second question: What is involved in being peacemakers? The word 'peacemakers' translates the Greek word **eirenopoios**, a straightforward combination of the noun **eirene** (peace) and the verb **poleo** (to make) and we must begin this section of our study by giving full weight to the latter. In the fourteenth century, the English Reformer John Wycliffe translated **eirenopoios** as 'peaceable men' and 200 years later the equally famous Reformer William Tyndale rendered it 'the maintainers of peace', but both of these phrases miss the point that peace is something which needs to be **made**. The ancient Greek writers Plutarch and Xenophon both confirm that **eirenopoios** was used of ambassadors commissioned to negotiate peace with alienated parties, a task which called for enterprise and effort.

As we saw at the beginning of this chapter, we live in a world in which peace is conspicuous by its absence. Writing to the Romans, Paul quotes several Old Testament authors and confirms the continuing truth of their diagnosis: 'As it is written: "There is no-one righteous, not even one; there is no-one who understands, no-one who seeks God. All have turned away, they have together become worthless; there is no-one who does good, not even one." "Their throats are open graves; their tongues practise deceit." "The poison of vipers is on their lips." "Their mouths are full of cursing and bitterness." "Their feet are swift to shed blood; ruin and misery mark their ways, and **the way of peace they do not know**"' (Romans 3:10-17). In his letter to Titus, he reminds him that 'at one time we too were foolish, disobedient, deceived and enslaved by all kinds of passions and pleasures. We lived in malice and envy, **being hated and hating one another'** (Titus 3:3).

Nothing has changed. Man's driving, dominating force remains the passion for self-gratification, whatever the cost, with the result that humanity is so deeply fractured that not even the most costly and sophisticated attempts at self-healing stand the remotest chance of success. It is into this situation that God sends his spiritual peace corps, the 'peacemakers' of whom Jesus speaks. This is the last description given in the Beatitudes of those who belong to the kingdom of heaven, and it is not difficult to see where it fits into the sequence. The poor in spirit grieve over sin, humbly accept God's providential over-ruling in their lives and hunger and thirst for right-eousness. As God graciously fills them they are merciful to others and honest and open in their dealings with them. Now, they do everything they can to bring them into a right relationship with each other, and above all with God.

This is no easy task. It goes far beyond loving peace or even yearning for it, both of which can go hand in hand with comfortable compromise. Making peace involves strenuous and determined effort and, as in every other area of seeking to live righteously, 'our struggle is not against flesh and blood, but against the rulers, against the authorities, against the powers of this dark world and against the spiritual forces of evil in the heavenly realms' (Ephesians 6:12). Satan and his agents are committed to a policy of discord and disruption in every part of society, with the result that peacemaking in a fallen and fractious world is as difficult a task as any that God has committed to his people. With this in mind, we can turn to look at some of the ways in which peacemakers are to operate.

## THE PERMANENT PRIORITY

First and foremost, peacemakers are to be people of prayer. After their return from many years of captivity and slavery, God's people were urged, 'Pray for the peace of Jerusalem' (Psalm 122:6). As used here, the word 'peace' would have included everything that made for the city's welfare and for the unity and stability of its inhabitants. This Old Testament commandment clearly points to a Christian citizen's responsibility wherever he lives in today's world. The New Testament makes that responsibility even clearer: 'I urge, then, first of all, that requests, prayers, intercession and thanksgiving be made for everyone - for kings and all those in authority, that we may live peaceful and quiet lives in all godliness and holiness. This is good, and pleases God our Saviour, who wants all men to be saved and to come to a knowledge of the truth' (1 Timothy 2:1-4).

The scope of the prayer urged on the peacemakers could not be more comprehensive. It includes 'all men', by which Paul means people of every nation and class. Specifically, he singles out 'kings and all those in authority'. Prayer is not to be limited to those in supreme authority, but is to include all who hold public office and thus influence the ethos of society. When Paul wrote these words the most powerful ruler in the world was Nero, the pagan Roman emperor, and we can be certain that scarcely any of 'those in authority' were believers. Nevertheless, Paul insists on the responsibility of Christians to pray for them, so that those under their leadership might live in conditions favourable to the furtherance of the gospel.

Those in God's peace corps have the same responsibility today, buttressed by the Bible's insistence that 'there is no authority except that which God has established' (Romans 13:1). But what is the point of praying for pagan politicians? What difference can the prayers of politically powerless Christians make? The answer to the first question is that God commands us to do so. The answer to the second lies hidden behind the Bible's assurance that 'The king's heart is in the hand of the Lord; he directs it like a watercourse wherever he pleases' (Proverbs 21:1). God can change rulers' policies as easily as a farmer can cut a channel to irrigate a field. Visiting the United Nations head-quarters in Geneva some years ago, I was fascinated to watch scores of people striding along the corridors of power clutching important-looking brief-cases and wearing facial expressions to match. As I wondered how many people's lives were affected all around the world by decisions taken in that building, I remembered an Old Testament verse I had read that morning: 'For the kingdom is the Lord's: and he is the governor among the nations' (Psalm 22:28, AV). The assurance that God governs all the world's governors should surely be an encouragement to pray for them?

Who can tell what benefits have accrued to people at large and to God's people in particular as a result of the prayers of believers for those in authority? Who can gauge to what extent God's wrath has been averted? Who knows how often or to what extent God has sovereignly intervened in the affairs of the nations in response to the prayers of his people? William Hendriksen says of this aspect of peacemaking, 'Is not the church the very cork on which the world remains afloat?' The American preacher Paul Billheimer is even more direct: 'If it were not for the church, Satan would already have turned this world into hell.'

The unquantifiable but unqualified certainty is that prayer is a powerful weapon in the hands of God's peacemakers.

## EVASIVE ACTION

The second way in which peacemakers operate is by avoiding causes of contention. As A W Pink writes, 'It is part of Christian duty to see to it that we so conduct ourselves as to give no just cause of complaint against us.' One statement in Scripture will be especially helpful in setting up this part of our study: 'Let the peace of Christ rule in your hearts, since as members of one body you were called to peace' (Colossians 3:15). The verb 'rule' translates the Greek **brabeuo**, which literally means 'to act as an umpire', and the application of Paul's words becomes crystal clear when we bear this in mind. An umpire only interferes when there has been infringement of the rules. As long as the rules are being obeyed the umpire keeps his mouth closed, his flag down, his whistle from his lips. It is only when someone has committed a foul that the umpire intervenes. Paul is saying that believers should act in such a way that the heavenly Umpire does not have to step in and call them to order. In other words, they are to seek in every part of life to have 'a good conscience towards God' (1 Peter 3:21). The Bible makes it clear not only that peacemakers are blessed but that peacebreakers are cursed. One Old Testament writer solemnly warns us that God detests 'a man who stirs up dissension among brothers' (Proverbs 6:19), and Thomas Watson is right to remind us that 'our murmuring is the devil's music'. There is something radically wrong with anyone who seems always to be looking for faults, unsettling relationships, or causing some kind of disturbance in the church or elsewhere. In Guy Appéré's assessment, 'Peace is to the soul what health is to the body, a sign of balance and order.'

What, then, are some of the causes of contention? There can be little doubt that pride is at the top of the list: 'Pride only breeds quarrels' (Proverbs 13:10). The entire history of sin is inextricably linked with pride. Paul's statement that someone promoted to leadership in the church too soon after his conversion 'may become conceited and fall under the same judgement as the devil' (1 Timothy 3:6), may be more than a hint that Satan's disastrous fall from heaven was the result of pride. The Old Testament is filled with the strife and bloodshed caused by the outrageous arrogance of a long succession of rulers. The early Roman, Persian, Egyptian and Greek empires reek of the disastrous consequences of pride. So do the Dark Ages and the Middle Ages. In modern times, millions have suffered as the result of the rampant megalomania of Adolf Hitler in Germany, the tyranny of Joseph Stalin in Russia and of Mao Tse Tung in China, and the pretentious claims of countless others. It would be no exaggeration to say that pride and peace are incompatible. That being the case, the peacemaker will be at pains to avoid pride like the plague.

Linked with pride are the unholy trinity of self-centred desires, the pursuit of personal pleasure and covetousness. We touched on these near the beginning of this chapter. We could paraphrase the statement from James 4 (and perhaps make the sense clearer by improving on the NIV's punctuation) like this: 'What causes fights and quarrels among you? Don't they come from your self-centred pleasure-seeking which is always stirring things up? You want something, but don't get it, so you kill. You covet something, you cannot have it, so you quarrel and fight.' There is no peace in the heart of the man who is self-centred and covetous and whose constant concern is to please himself. He is always envious, pushing, striving, pressing, agitated and restless. The American missionary E Stanley Jones once wrote, 'The self-centred are the self-disrupted.' That being the case, they are not likely to be effective in bringing peace to others.

Anger is another constant cause of contention: 'A hot-tempered man stirs up dissension' (Proverbs 15:18). The same writer later adds a graphic endorsement of this: 'For as churning the milk produces butter, and as twisting the nose produces blood, so stirring up anger produces strife' (Proverbs 30:33). Anger is a major enemy of peace, not least because it disengages truth. In C S Lewis' words, 'When passion enters a situation, human reasoning (unassisted by grace) has as much chance of its retaining its hold on truth as a snowflake in the mouth of a blast furnace.' In striking contrast to those who have a reputation for resentment, peacemakers are those who, as someone has beautifully put it, 'carry about with them an atmosphere in which quarrels die a natural death'.

This is not to say that anger is always out of place. Writing to the Ephesians, Paul quotes David's dictum: 'In your anger do not sin' (Ephesians 4:26), showing clearly that there is a place for righteous anger. The Bible tells us that 'God is a righteous judge, a God who expresses his wrath every day' (Psalm 7:11) and that 'The wrath of God is being revealed from heaven against all the godlessness and wickedness of men who suppress the truth by their wickedness' (Romans 1:18). There are so many references to God's anger in Scripture (some 600 in the Old Testament alone) that J I Packer goes so far as to say, 'The Bible could be called the book of God's wrath.' It is this righteous wrath that his people are to reflect. There is something radically defective in someone who never has the courage to be angry. There is no virtue in spineless silence in the face of sin. Charles Colson is right to say, 'If Christ is Lord of all, Christians must recover their sense of moral outrage.' It is right to be angry with things that are wrong. Preaching on Ephesians 4:26, C H Spurgeon said, 'Anger is one of the holy feet of the soul when it goes in the right direction.' The qualification is important. We need to be sure that we are not angry merely because we have been contradicted, inconvenienced or hurt. There is sometimes a very fine line between righteous anger and personal offence, but the line is there and the peacemaker will make every effort to ensure that he does not get on the wrong side of it.

One further and equally obvious cause of contention is the wrong use of the tongue, and a familiar Old Testament writer again points us in the right direction: 'A gentle answer turns away wrath, but a harsh word stirs up anger' (Proverbs 15:1); 'A gossip separates close friends' (Proverbs 16:28). It would be easy to show that most of the strife, restlessness and turmoil in society at large, in business life, in church life, in family life and in other personal relationships is caused by people allowing their mouths to stay open when they ought to be kept closed. While I was leading a houseparty in Norway some years ago, our group took a boat trip along one of that country's beautiful fjords. Looking up at the steep mountain slopes on either side, I asked our guide whether there was ever a danger of avalanches when the snow melted in the Spring. 'Of course,' he replied, 'and there are times when the snow is so delicately poised that it can be brought down by the sound of a human voice.' I have never forgotten that. There are moments in our lives when a situation is so delicately balanced that the sound of a human voice can bring down an avalanche of disruption, misunderstanding and pain. Peacemakers are careful to pray with David, 'Set a guard over my mouth, O Lord; keep watch over the door of my lips' (Psalm 141:3).

## STEPS IN THE RIGHT DIRECTION

United States President Abraham Lincoln once wrote, 'Die when I may, I would like it to be said of me that I always pulled up a weed and planted a flower where I thought a flower would grow.' This is hardly an adequate expression of what is meant by the Beatitude we are studying in this chapter, but it helps us to realize that peacemaking involves taking positive action to deal with situations where there is ill-feeling, misunderstanding, conflict or alienation. The Bible urges us, 'Make every effort to live in peace with all men' (Hebrews 12:14) and that we should 'make every effort to do what leads to peace and to mutual edification' (Romans 14:19). Both statements underline our earlier discovery that peacemaking requires effort. It is sometimes difficult to overcome our prejudices, to suppress our natural feelings or even, at times, to yield ground over an issue in which no principle is involved. Again, it is often hard work to have a peaceable relationship with those who are temperamentally different from us, or whose lifestyle is out of kilter with ours. Yet we have a biblical responsibility to 'make every effort'. In the early part of the nineteenth century the British engineer Isambard Kingdom Brunel had a vision of building a massive bridge across the Avon Gorge at Clifton, on the outskirts of Bristol. His plans met with fierce opposition and it took years of patient negotiation before he was eventually given permission to go ahead. Today, Clifton Suspension Bridge stands as a superb and serviceable monument to its designer.

There are times when it takes courage and a great deal of patience to build bridges across to the ungodly, the unlovely, the awkward and those who oppose us. The Bible understands this, and is perfectly realistic about the issue: 'If it is possible, as far as it depends on you, live at peace with everyone' (Romans 12:18). The command to live at peace is qualified. The Bible recognizes that there will be times when this is impossible, that there will be those who stubbornly refuse to be at peace with us. In cases like this, we are not to sacrifice truth or compromise principle in order to find some **via media**. As John Stott reminds us, 'The words "peace" and "appeasement" are not synonyms.' We must never settle for peace at the expense of holiness or truth. We have to accept the fact that peace must always give way to principles, but we must be quite sure that we have done everything we possibly can to handle the situation with love and grace as well as in righteousness and truth. What is more, we must never walk away from a situation in an unforgiving frame of mind. When the Puritan preacher Cotton Mather received a number of letters in which he was falsely accused he fastened them together and put them on a shelf with a label on which he wrote, 'Father, forgive them.' Genuine peacemakers never surrender the last possibility of peace, but always leave room for the grace of God to work.

There are times when peacemaking involves trying to reconcile those who are estranged from each other, and these situations also demand a great deal of sensitive effort. As John Stott wisely warns: 'In this case there will be the pain of listening, of ridding ourselves of prejudice, of striving sympathetically to understand both the opposing points of view, and of risking misunderstanding, ingratitude or failure.' This takes peacemaking far beyond spineless compromising and the self-serving attempt to please everybody concerned. It involves the peacemaker in doing whatever he can to understand the facts, lessen tension, break down barriers and help people to communicate with each other.

## THE MESSAGE AND THE MINISTRY

Yet the greatest activity in which God's peacemakers can get involved is in the work of evangelism. Christians are ambassadors, and it is important to notice the context in which they are given this title: 'Therefore, if anyone is in Christ, he is a new creation; the old has gone, the new has come! All this is from God, who reconciled us to himself through Christ and gave us the ministry of reconciliation: that God was reconciling the world to himself in Christ, not counting men's sins against them. And he committed to us the message of reconciliation. We are therefore Christ's ambassadors, as though God were making his appeal through us. We implore you on Christ's behalf: Be reconciled to God' (2 Corinthians 5:17-20).

In this great passage, Paul makes two key statements about the doctrine of reconciliation. The first is that 'God ... reconciled us to himself in Christ.' In the death of Christ, God did something to enable man to return to him in peace. He took the initiative and dealt with the root of the problem. When Christ took upon himself the sin, guilt and condemnation of those on whose behalf he died, God removed the barrier which separated him from the sinner. As Paul joyfully told the Romans, 'We were reconciled to (God) through the death of his Son' (Romans 5:10). The claims of God's law were met, his anger was turned away, the barrier between the Sovereign and the sinner was broken down, so that on behalf of all reconciled sinners Paul can say that 'we have peace with God through our Lord Jesus Christ' (Romans 5:1).

In the second statement Paul says that God 'gave us the ministry of reconciliation'. Reconciled sinners have been given the privilege and the responsibility of announcing the message of reconciliation to those who remain under God's righteous wrath. Writing about the work of the preacher, the well-known Methodist minister W E Sangster, who died in 1960, said this: 'It is the sheer work of the herald who goes in the name of the King to the people who, either openly or by their indifference, deny their allegiance to their rightful Lord. He blows the trumpet and demands to be heard. He tells the people in plain words of the melting clemency of their offended King and the things that belong to their peace.' Nor is this task limited to full-time Christian preachers. At one point in the life of the early church a fierce persecution broke out in Jerusalem 'and all except the apostles were scattered throughout Judea and Samaria' (Acts 8:1). But three verses later we read this very significant statement: 'Those who had been scattered abroad preached the word wherever they went' (Acts 8:4). The professional preachers remained in Jerusalem, but that did not prevent the gospel being preached; it continued to be preached by the non-preachers. This does not mean that they held formal services or produced structured sermons but that, as someone has put it, they 'gossiped the gospel' wherever they went. In Michael Green's words, 'There is no hint among ancient records that the early church saw evangelism as the task of the leadership alone. It was too good to leave to the professionals.'

There is no greater means of bringing peace than by spreading the gospel, the good news that 'God was in Christ reconciling the world unto himself'. Nor is there any surer way of breaking down the barriers of race, colour, culture and economics that separate men from each other. When tribal, social and political hatred erupted into bloody violence in Nigeria in the late nineteen-sixties, there was a period when the officers of the Scripture Union in that country were drawn from the three tribes which were at each other's throats. The president was a Hausa from the northern part of the country, the chairman a Yoruba from the west and the secretary an Ibo from the east. The gospel is a message which brings peace between man and God and between man and his fellow men, and it is the peacemaker's privilege to announce this glorious gospel to the world.

Yet as with other areas of peacemaking, evangelism must not be compromised in the interests of achieving some kind of success. The peacemaker who is true to Scripture will not dilute the message until it becomes an anaemic statement of 'easy believism', the notion that all one has to do to be saved is to believe that the gospel is true. Instead, the biblical peacemaker will insist on genuine repentance and whole-hearted faith and will give full weight to Jesus' warning that 'anyone who does not carry his cross and follow me cannot be my disciple' (Luke 14:27).

## FAMILY LIKENESS

The third major question in our study concerns the particular way in which peacemakers are blessed: What does it mean to say that peacemakers 'shall be called sons of God'?

At the beginning of this chapter I suggested that this Beatitude would be seen by most people as the least controversial and the least revolutionary. This needs to be qualified, however, by the fact that many of those who heard Jesus deliver it would have thought otherwise. Most Jews regarded Gentile nations with contempt and believed that when Messiah came he would lead a succession of attacks against them until they were completely destroyed or brought into subjection to God's people. This idea seeps through the New Testament again and again. For example, 'After the people saw the miraculous sign that Jesus did, they began to say, "Surely this is the Prophet who should come into the world." Jesus, knowing that they intended to come and make him king by force, withdrew again to a mountain by himself' (John 6:14-15). By doing so, Jesus thwarted a revolutionary coup which the people hoped would lead to the overthrow of the occupying Roman power, an all-out attack on the Gentile nations and the setting up of the kingdom of God on earth. Many believed that, as this exciting scenario developed, the greatest blessing would come to those who were in the front line, fighting for God and for the good of his people. In that particular context, this Beatitude would have sounded as revolutionary as any of the others; Jesus did not say 'Blessed are the warmongers' but 'Blessed are the peacemakers.'

The peacemakers' specific blessing is to be called 'sons of God' (not 'children of God', as in the AV). The difference is slight but significant. The Greek word for 'children' (**teknon**) places the emphasis on one's position within the family, whereas the word for 'sons' (**huioi**) places the emphasis on character and behaviour. The phrase 'sons of God' is a typically Jewish way of using a noun to do the work of an adjective, which then takes its significance from the noun to which it is linked. We are told that Jesus gave James and John the name Boanerges, 'which means Sons of Thunder' (Mark 3:17), a title probably referring to their ardent or fiery natures. His fellow apostles gave Joseph the nickname Barnabas, 'which means Son of Encouragement' (Acts 4:36), a clear reference to his helpful, supportive nature.

In calling peacemakers 'sons of God' Jesus is saying that they reflect God's peacemaking character. In J C Ryle's words, 'They are doing the very work which the Son of God began when he came to earth for the first time and which he will finish when he returns for the second time.' Breaking down barriers, easing tensions and seeking reconciliation are actions that flow from the hearts of those whose alienation from God has been brought to an end. As R V G Tasker puts it, 'The peacemakers are those who are at peace with God ... and who show that they are truly children of God by striving to use every opportunity open to them to effect reconciliation between others who are at variance.'

Later in the Sermon on the Mount, Jesus gives a wonderfully clear illustration of this principle: 'You have heard that it was said, "Love your neighbour and hate your enemy." But I tell you: Love your enemies and pray for those who persecute you, that you may be sons of your Father in heaven. He causes his sun to rise on the evil and the good, and sends rain on the righteous and the unrighteous' (Matthew 5:43-45). The point is clear. In sending rain and sunshine God does not discriminate between the godly and the ungodly. In an expression of common grace, the crops of downright sinners are as favoured as those of upright saints. Those who wish to be seen to be sons of God (the meaning of the phrase 'that you may be sons of God') must see to it that they treat people indiscriminately and seek to express practical love to them without distinction. In this Beatitude, the same principle applies: the Puritan preacher Richard Baxter went so far as to say, 'He that is not a son of peace is not a son of God'. Peacemaking is a defining duty.

## MANIFESTATION

Yet we must note Jesus' words that peacemakers 'will be **called** sons of God'. As used in this Beatitude, the word 'called' has the sense of 'owned' or 'acknowledged', and one aspect of the blessing Jesus had in mind is reflected in Paul's statement that 'those who are led by the Spirit of God are the sons (**huioi**) of God ... The Spirit himself testifies with our spirit that we are God's children (**teknon**) (Romans 8:14,16). This is an experience unique to God's people and Paul's words make nonsense to those who are not. Generations of expositors have tried to capture the warmth and depth of this experience and though none have succeeded these comments by the Puritan preacher Thomas Goodwin (which I have slightly modernized) on a related phrase elsewhere in the New Testament will give some idea of what they mean: 'There is a light which comes and overpowers a man's soul and assures him that God is his, and he is God's, and that God loves him from everlasting ... It is a light beyond the light of ordinary faith ... the next thing to heaven; you have no more, you can have no more, till you reach there ... It is faith elevated and raised up above its ordinary rate, it is electing love of God brought home to the soul.' This intimate ministry of the Holy Spirit in the hearts of believers is one way in which they are called sons of God.

Another sense in which the words of this Beatitude are fulfilled in this life is the way in which genuine peacemakers are recognized as such by their peers. The **Biblical Museum** tells of a Birmingham man by the name of Dickinson who was commonly known as 'the peacemaker' and of whom this was said: 'Such was his anxiety to keep the bonds of peace from being broken, such was his solicitude to heal the breach when made, that he would stoop to any act but that of meanness, make any sacrifice but that of principle, and endure any mode of treatment, not excepting even insult and reproach. From the high estimate in which his character was held, he was often called upon to act as umpire in cases of arbitration; and it was rarely, if ever, that the equity of his decisions was impeached.' The record goes on to tell of two men arguing over a decision that had been made over a certain issue. As soon as they heard John Dickinson's judgement on the matter their argument was over. We need a whole generation of John Dickinsons in today's world!

Yet as so often in the Beatitudes the final fulfilment of Jesus' words comes not in this world but in the next. Paul pinpoints this in his letter to the Romans: 'The creation waits in eager expectation for the sons of God to be revealed ... Not only so, but we ourselves, who have the first-fruits of the Spirit, groan inwardly as we wait eagerly for our adoption as sons' (Romans 8:19,23). The visible church on earth is a very mixed bag of truth and error, the holy and the hypocrites, the faithful and the formalists, the converted and the unconverted, those trusting in Christ and those trusting in their religion, a situation which has led to centuries of misunderstanding and conflict. The church in heaven will be vastly different! There will be no misunderstanding on the issue in the world to come, when the identity of the sons of God will be revealed. The word 'revealed' translates the noun **apokalupsin** which, as Spiros Zodhiates explains, 'includes not merely the thing shown and seen but the interpretation, the unveiling of the same'. When humanity is brought before the bar of divine judgement those who are truly the sons of God will be certified in public for all the world to see. False claims on the one side and false accusations on the other will disintegrate in the light of God's infallible declaration of men's eternal destinies.

Nearly 2,000 years ago John reminded fellow believers that although they truly were God's children 'the world does not know us' (1 John 3:1). That ignorance will not last for ever. At the present time, even though believers have what Paul calls 'the firstfruits of the Spirit' (that is, the Holy Spirit himself as a pledge and 'down payment' of their future inheritance) their true identity as sons of God is frequently blurred, not least by their own moral and spiritual inconsistencies. This is why, as Paul puts it, 'we groan inwardly and we wait eagerly for our adoption as sons', for the time when Christ will 'transform our lowly bodies so that they will be like his glorious body' (Philippians 3:21) and when 'we shall be like him' (1 John 3:2). There will be no cases of mistaken identity then! The contemporary British preacher Stuart Olyott makes the point well: 'It will be quite clear who are the children of God. It will be manifestly obvious. Until then we cannot be infallibly certain who is a child of God and who is not, for there are many counterfeits and apostates in the world. But then it will be plain to see. Creation is longing for that day. It is straining at the neck, like someone in a crowd, longing to see exactly who are the sons of God.'

What wonderful encouragement this should be to God's peacemakers, who so often seem to be brushed aside by pushy schemers in the church and powerful sceptics in the world. J C Ryle offers excellent advice: 'Those who try to do good must look forward to the Day of Judgement with patience. They must be content in this present world to be misunderstood, misrepresented, vilified, slandered and abused. They must not cease to work because their motives are mistaken and their characters are fiercely assailed. They must remember that all will be set right at the last day. The secrets of all hearts will then be revealed. The purity of their intentions, the wisdom of their labours and the rightfulness of their cause shall at length be manifest to all the world.'

In today's fallen world, the true sons of God, however feebly at times, reflect something of their family likeness by the quality of their lives, not least in their concern to be peacemakers. One day, as Jesus promised, they will 'shine like the sun in the kingdom of their Father' (Matthew 13:43).

# Chapter 13

# Blessings out of buffetings

Blessed are those who are persecuted because of right-eousness, for theirs is the kingdom of heaven. Blessed are you when people insult you, persecute you and falsely say all kinds of evil against you because of me. Rejoice and be glad, because great is your reward in heaven, for in the same way they persecuted the prophets who were before you' (Matthew 5:10-12).

At one period during his pastorate of Moody Bible Church, Chicago, the British preacher Alan Redpath led the congregation in a series of studies based on Paul's Second Letter to the Corinthians. Later, when pastor of Charlotte Chapel, Edinburgh, he was in the course of going through the series again when he was taken seriously ill. This came as a severe blow to him but, as he later testified, the contents of Paul's letter 'began to live in a new way, and truths which I had thought to be well learned became part of my experience'. His studies were eventually published in a book which he called **Blessings out of Buffetings**. The title was not original (the poet Avis Christiansen had coined it earlier) but it touches a deep chord of biblical truth and is an apt introduction to our final study in the Beatitudes. The relevance of the phrase will be seen throughout this chapter and will be indelibly underlined when we look at a key statement from 2 Corinthians towards the end of our study.

## SAME PEOPLE; NEW POINT

It is immediately obvious that the Beatitude now before us is couched in very different terms from all the others. Each of the first seven Beatitudes speaks of a particular characteristic found in God's people, such as poverty of spirit, meekness and purity of heart. Jesus now turns to highlight not another characteristic, but the fact that those whose lives consistently display these godly virtues in a godless world will inevitably run into all kinds of opposition, some of it so bitter and fierce as to warrant being called persecution.

The verb 'persecuted' used in this Beatitude comes from the Greek **dio**, which carries a wide range of meanings, such as 'to pursue', 'to prosecute', 'to persecute', 'to pursue with repeated acts of enmity', 'to drive away', 'to harass' and 'to treat wrongly'. In a nutshell, Jesus was saying that as long as they lived here on earth members of the kingdom of heaven could expect endless difficulties of one kind or another as Satan attacked them through the spiritual and human agencies under his control.

We have noticed time and again that the teaching given in the Beatitudes would have sounded revolutionary to its hearers, and this final Beatitude would have been no exception. The idea that people being persecuted, insulted and slandered (whatever the qualifications) could count themselves 'blessed' would have sounded nonsensical. The common conception among Jews and Gentiles alike was that any kind of suffering (persecution would qualify) was a sign that the person on the receiving end had incurred divine displeasure.

There is a glimpse of this philosophy in an incident which occurred after Paul and his companions were shipwrecked on the Island of Malta: 'Paul gathered a pile of brushwood and, as he put it on the fire, a viper, driven out by the heat, fastened itself on his hand. When the islanders saw the snake hanging from his hand, they said to each other, "This man must be a murderer; for though he escaped from the sea, Justice has not allowed him to live"' (Acts 28:3-4). The ignorant islanders were caught up in such a web of baseless superstitions that they could draw only one conclusion from Paul's predicament: the deities (in particular the goddess Dike, the personification of justice and revenge) were ensuring that Paul got his just deserts. When Paul shook the snake off and suffered no ill effects, 'they changed their minds and said he was a god' (Acts 28:6). This sudden U-turn may have fitted into their philosophy, but it did nothing to rescue it from being outright ignorance.

There were times when the Jews showed a similar lack of understanding. John tells us of an occasion when Jesus met a man who had been blind from birth: 'His disciples asked him, "Rabbi, who sinned, this man or his parents, that he was born blind?"' (John 9:2). The Jews went far beyond the orthodox biblical doctrine that all human suffering stems from the entry of sin into the world. They saw a link between any given suffering and specific sin, and in this case wanted to know who was responsible for the man's catastrophic blindness. It seems more than unfair to raise the possibility that the man himself was to blame, as he had been born blind, but this was suggested because some Rabbis taught that an embryonic child could begin sinning while still in the womb. If in this case the man concerned had not been responsible for bringing blindness upon himself, then they imagined that the blame must lie with his parents. Jesus immediately dismissed both speculations by telling them that neither the man nor his parents were responsible, declaring that the man's disability had come about 'so that the work of God might be displayed in his life' (John 9:3) and immediately restored the blind man's sight.

There was another side to the coin of the Jews' confusion in the area of life's changing circumstances. This was the idea that when Messiah came and set up the kingdom of God on earth their years of oppression, persecution and poverty would come to an end and they would enter a time of unimaginable freedom, peace and prosperity. There is nothing new about today's so-called 'prosperity gospel', which promises Christians instant solutions to their physical, material or economic problems if only they will exercise sufficient faith. This modern monstrosity twists Scripture just as violently as did those who taught that by lining up with Messiah they would be guaranteed deliverance from all the woes that plagued the lives of others.

What a different picture Jesus presented in the Beatitudes! He taught that Messianic blessings were not for the nation of Israel as a whole but rather for a group of people changed by the grace of God. That change would bring blessings vastly different from those commonly imagined. It would make them poor in spirit; they would grieve over sin; they would meekly accept life's circumstances; they would hunger and thirst for righteousness; they would be merciful to others; they would be pure in heart; and they would be known as peacemakers in society. What is more, as a direct result of their transformed lives, they would be persecuted, and this too would make them blessed. To those who heard Jesus on that mountainside, this must have sounded like religious nonsense. Why would virtue be met with vitriol and violence? Why would the kingdom of heaven run into such opposition on earth? What blessing could come from persecution? Many would ask the same questions today. It is important that we discover the answers.

## KINGDOMS IN CONFLICT

The first major lesson to be drawn from this Beatitude is that **the persecution of God's people is one of the best attested facts in history**. According to the notable historian Kenneth Scott Latourette, 'No other of the faiths of mankind, religious or political, has quite so extensive a record of violent and bitter opposition to its growth.' A broad sweep over the Bible confirms his assessment. Violent opposition to God's people began in Genesis 4, when Cain murdered his brother Abel, a point picked up by Jesus when he spoke of 'all the righteous blood that has been shed on earth, from the blood of righteous Abel to the blood of Zechariah son of Berakiah, whom you murdered between the temple and the altar' (Matthew 23:35). The very names Jesus mentioned, Abel and Zechariah, serve as an unintentional reminder to us that the list of those persecuted for the faith runs from A to Z. Within this saga of suffering, prophets were among the main targets. In our Beatitude, Jesus speaks of the persecution of '**the** prophets', as if to make it clear that none escaped. Persecution of the prophets was proverbial. At his own martyrdom, Stephen courageously told his executioners that they were running true to type and asked, 'Was there ever a prophet your fathers did not persecute? They even killed those who predicted the coming of the Righteous One' (Acts 7:52). When James wanted to give an example of how to be patient in the face of suffering he encouraged his readers to consider 'the prophets who spoke in the name of the Lord' (James 5:10).

The Old Testament provides centuries of evidence to back this up. Moses was constantly harassed by grumbling and unbelieving elements among the Israelites. Samuel knew what it was to be rejected. David's life was frequently in danger. Elijah was hounded by Jezebel, who threatened to kill him. Nehemiah had running feuds with Sanballat, Tobiah, the Arabs, the Ammonites and the men of Ashdod. God encouraged Ezekiel not to be afraid, 'though briers and thorns are all around you and you live among scorpions' (Ezekiel 2:6). Jeremiah was beaten, put into stocks, thrown into a cistern of mud, threatened with execution and eventually martyred. The second-century apologist Justyn Martyr says that Isaiah was dismembered with a wooden saw.

These are some of the high-profile names. Many others were relentlessly persecuted for their faith, and are anonymously honoured in the New Testament's 'Hall of Fame': 'Some faced jeers and flogging, while still others were chained and put in prison. They were stoned; they were sawn in two; they were put to death by the sword. They went about in sheepskins and goatskins, destitute, persecuted and ill-treated - the world was not worthy of them. They wandered in deserts and mountains, and in caves and holes in the ground' (Hebrews 11:36-38).

When we turn to New Testament history, two strands are intertwined, the general persecution of the Christian church and the particular persecution of its preachers. The first sermon preached by an apostle in the history of the Christian church was on the Day of Pentecost, but he had not even started before he and his colleagues were accused of being drunk. Shortly afterwards, Peter and John were arrested and imprisoned and commanded 'not to speak or teach at all in the name of Jesus' (Acts 4:18). We are told that the religious authorities 'arrested the apostles and put them in the public jail' (Acts 5:18), and, after they had been miraculously released, re-arrested them 'and had them flogged' (Acts 5:40). Stephen, 'a man full of God's grace and power' who 'did great wonders and miraculous signs among the people' (Acts 6:8) was stoned to death. On that very day, 'a great persecution broke out against the church at Jerusalem' (Acts 8:1) and from then on there is scarcely a page in Acts which is not punctuated with persecution of one kind or another. In reading through Acts I found no fewer than 56 instances of persecution in 28 chapters.

Paul underlines this when ironically contrasting the apostles' experience with false claims made by some church members in Corinth: 'For it seems to me that God has put us apostles on display at the end of the procession, like men condemned to die in the arena. We have been made a spectacle to the whole universe, to angels as well as to men. We are fools for Christ, but you are so wise in Christ! We are weak, but you are strong! You are honoured, we are dishonoured! To this very hour we go hungry and thirsty, we are in rags, we are brutally treated, we are homeless. We work hard with our own hands. When we are cursed, we bless; when we are persecuted, we endure it; when we are slandered, we answer kindly. Up to this moment we have become the scum of the earth, the refuse of the world' (1 Corinthians 4:9-13). Paul uses strong language here. The word 'scum' translates **perikatharma**, something wiped out or swept away as being worthless, while 'refuse' translates **peripsema**, something rubbed or scraped off for the same reason. As far as the world was concerned, the apostles were no better than garbage, and were treated accordingly. Tradition has it that Andrew was executed by being tied to a cross and left to die and that Peter was crucified upside down. Others have suggested that every one of the apostles was executed except John, who died in lonely exile on the island of Patmos. So much for the 'prosperity gospel'!

As the apostle with the highest profile of all, Paul attracted prolonged persecution, as he testified when writing to the church in Corinth: 'I have worked much harder, been in prison more frequently, been flogged more severely, and been exposed to death again and again. Five times I received from the Jews the forty lashes minus one. Three times I was beaten with rods, once I was stoned, three times I was shipwrecked, I spent a night and a day in the open sea, I have been constantly on the move. I have been in danger from rivers, in danger from bandits, in danger from my own countrymen, in danger from Gentiles; in danger in the city, in danger in the country, in danger at sea; and in danger from false brothers ... Who is weak, and I do not feel weak?' (2 Corinthians 11:23-26,29)

## THE LONG WAR AGAINST GOD

Nor was persecution limited to apostles, disciples and other church leaders. In those early days Christians were accused of atheism, because they worshipped an invisible God. They were accused of cannibalism, because in taking the Lord's Supper they quoted Christ's words, 'This is my body' and 'This cup is the new covenant in my blood' (1 Corinthians 11:24-25). Others accused them of sacrificing their own children before eating their flesh. Above all, they were accused of being political outlaws by their refusal to make the mandatory annual declaration 'Caesar is Lord' and their insistence that 'Jesus is Lord' (Romans 10:9). Meeting together for public worship was not only difficult but dangerous; one poet wrote of them as 'the panting, huddled flock whose crime was Christ'.

Vicious opposition to those early Christians was personified in Nero, who was Roman Emperor for fourteen years from A D 54. Under his instructions, thousands of Christians were flung to the lions or burned at the stake, but in reminding us that 'these were kindly deaths' William Barclay gives us a fuller picture: 'Nero wrapped the Christians in pitch and set them alight, and used them as living torches to light his gardens. He sewed them in the skins of wild animals and set his hunting dogs upon them to tear them to death. They were tortured on the rack; they were scraped with pincers; molten lead was poured hissing upon them; red hot brass plates were affixed to the tenderest parts of their bodies; eyes were torn out; parts of their bodies were cut off and roasted before their eyes; their hands and feet were burned while cold water was poured over them to lengthen the agony.' It is chilling to read and write these things, but they serve as powerful reminders that the world is implacably opposed to genuine Christianity and that God's children can expect no favours from those who are his enemies.

In the years which followed, successive Emperors, including Domitian, Trajan, Marcus Aurelius, Decius, Gallus, Valerian and Diocletian continued the policy of ruthless persecution. As the Roman Empire declined, so did the wholesale, systematic attacks on the Christian church, though no substantial period of time since then has been free from shocking examples of brutality against God's people. To avoid too long a litany, we can pick up the story in the fourteenth century, with the relentless suppression of John Wycliffe and his followers, the Lollards. In the fifteenth century, examples included the great Reformer Jan Hus, who was burned at the stake in Bohemia and the courageous preacher Girolamo Savonarola, who was executed in Italy. In the sixteenth century thousands of Anabaptists were slaughtered in Europe, Martin Luther was condemned and outlawed and William Tyndale was strangled and burned to death in Belgium. In the same century, Henry VIII's daughter Mary Tudor (justifiably known as 'Bloody Mary') had hundreds of Christians, including great evangelical leaders like Thomas Cranmer, Hugh Latimer and Nicholas Ridley, burned at the stake for their loyalty to the gospel.

The list is seemingly endless and includes the persecution of the Puritans and the Pilgrim Fathers in the seventeenth century, faithful preachers such as George Whitefield and John Wesley in the eighteenth century, and pioneer missionaries like Adoniram Judson and J Hudson Taylor in the century that followed. One comparatively little-known hero from that last era will form a natural bridge into our present century. In 1838 Dr Robert Reid Kalley set sail from Scotland for the Portuguese colony of Madeira, where he devoted himself to the healing of men's bodies and souls. He concentrated his attention on the poor and treated up to 50 patients a day, offering them free treatment, medication and hospital care. In addition he taught Scripture, founded schools (where education was given without charge) and wrote Christian hymns, tracts and leaflets. His energies, output and contribution to the island's welfare were such that he became known as 'the English saint' (a title he no doubt disowned, not least because he was a

Scot!). Within four years, he was preaching to congregations of up to 5,000. Yet when the Roman Catholic church began to suffer from the effects of his ministry, church and state combined in turning their fury on him. He was denounced as a heretic and lawbreaker and prohibited from dispensing medicine. Many of the schools he had founded were closed down. Believers were arrested and imprisoned, their Bibles burned and their homes destroyed. Eventually, Kalley was forced to leave the island, barely escaping with his life. This is an outline of just one part of Kalley's remarkable story, which is told by William Forsyth in **The Wolf from Scotland**, but it is a telling illustration of the fact that nothing rouses the world's fury like uncompromising biblical truth and the purity and power of the gospel seen in the lives of God's people.

In the same year that Kalley landed in Madeira the German philosopher Karl Marx wrote these words: 'Man makes religion: religion does not make man … It is the opiate of the people … The people cannot really be happy until it has been deprived of illusory happiness by the abolition of religion.' Some 80 years later the Russian revolutionary leader Nikolai Lenin, Marx's most influential follower, endorsed this philosophy: 'Everyone must be an atheist. We will never achieve our goal until the myth of God has been removed from the thoughts of man.' Who can tell how many hundreds of thousands of Christians have been imprisoned, tortured, persecuted and executed by those who have embraced the philosophies of Marx and Lenin, not only in Eastern Europe but in China, Latin America and in many other places?

Yet atheistic Communism is only one of the elements contributing to the fact that there have been more Christian martyrs in the twentieth century than in any other. In 1915 some 700,000 Armenians were slaughtered by the Ottoman militia in Turkey. Records tell of soldiers lining whole villages up and asking each person in turn, 'Mohammed or Christ?' Those who answered 'Christ' were either bayoneted or shot. Many of the 500,000 Ugandans killed under the dictatorship of Idi Amin in the nineteen-seventies were Christians. David Barrett, Editor of **World Christian Encyclopaedia**, published in 1982, has said that one in every 200 Christian workers is being killed on the mission fields of the world and is on record as saying 'In recent years the average number of believers who have been martyred for their faith is 300,000 per year.'

The long war against God is a sickening saga. The history of Christianity is written in the blood of its martyrs and spoken with the voice of its suffering.

## THE HALLMARK

This brings us to the second major lesson to be drawn from this Beatitude: **persecution of one kind or another is one of God's promises to his people.** In the course of strengthening new converts in Lystra, Iconium and Antioch, and 'encouraging them to remain true to the faith', Paul and Barnabas made no attempt to hide the problems they would face in a hostile world: 'We must go through many hardships to enter the kingdom of God' (Acts 14:22). 'Hardships' translates the Greek **thlipsis**, a word which speaks of tribulation, trouble, distress, affliction, anguish and pressure. It is often used in the New Testament to describe the experiences of God's people at that time. Paul reminds one group of believers that they had embraced the gospel 'in spite of severe suffering' (**thlipsis**) (1 Thessalonians 1:6) and later wrote to them about 'all the persecutions and trials (**thlipsis**) you are enduring' (2 Thessalonians 1:4). Elsewhere he wrote of the 'severe trial (**thlipsis**)' being endured by the churches in Macedonia (2 Corinthians 8:2). Yet Paul did not consider these trials surprising, but quite the reverse. He tells the Thessalonians, 'You know quite well that we were destined for them. In fact, when we were with you, we kept telling you that we would be persecuted (**thlibo**)' (1 Thessalonians 3:3-4). This is an apostolic echo of Jesus' promise to his disciples: 'In this world you will have trouble (**thlipsis**)' (John 16:33). In one form or another persecution is, as Thomas Watson put it, 'the legacy bequeathed by Christ to his people'.

Genuine Christianity will always attract persecution. As J C Ryle commented: 'Persecution ... is like the goldsmith's hallmark on real silver and gold; it is one of the marks of a converted man.' This is light years away from the kind of preaching sometimes heard today, in which

Christianity is offered as an instant solution to the pressures and problems of twentieth century life and as a guarantee of uninterrupted pleasure and happiness. This pragmatic, materialistic, man-centred substitute is a perfect match for today's world. In a recent survey in the United States three out of ten professing Christians agreed that 'nothing in life is more important than having fun and being happy', but this philosophy bears no resemblance at all to what the Bible teaches. The idea that genuine Christianity can happily and cosily co-exist with common human values, ethics and life-styles is a travesty of the truth. John MacArthur is right on the mark in saying, 'When the world runs into Christianity there is always conflict, conviction, guilt, resentment and persecution.'

Why is this the case? Why do we have this sad irony that the people most likely to be persecuted are the humble, the meek, the pure in heart, and those who sincerely seek to be peacemakers? The straightforward answer is that every one of the characteristics commended in the Beatitudes grates against the spirit of the world. Poverty of spirit clashes headlong with human pride. Mourning for sin is anathema to the happy-go-lucky. Meekness is derided by the self-assertive. Hungering and thirsting for righteousness makes nonsense in today's permissive culture. A merciful spirit conflicts with hard-headed self-centredness. Purity of heart is the exact opposite of hypocrisy and compromise. Peacemaking is scorned by the contentious and argumentative. At every point, genuine Christianity is at odds with the world and by implication condemns hypocrisy and godlessness alike. The virtues which Jesus dignified, the world derides. The characteristics of the godly are living protests against common standards in modern society and the backlash is inevitable. As John Stott puts it, 'Persecution is simply the clash between two irreconcilable value-systems.' The only way for a professing Christian to escape persecution in any form is to go along with the world, raise no objection when it mocks God, laughs at sin, glories in self-indulgence and deifies materialism; but in doing so he forfeits any right to be called a Christian. By the same token, the professing Christian who never faces persecution of any kind should ask why this is so when persecution is guaranteed to the godly.

## QUALIFICATIONS

None of this should be taken to mean that persecution guarantees the spiritual standing of the person being persecuted. In the Beatitude we are studying, Jesus inserts three qualifications which need to be carefully noted. In the first place, Jesus speaks of those who are persecuted '**because of righteousness**'. The blessing of this Beatitude clearly has no relevance to the unrighteous. In his first New Testament letter Peter tells his readers, 'If you suffer, it should not be as a murderer or thief or any other kind of criminal, or even as a meddler' (1 Peter 4:15). In passing, we should notice that murder and meddling (poking one's nose into other people's affairs) are lumped together as being reprehensible for God's people. Peter's principle is that there is no virtue in being punished for wrongdoing. This underlines a point he makes earlier in the same letter when addressing those who were slaves: 'For it is commendable if a man bears up under the pain of unjust suffering because he is conscious of God. But how is it to your credit if you receive a beating for doing wrong and endure it?' (1 Peter 2:19-20). The criminal can hardly claim the blessing mentioned in the Beatitudes if he is punished for his crime, nor can the busybody who disrupts relationships and finds himself suffering as a result.

Peter's principle can be extended because, as William Hendriksen says, 'The persecution to which Jesus refers does not spring from purely social, racial, economic or political causes, but is rooted in religion. It is distinctly a persecution "for righteousness".' R V G Tasker takes this one step further: 'Those who are persecuted for righteousness' sake suffer solely because they uphold God's standards of truth, justice and purity, and refuse to compromise with paganism or bow the knee to the idols that men tend to erect as substitutes for God.' This helps us to give full weight to the first qualification Jesus mentions. As we saw in Chapter 9, 'righteousness' embodies the character and quality of being right, something that applies both to doctrine and to behaviour. When so-called Jehovah's Witnesses are cold-shouldered in their attempts to proselytize they look to this Beatitude as confirmation that they enjoy God's favour, but as they deny the deity of Christ this cannot possibly be the case. Augustine wisely remarked that it is 'not the punishment, but the cause which makes the martyr'.

The qualification 'for righteousness' also rules out those who suffer because they are angular and awkward in their approach to others. There is no virtue in being ostracised or ignored because of one's prickly personality, or because enthusiasm outruns common sense or refuses to submit to proper authority. A few years ago I met a student in the United States who was convinced that God had called him to preach in the open air at the university he was then attending. As this kind of thing was forbidden, the leaders of the Christian group within the university urged him not to go ahead with his plan but to get involved in other opportunities for evangelism, such as discussion groups, literature and properly authorized meetings. The young man would have none of it, insisted on going ahead, and was duly punished for doing so. His zeal was not in question, but stubbornness is not the same as righteousness. In the same way, the Christian who is criticised, ostracised or treated badly because of his arrogance, censoriousness or constantly negative criticism of others has only himself to blame and cannot take refuge in this Beatitude.

The second qualification Jesus mentions centres on the phrase 'Blessed are you when people insult you, persecute you, and **falsely say all kinds of evil against you'**. Before coming to the main point here, we should notice that persecution is not limited to being hounded to death. The word 'insult' translates the Greek **oneidizo**, which means to defame, disparage, reproach or attack with abusive words. Persecution can take the form of slander as well as slaughter and there are times when the tongue inflicts deeper wounds than any sword. The key to this second qualification is the word 'falsely', a point which Peter specifically addresses when warning new Christians of the problems they would face because of the radical change in their life-style: 'For you have spent enough time in the past doing what pagans choose to do - living in debauchery, lust, drunkenness, orgies, carousing and detestable idolatry. They think it strange that you do not plunge with them in the same flood of dissipation, **and they heap abuse on you'** (1 Peter 4:3-4). The expression 'heap abuse on you' translates **blas-**

**phemeo,** from which we get our English word 'blaspheme'. Its meaning is not solely related to impious irreverence about God, but has the more general sense of what Spiros Zodhiates calls 'the very worst type of slander', false statements aimed at damaging a person's reputation.

Nothing infuriates the ungodly more than losing one of their own number. When a new Christian breaks off from the kind of loose behaviour Peter mentions and begins to live a life of disciplined godliness he is heading for trouble. When a man no longer uses foul language or swaps dirty jokes, when a businessman refuses any longer to engage in sharp practice, when a trader stops cutting corners, when Sunday is suddenly set apart for public worship, it will not be long before the world reacts. Those who begin living transformed lives are likely to be accused of everything from fanaticism to Pharisaism. Yet none of this should move them. Their great concern should be to ensure that the accusations are false and that they are humbly seeking to live 'in a manner worthy of the gospel of Christ' (Philippians 1:27). If they are, they can lean without hesitation on the words of the Beatitude we are studying.

This leads us to the third way in which the persecution Jesus mentions is qualified. He says it must be '**because of me**'. It is impossible to miss the link between the phrases 'because of righteousness' and 'because of me'. None of the Old Testament prophets would have dared to use such an expression, nor would Paul, Peter, John or any of the other New Testament writers or leaders. Jesus was able to do so because he was the very embodiment of righteousness; he was 'the sun of righteousness' (Malachi 4:2), 'the Holy and Righteous One' (Acts 3:14). Once again, the qualification is important. We are not told that people are blessed when persecuted for a cause or a conviction but for Christ. This Beatitude has nothing to say about persecution because of political allegiance, loyalty to one's country or the colour of one's skin.

## MASTER AND SERVANTS

At this point in the Beatitude, Jesus switches from the third person -

'those' - to the second person - 'you'. One can imagine him turning directly to his disciples, those sitting nearest to him on the mountainside, as if to emphasize the importance of what he was saying and its relevance to them in the days that were to follow. It is also significant that he does not speculate on the possibility of their being persecuted but says 'Blessed are you **when** people insult you, persecute you and falsely say all kinds of evil against you because of me'. The word 'when' is an aorist subjunctive, giving the phrase a meaning akin to 'Blessed are you if people insult you, which they certainly will ...'

The certainty that the followers of Jesus would be persecuted was based on the way the world treated him: 'He was in the world, and though the world was made by him, the world did not recognize him. He came to that which was his own, but his own did not receive him' (John 1:10-11). This had been clearly foreseen hundreds of years earlier, when Isaiah prophesied that Messiah would be 'despised and rejected by men' (Isaiah 53:3), words fulfilled to the letter. Herod tried to kill Jesus while he was still a babe in arms. He was called 'a glutton and a drunkard' (Matthew 11:19). On one occasion, Jews said, 'Aren't we right in saying that you are a Samaritan and demon-possessed?' (John 8:48) and the bitter hatred between Jews and Samaritans made the first accusation nearly as bad as the second. Pharisees once told him bluntly, 'You were steeped in sin at birth' (John 9:34), while other religious leaders complained, 'This fellow is blaspheming!' (Matthew 9:3). On more than one occasion people 'took up stones to stone him' (John 8:59, 10:31). Eventually, he was arrested on a trumped-up charge, condemned by a corrupt court, mocked, spat upon, and tortured before being stripped naked and put to death on a cross, the cruellest form of execution that had ever been devised.

This is the context in which believers must read the warning Jesus gave his early followers: 'If the world hates you, keep in mind that it hated me first. If you belonged to the world, it would love you as its own. As it is, you do not belong to the world, but I have chosen you out of the world. That is why the world hates you. Remember the words I spoke to you: "No servant is greater than his master." If they persecute me, they will persecute you also' (John 15:18-20). How tragically true those words have proved! When Messiah left the world, his enemies vented their spleen on his followers, and they have been doing so for 2,000 years.

The world has no great difficulty in accepting generally decent moral standards, but it cannot stomach the blazing righteousness of Christ reflected in Christians. As the English preacher Thomas Scott put it nearly 200 years ago, 'The wicked hate the holy image of God and those who bear it; his holy truth and those who profess and preach it; his holy law and those who stand up for its obligations and authority; his holy ordinances and those who attend on them.'

As we have seen, Jesus qualified the persecution mentioned in this Beatitude by the phrases 'because of righteousness', 'falsely' and 'because of me'. Yet even with these qualifications in place persecution of one kind or another is a gilt-edged guarantee for those prepared to take their stand and live wholeheartedly for Christ. The Bible could not be clearer on the point: 'In fact, everyone who wants to live a godly life in Christ Jesus will be persecuted' (2 Timothy 3:12). The verb 'wants' which Paul uses here is **thelo**, which signifies not merely desire but determination to carry that desire through to completion. Surely this should be true of all who profess to be Christ's followers? Does this statement of Paul's not say something very serious and searching to those who call themselves Christians yet go through life without so much as a pinprick of persecution? Christians never make a bigger mistake than when they try to fit comfortably into the world's style and standards. The Christian's calling is not to be popular but to be pure, yet if he is pure he will be unpopular because, as Jesus said, 'Everyone who does evil hates the light' (John 3:20).

The world can stand any amount of wishy-washy religion, but it can no more stand genuine, biblical Christianity than it could stand its Founder. Nor must we forget that over the centuries a great deal of the persecution of God's people has come from religious groupings. Religious persecution began with the first recorded murder in history, when Cain, angered at the fact that his brother's offerings found favour with God while his did not, 'attacked his brother Abel and killed him' (Genesis 4:8). Much of the persecution of God's people in the Old

Testament had a religious context, and the same was true in the New Testament. Today, the pure gospel of the grace of God remains anathema not only to the blatantly godless but to countless sects and cults, to hard-line Roman Catholicism which insists that man must contribute to his own salvation, and to liberalism, which robs the Bible of its authority, Christ of his deity, his miracles of their integrity and his substitutionary death of its efficacy.

Sadly, persecution sometimes comes from unexpected quarters. As I was writing this chapter I received a letter from a godly fellow preacher in the United States, telling me of a recent experience in New England. He had been invited to one of the larger churches in the region and preached in the morning on the text, 'Will you not revive us again, that your people may rejoice in you?' (Psalm 85:6). Knowing him as I do, I am sure that he expounded the text faithfully and applied it warmly. Yet when he returned for the evening service he was met by a deacon who denounced him as a heretic. When my friend protested his love for Christ and the gospel he was told, 'Mormons say they love Jesus and are lost just like you!' Other deacons were hastily brought into the discussion and with the service already under way, my friend was told to leave the church and not to return. His life was not threatened, nor was he physically assaulted, yet this was a clear case of persecution for the cause of righteousness.

Many other examples could be given: Christian teenagers facing derision from their friends, Christians at work cold-shouldered by their colleagues or discriminated against by their employers, faithful businessmen short-changed by those who take advantage of their meekness and young believers misunderstood or maligned by their parents are all part of the same pattern - and all share in the promise Jesus makes in the Beatitude we are studying.

### '... A PASSION UNBECOMING...'

Before going on to the next section of our study, one other important point can be made from a technicality in the text. The phrase 'those who are persecuted' is rendered as a passive perfect participle. The perfect tense in Greek has no exact equivalent in English, but the phrase has the sense of referring to something that is constantly being allowed to happen. This carries with it the inference that there is to be no retaliation by those being persecuted. Christians should obviously never provoke opposition, nor welcome it with foolish bravado, but neither should they retaliate in kind or seek to take revenge.

Several years ago I met a young Latvian with an extraordinary story. Some time earlier he had been taken seriously ill and pledged that if his life was spared he would devote himself to God. After his recovery he was converted to Christ while reading the New Testament. At that time his widowed father was living with a German countess, and became incensed at his son's new-found faith and the moral revolution which had taken place in his life. He threatened him with severe punishment if he persisted in his Christian commitment. Every evening, when the son returned from working in the fields, his father asked him whether he had recanted. When he received a negative answer, as he always did, he ordered his son to strip, then lashed him with a belt until he bled. When I asked how he had coped with this kind of treatment he told me, 'I prayed to God to help me bear the pain without resentment. And while I lay on the floor being whipped I would think of those who had laid down their lives for the faith and say, "Thank you, Lord, for allowing me the privilege of this small sacrifice".' This example of true meekness is made all the more remarkable by the fact that he was a powerfully built young man who could easily have prevented his father from laying a finger on him or retaliated violently when he did.

John Calvin called revenge, 'a passion unbecoming to the children of God'. It is certainly out of kilter with the example given by Christ: 'When they hurled their insults at him, he did not retaliate; when he suffered, he made no threats. Instead, he entrusted himself to him who judges justly' (1 Peter 2:23). Those who suffer for Christ should pray for grace to submit to it.

## FAITH AND FRICTION

The third major lesson to be drawn from this Beatitude is that **blessing**

**attaches to the persecution to which Jesus refers.** Earlier in this chapter we noted the 'prosperity gospel' heresy which teaches that health, wealth and other material benefits are available 'on tap' for God's people, so that all they have to do is to bring their need to God and 'claim' the appropriate blessing. The idea that we can 'name it and claim it' has understandable attraction, but it has no biblical basis. Nowhere in Scripture are we told that we can 'claim' things such as healing, prosperity, success at work or the conversion of family members or friends - nor can we 'claim' deliverance from persecution or pressure which may come to us as Christians.

Far from helping Christians to get a biblical perspective on things, such teaching does exactly the opposite, as Sinclair Ferguson points out: 'Instead of delivering us from our fascination with this world, such teaching only immerses us further in it. We fall into the error of taking material prosperity as the ultimate mark of God's blessing, whereas Jesus tells us that the marks of God's blessing are poverty of spirit, mourning for sin and persecution for the sake of righteousness.' In the Beatitude we are presently studying, Jesus says that far from being something from which we should 'claim' deliverance, persecution (qualified in the ways we have noted) is a token of God's blessing. Incomprehensible as it may seem to unbelievers, persecution is a special favour which God grants to his people. Encouraging the Christians at Philippi to stand firm in the face of opposition, Paul writes, 'For it has been granted to you on behalf of Christ not only to believe on him, but also to suffer for him' (Philippians 1:29). The word 'granted' comes from the Greek **charis**, meaning 'grace', and the significance of the word can be seen in something Paul says elsewhere: 'For it is by grace (**charis**) you have been saved, through faith - and this not from yourselves, it is the gift of God - not by works, so that no-one can boast' (Ephesians 2:8-9). Bringing these two statements from Scripture together, we can dare to say that just as faith in Christ is something graciously granted by God, so is persecution for the sake of Christ. As Alec Motyer confirms: 'The suffering which comes to a Christian as a Christian, far from being evidence of divine forgetfulness, as we in our easy rebellion often understand it, is rather "sign, omen and proof" of the reality of the work of grace.'

Paul is using another great salvation word when he says that such suffering is 'for' Christ. 'For' translates the Greek **huper,** the very word we have in Peter's great statement that 'Christ died for sins once for all, the righteous for (**huper)** the unrighteous, to bring you to God' (1 Peter 3:18). The word means not merely 'for the sake of' but 'in the place of'. There is no suggestion in Paul's statement to the Philippians that there is any atoning value in the persecution suffered by Christians, not even in the death of the martyrs. Yet just as Jesus suffered for the cause of righteousness during his earthly lifetime, so his followers should expect to do so during theirs. When honesty, purity and integrity are at stake, so is Christ's name. In his absence he gives Christians the privilege of taking his place and being subjected to the kind of treatment he would receive were he still here in the flesh. No honour in the world can equal that of standing in for Christ and standing up for him against all the opposition of a cynical and sceptical world.

The response Christians should make to this privilege is given in the Beatitudes' only imperative - 'Rejoice and be glad'. This is a rather tame translation, in that 'be glad' (a more intense word than 'rejoice') is based on the Greek verb **agalliao,** which Spiros Zodhiates says means 'to exult, leap for joy, show one's joy by leaping and skipping, denoting excessive joy and delight'. Luke uses the word in writing of an occasion when Jesus was 'full of joy (**agalliao**) through the Holy Spirit' (Luke 10:21), and of a converted jailer's family being 'filled with joy' (**agalliao**), because they had come to believe in God (Acts 16:34). There is no warrant in these words for orchestrated gymnastics in public worship, but they do speak of intense, deep, fervent joy, what Peter elsewhere calls 'an inexpressible and glorious joy' (1 Peter 1:8). In **Letters to Young Churches**, his paraphrase of the New Testament Epistles, J B Phillips renders this 'a joy that words cannot express and which has in it a hint of the glories of heaven'. Phillips' phrase points us towards the double-barrelled reason **why** Christians should rejoice under pressure. Jesus says that those who are persecuted are blessed 'because theirs is the kingdom of heaven' and that when his followers are insulted, persecuted and slandered they are to rejoice 'because great is your reward in heaven'. The second phrase clearly looks forward to eternity but, as we saw in an earlier chapter, Christians enter the kingdom of heaven not at death but at the moment of their conversion. This being the case, the joy produced by persecution is not put on 'hold' until they die, but is something they experience here and now as members of God's eternal kingdom. There are at least five reasons why God's people can 'rejoice and be glad' when their faith produces friction.

## REASONS FOR REJOICING

First, **it identifies them with Christ**. Peter has a great word of encouragement about this: 'Dear friends, do not be surprised at the painful trial you are suffering, as though something strange were happening to you. But rejoice that you participate in the sufferings of Christ, so that you may be overjoyed when his glory is revealed. If you are insulted because of the name of Christ, you are blessed, for the Spirit of glory and of God rests on you' (1 Peter 4:12-14). Jesus constantly faced opposition from the ungodly, and his followers should rejoice whenever they are called upon to share with him in that which he suffered for them. After the apostles had been flogged on the orders of the Sanhedrin for preaching the gospel, they walked away 'rejoicing because they had been counted worthy of suffering disgrace for the name' (Acts 5:41). As far as they were concerned, they counted it an honour to be dishonoured and were given grace to accept disgrace. Nearly 1,800 years later John Wesley often faced hostile crowds when preaching the gospel in the open air. In his diary he tells of an open air service held at Moorfields, in London, when 'I was honoured by having stones, dirt, rotten eggs and pieces of dead cats thrown at me'. Only his identification with Christ could turn these missiles into medals.

Secondly, **it identifies them with the prophets**. Jesus specifically told his disciples to rejoice in the opposition they faced, 'for in the same way they persecuted the prophets who were before you'. Writing to pressurized Christians in his day, James encouraged them to look to the prophets 'as an example in the face of suffering' and reminded them that 'we consider **blessed** those who have persevered' (James 5:10-11). Christians who suffer for their faith join an illustrious roll of honour, one by no means limited to those who wrote prophetical books. Noah, Abraham, Jacob, Moses, Elijah, Isaiah, Jeremiah and Daniel were among those who persevered in the face of persecution and are now considered 'blessed'. It is surely a cause for rejoicing to read in Scripture that God has added one's name to such a list?

Thirdly, **it strengthens their assurance of salvation**. This is brought out by the phrase 'for theirs **is** the kingdom of heaven', and is underlined by something Jesus told his disciples shortly before his death: 'If the world hates you, keep in mind that it hated me first ... you do not belong to the world, but I have chosen you out of the world. That is why the world hates you' (John 15:18-19). The world cannot tolerate the idea that God has a chosen people and is enraged when God's people refuse to conform to its standards. Yet even that fury becomes a means of blessing to those who belong to the kingdom of heaven because it helps to endorse their membership. It provides them with a certificate of authenticity. In John Calvin's words, 'Persecutions are in a way seals of adoption to the children of God.' The persecution of those who seek to live godly lives in a godless world is a sign of their salvation, evidence of their election. Far from being a cause of depression, this should be a cause for delight because, as Don Carson says, 'Their suffering under persecution, which has been prompted by their right-eousness, becomes a triumphant sign that the kingdom is theirs.'

Fourthly, **it helps them to grow in grace**. When Christians face opposition in the cause of the kingdom they have a great opportunity to make progress in the things of God. James is quite clear about this: 'Consider it pure joy, my brothers, whenever you face trials of many kinds, because you know that the testing of your faith develops perse-verance. Perseverance must finish its work so that you may be mature and complete, not lacking anything' (James 1:2-4). When James speaks of 'trials of many kinds' he is clearly not thinking only of what we might call 'persecution', but neither is he excluding it. Instead, he was saying that all the pressures faced by the Christian should be seen as instruments in God's hands intended for the believer's blessing. D

Edmond Hiebert makes the point well: 'James was not inculcating a stoic resignation, which when engulfed by trials wears a forced smile and seeks to ignore the pain. Rather, James is calling for a positive attitude towards trials which he views as opportunities, under God's grace, for growth and development in the Christian life. Christian faith must apprehend that beneficial results are to be derived from such experiences and so accept them as occasions for rejoicing.' Many of the finest Christians I know have suffered significantly for the cause of Christ.

Paul makes much the same point when writing to the Romans: 'Therefore, since we have been justified through faith, we have peace with God through our Lord Jesus Christ, through whom we have gained access by faith into this grace in which we now stand. And we rejoice in the hope of the glory of God. Not only so, but we also rejoice in our sufferings, because we know that suffering produces perseverance; perseverance, character; and character, hope' (Romans 5:1-4). We dare not miss the significance of the apostle's testimony. Not only did he rejoice 'in the hope of the glory of God' (what J B Phillips calls 'the happy certainty of the glorious things he has in store for us') but also in his sufferings - '**because ... suffering produces**'. Suffering (including persecution of whatever kind) drives the believer to Christ, makes him more consciously dependent on the grace of God and helps to develop spiritual muscle. What is more, as he grows in his knowledge of Scripture, suffering gives him a greater vision of the purposes of God in his life. No Christian invites pressure, suffering or persecution, nor does he ever find these things enjoyable. Nevertheless, all who see them through the lens of Scripture gratefully endorse the Psalmist's testimony: 'It was good for me to be afflicted so that I might learn your decrees' (Psalm 119:71).

Fifthly, **it opens a door for the gospel**. Paul's letter to the Philippians was sent while he was in prison (probably in Rome) yet far from complaining about having his ministry curtailed, he wrote, 'Now I want you to know, brothers, that what has happened to me has really served to advance the gospel. As a result, it has become clear throughout the whole palace guard and to everyone else that I am in chains for Christ' (Philippians 1:12-13). Paul's imprisonment gave an unexpected opportunity of sharing the gospel with people who would otherwise have remained unreached. His throwaway phrase 'what has happened to me' covered false accusations, insults, malicious misrepresentation, floggings, stonings, imprisonments and death threats. Yet he could look back on all of these things and rejoice that they 'served to advance the gospel'. What some might have considered road-blocks he considered stepping-stones. Yet even that is not the whole story. The phrase 'that happened' is not in the original text and tends to obscure the important point that for the Christian nothing 'just happens'. No circumstances in the believer's life are accidental or incidental, but are ordained by God to serve his eternal purposes. As Alec Motyer finely puts it, 'God is too great to be knocked off course by the malpractice of wicked men.'

Even if we confined our thinking to the advance of the gospel through the imprisonment of preachers, history would provide thousands of examples. To give just one, the Romanian pastor Richard Wurmbrand was incarcerated by the Communists for 14 years and frequently tortured for his faith, yet during that time he was instrumental in leading many of his fellow-prisoners to Christ. These high profile cases are remarkable illustrations of a principle that applies to all believers: persecution opens a door for the gospel. When Christians are criticized, slandered, vilified, misrepresented or attacked they are always presented with a golden opportunity to react in ways that demonstrate the reality of the power of the gospel and often to share its truth with their persecutors.

These are some of the ways in which persecution becomes a means of blessing to those who belong to the kingdom of heaven; but the best is yet to be ...

## THE VICTOR'S SONG

The Beatitudes come to a triumphant conclusion with Jesus' promise to believers who are persecuted for their faithfulness: **'great is your reward in heaven'**. The New Testament writers are unanimous in endorsing this. Paul tells the Christians in Rome, 'I consider that our present sufferings are not worth comparing with the glory that will be revealed in us' (Romans 8:18). The word 'consider' (**logizomai** in Greek) is an accountant's word and has to do with reckonings and calculations. It is as if Paul puts 'our sufferings' in one column and 'the glory that will be revealed in us' in another, adds them both up and comes to the conclusion that the first total is 'not worth comparing' with the second. He says much the same thing to the Christians in Corinth when he assures them that 'our light and momentary troubles are achieving for us an eternal glory that far outweighs them all' (2 Corinthians 4:17). There is as great a difference in 'weight' between the Christian's present persecution and his future glory as there is between time and eternity. James puts the point in the form of a beatitude of his own: 'Blessed is the man who perseveres under trial, because when he has stood the test, he will receive the crown of life that God has promised to those who love him' (James 1:12). Peter emphasizes the reason for rejoicing under pressure and encourages his readers to 'rejoice that you participate in the sufferings of Christ, so that you may be overjoyed when his glory is revealed' (1 Peter 4:13).

No Christian relishes opposition or persecution of any kind, but the more he understands their true significance the more he will learn to rejoice in them. As Stuart Olyott says, 'Our present sufferings are like an ugly porch which leads to the threshold of an unspeakably glorious mansion.' This certainty of future glory was a major motivation in the life of Moses: 'By faith Moses, when he had grown up, refused to be known as the son of Pharaoh's daughter. He chose to be ill-treated along with the people of God rather than enjoy the pleasures of sin for a short time. He regarded disgrace for the sake of Christ as of greater value than the treasures of Egypt, because he was looking ahead to his reward' (Hebrews 11:24-26). Surrounded with immense luxury and privilege, Moses could have relaxed and revelled in it all. In the modern phrase, he 'had it made'. Yet he deliberately turned his back on it all and threw in his lot with the despised, ill-treated Israelite slaves, laying himself open to Pharaoh's scorn, hatred and abuse. The word 'regarded' (**hegeomai**) tells us that this was not a sudden decision made on the spur of the moment as the result of some emotional impulse. Moses carefully weighed up the pros and cons and came to the conclusion that God's reward for faithfulness was infinitely preferable to anything that Egypt had to offer.

The author of Hebrews gives God's people an even greater example in encouraging them to persevere: 'Let us fix our eyes on Jesus, the author and perfecter of our faith, who for the joy set before him endured the cross, scorning its shame, and sat down at the right hand of the throne of God' (Hebrews 12:2). Jesus had before him all the Messianic promises of eternal glory, and throughout the terrible treatment meted out to him by his enemies he clung to these with unwavering faith.

When the pressures mount, it is sometimes difficult not to be discouraged or depressed and to ask, 'Why is this happening to me?' In times like these we need to focus on the fact that persecution is proof of our destiny. As Martyn Lloyd-Jones writes, 'By thus persecuting you the world is just telling you that you do not belong to it, that you are a man apart; you belong to another realm, thus proving the fact that you are going to heaven.' When preaching in Norway some years ago, I stayed talking with the manager of our hotel on the Hardangerfjord long after the other guests had gone to bed. Noticing that he looked very tired, I said, 'It's been a very long day for you, hasn't it?' I have never forgotten the exact words of his reply, 'Yes, a very long day, but a very short season'. There are times when, to Christians facing misunderstanding, opposition, persecution and the constant pressure of countering a pervasive, godless culture, life seems 'a very long day'. Yet it is a very short season, and the day is coming when all their pressures and problems will end and they will hear their Saviour's invitation, 'Come, you who are blessed by my Father; take your inheritance, the kingdom prepared for you since the creation of the world' (Matthew 25:34).

When John Bradford, one of the godly Marian martyrs, was being burned at the stake in London on 1 July 1555, he turned to another Christian being executed with him and said, 'Be of good comfort, brother, for we shall have a merry supper with the Lord this night'.

Christians are never far from home and from the eternal joy and glory which will be their 'reward in heaven'. The reward will not be something they have earned because, in John Calvin's words, 'The promise of the reward is free'. All the Christian's rewards in heaven are his by the sovereign grace of a loving Father. What those rewards will be are beyond our imagining or understanding - as Thomas Watson says, 'The reward is as far above your thoughts as it is beyond your deserts.' In the last book in the Bible, however, God turns back a corner of the curtain and in a series of metaphors gives us a glimpse of the glory that awaits those who have faithfully passed through the pressures of life: 'Therefore, they are before the throne of God and serve him day and night in his temple; and he who sits on the throne will spread his tent over them. Never again will they hunger; never again will they thirst. The sun will not beat upon them, nor any scorching heat. For the Lamb at the centre of the throne will be their shepherd; he will lead them to springs of living water. And God will wipe away every tear from their eyes' (Revelation 7:15-17).

Nothing that has ruined man's life on earth will be allowed to do so in heaven and opposition to God's people will be a thing of the past there. In A W Pink's phrase, 'One breath of paradise will extinguish all the adverse winds of earth.' This is the only context within which the persecution of God's people can be properly seen. In 1858 a young American clergyman by the name of Dudley Tyng died as the result of an accident on his parents' farm. In his last words to his father he asked him to tell all his fellow ministers to 'stand up for Jesus'. A few days after his death, one of his closest friends, fellow minister George Duffield, wrote a poem based on Tyng's last words. Duffield's poem eventually became a well-known Christian hymn, and the exhortation and encouragement of its closing lines provide the perfect climax to our study of the Beatitudes:

Stand up, stand up for Jesus!     To him that overcometh
The strife will not be long;       A crown of life shall be;
This day the noise of battle,      He with the King of glory
The next the victor's song.        Shall reign eternally.